EVENTUALLY
CRICKET

EVENTUALLY
CRICKET

MORE
unpredictable
performances from the
Outcasts C.C.

To Mark

With best wishes

Alan Haselhurst

Illustrations by 'Hoby'

(David Haselhurst)

Queen Anne Press

First published in Great Britain in 2001 by
Queen Anne Press
a division of Lennard Associates Limited
Mackerye End, Harpenden
Hertfordshire AL5 5DR

A CIP catalogue record for this book
is available from the British Library

ISBN 1 85291 637 0

Editor: Michael Leitch
Jacket design: Paul Cooper

Printed and bound in Great Britain by
Hackman Printers

CONTENTS

With love and my most grateful thanks to my wife Angela who,
as she typed and interpreted every longhand word, may be forgiven
for wondering – perhaps with countless others – whether it was
all really necessary.

ACKNOWLEDGEMENTS

The people to whom I owe a real debt of gratitude are those who read *Occasionally Cricket*, approved and asked if there would be a sequel. I will not name them as I am sure they do not want bricks through their windows. But they were the main reason why I was encouraged to pick up my pen once again.

I admit to enjoying the writing experience. It proves an effective antidote to the day job as it allows me in rest periods to devote my mind to my characters and to unlikely situations into which I might pitch them. There is a sense of ownership and manipulation which is pure escapism.

Positive critics of *Occasionally Cricket* claimed to see in my prose style shades of other more distinguished authors, some of whom I have never actually read. In introducing my first book I freely admitted to being influenced by those writers of cricket fiction whose works I had read. We are what we absorb. There has been no intended plagiarism. As a composer of fiction I am my own man, even if I still wear my L plates.

Outside the family only two people have examined the text of this book. I am indebted to one friend, who was a huge enthusiast for *Occasionally Cricket*. He offered me some wise guidance in editing and finalising the content. If I attract opprobrium for not adopting all his comments, it is entirely my own fault. I will not acknowledge him by name because he is a candidate for membership of the House of Lords and I would not wish to damn his chances of selection.

I am also indebted to my publisher whose decision to back this unknown author has fortunately not led to his bankruptcy. He has been friend as well as adviser and I regard it as mighty indulgence on his part that he has been ready and willing to take another book from me. I hope his faith will once again be repaid.

I owe a particular debt to Malcolm Field of Essex County Cricket Club who patiently helped me to understand sufficient (I hope) of the Duckworth/Lewis system to (mis)apply it in this book. Any unforeseen error is mine, not his.

I have managed to coax another set of drawings out of my son, David ('Hoby'), before he went into preparation for his university finals. I think he has responded well with a growing talent which comes from we know not where. Should the editor of any national newspaper read this book, please note that David leaves university in the summer with an ambition to have his own strip cartoon.

I cannot thank my wife enough for all the work she has done in preparing my words for publication. Draft has followed draft as I have played around with the text adding a whim here and eliminating an inconsistency there. She has been monumentally patient in deciphering my handwriting and correcting my errors. Any which remain are entirely down to me.

Outside politics and family, cricket is my passion. I hope it shows through these pages. I equally hope that I respect the game sufficiently to have avoided any glaring mistakes in the compilation of match details. At close of play, so to speak, it is just meant to be good fun. I realise that I am putting my sense of humour on trial without knowing how large and how forgiving the jury is.

MEMBERS OF THE OUTCASTS CRICKET CLUB

Alan Birch

Stewart Thorogood

Dean Faulds

Jon Palmer

Winston Jenkins

Phil Cole

Colin Banks

Greg Roberts

Tom Redman

Nigel Redman

Basil Smith

John Furness

Kevin Newton

Charlie Colson

David Pelham

Rashid Ali

Tim Jackson

Ray Burrill

Simon Crossley (Scorer)

Syd Breakwell (Umpire)

Late arrival: Harry Northwood

OUTCASTS C.C.

versus

ROCKCLIFFE SCHOOL

THE TWO TEAMS
(in batting order)

ROCKCLIFFE SCHOOL
Tom Barnes (c)
Douglas Hamerskill
Philip Bond
William Briggs
Wayne Tibbins
Angus Flabert (w/k)
Derek Orman
David Simms
Charlie Burns
Jack Dolland
Cooperbatch T Gulfstrode

OUTCASTS C.C.
Stewart Thorogood
David Pelham
Dean Faulds
Charlie Colson
Ray Burrill (c)
John Furness
Kevin Newton (w/k)
Rashid Ali
Greg Roberts
Nigel Redman
Tom Redman

PRELIMINARIES

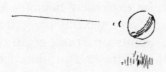

Neil Danby burst into the room in disarray. He had been suspended. Until that moment Rashid Ali, to whose office he came for legal advice, had never heard of Rockcliffe School. He would take a long time to forget it.

The offences alleged against the teacher, and they were certainly not minor misdemeanours, took several sheets of paper to detail. Just taking the notes was a harrowing experience. When the tale was complete, Rashid Ali leant back in his chair and surveyed his client. On first impressions, Neil Danby gave no suggestion that he was capable of a quarter of what had been said against him. But looks, thought Rashid Ali, who recognised himself as still only an apprentice judge of human nature, were not everything. He allowed Neil Danby to talk on and his feeling grew that there was far more to this than met the eye.

It did not take too long for cricket to enter the discussion. It never usually did. Directly behind the solicitor's chair and in the client's line of vision was a row of Wisdens going back to 1970, their yellow jackets contrasting sharply with the more sombre legal tomes which occupied the other shelves. Nor were the walls of Rashid Ali's office the exclusive preserve of luminaries of the legal world. Amid the odd wig and gown could be seen Compton sweeping, Dexter driving, Botham hooking and Trueman pounding. The atmosphere was more willow than quill.

Rockcliffe School in Essex was a minor public school catering for around two hundred boys from the age of eleven to eighteen. One of its not too numerous strengths was cricket, which it played hard and uncompromisingly. Rockcliffe had weathered variations in the economic climate better than many schools in the independent sector, because its cricketing prowess had continued to attract an undiminished core of parents who saw, in their sons, future lions of English cricket. It helped in such cases that the school's nominal entry requirements proved to be extremely flexible. A good cover drive or an extra yard of pace were seen as more than adequate compensation for low reading ability or a poor grasp of spelling.

The record showed that Rockcliffe had produced more than a handful of players to represent their country if barely anyone capable of benefiting from higher education. The school's tough approach to the game had gained them some grudging admiration, but in recent times the fixture list had thinned. Word was spreading round the school circuit that teams might go to Rockcliffe in mini-buses, but would very likely return in ambulances. That, at any rate, was the rumour, but it was a rumour as yet unknown to the Outcasts Cricket Club of which Rashid Ali was a leading member.

The remainder of Rashid Ali's professional day did not measure up to the images created by the consultation with Neil Danby. Cases of shoplifting, petty larceny and speeding (even at 135 mph on the North Circular) did nothing to banish from Rashid Ali's mind the events at Rockcliffe School to which his client had allegedly been party. It was a relief when six o'clock came. He felt doubly glad that Alan Birch, senior member of the Outcasts and their steadiest batsman, had suggested meeting for a drink at the Morose Macaw. An end-of-day loosener – not his usual style – seemed to have particular attraction.

Rashid Ali, whose ale consumption never challenged the Outcasts' records either in the sprint (pints per session) or long-distance (gallons per season), was into his third pint of Eggleton's Marauder Bitter before he and Alan had completed their assessment of England's winter tours. The beer was of greater solace than the analysis.

As far as England in the West Indies was concerned, it had been a case of another captain, another tour. Things had never really recovered after the umpiring incident in Barbados. The visitors had indeed been unlucky with injuries, but those sustained in the post-match brawl in Port of Spain had been wholly unnecessary. The 'A' team's tour of India had been a sad affair. Racked by food poisoning and other maladies, the team had needed to call on the services of as many as thirty-three players – and almost as many doctors – to complete the itinerary. Even now, five of the team were still occupying hospital beds in Madras and Calcutta. No comfort could be gleaned from the Under-19s in Canada where a number of diplomatic gaffes had led to early abandonment and the recall of the High Commissioner. In fact the one bright spot in the whole scene was the plucky performance of the Under-17 girls in Papua New Guinea.

So, by natural progression, Alan Birch and Rashid Ali turned to the winter activities of members of the Outcasts CC. None of them had involved cricket or anything remotely athletic in the ordinary sense of that word. Alan seemed to be suggesting that some kind of pre-season training might be considered. Rash thought this a little rich coming from the team's prominent gourmet whose girth bore signs of close season indulgence in good food and fine wine. As the conversation progressed, the chances of getting their friends jogging and exercising were variously examined. At which point the two elements came together was not clear – it was probably after the fourth pint. Alan had got as far as mentioning a nine-a-side practice match when Rockcliffe School floated back into Rash's mind. That was it. A gentle outing against a school side would give the Outcasts an opportunity to stretch their limbs and, as a useful bonus, Rash would have the opportunity to dig for information which might help his client. Alan was dubious (the thought of school food was not an inducement), but their session ended with Rash being charged with undertaking a feasibility study.

It took Rashid Ali only three phone calls the following morning to appreciate that the beer must have been doing the thinking. Feasibility rapidly began to look remote, and that was without anyone actually knowing anything about Rockcliffe School. Rather than offering excuses, Stewart Thorogood, Winston Jenkins and Phil Cole were completely dismissive. The theme was very much 'Playing schoolkids? No way.' This was disappointing if not embarrassing, because, before speaking with his colleagues, Rashid Ali had obtained a favourable reaction from the school itself. He thought it prudent to put in a qualifying call to the cricket coach at the school lest his first conversation had given the impression of a commitment which he might not be able to fulfil. 'I'm afraid he's gone out,' said the lady who answered. And had she said no more than that she would take a message, Rashid Ali might well have abandoned the project. But what she did add was, 'He's just dropped round to the brewery,' and that put a different complexion on the whole matter.

Rashid Ali reached for his copy of the *A-Z of British Brewing*. It was not a volume to which he gave daily study, but every Outcast had to have one. And there it was: the Rockcliffe Brewery, producing Rockcliffe Rugged Ales for a limited but discerning public. The brewery had only four outlets. The most noted beer in its range was 'Old Rocky', described as having the complementary attributes of winter warmer and summer comfort. The outlet in Rockcliffe itself was called, appropriately enough, the Brewery Tavern and its close proximity to the school appeared to be confirmed by its sharing the same postal address and code. Armed with this information and on the basis that knowledge is power, Rashid Ali took to his telephone again.

This time there was progress, but when he sat back to consider the list of acceptances (some of them tentative) Rashid Ali realised that he might have achieved quantity, but he was more doubtful about the quality. On a scale of talent he had procured the services of the most prodigious drinkers, but their playing power was of a different order. Having both Redman twins was in itself unusual. (It transpired that their frequently ailing mother had been persuaded to visit her sister in Australia and would be away for some weeks. It was still a mystery to Nigel and Tom how their sister and aunt between them had pulled off this remarkable coup because for the last couple of years Muriel Redman had been unable to venture as far from home as the local supermarket.) Alan Birch had felt some obligation to play having been partner to the original discussion. However, a side lacking Jon Palmer, Stewart Thorogood, Dean Faulds and Phil Cole looked distinctly unbalanced. Those four Outcasts could make some sort of claim to batting honours. Beyond Rashid Ali himself that left no more than two others on his list who could half seriously make the same claim. After a further consultation with his client, Rashid Ali realised that the situation was not even as good as that.

Neil Danby returned to his solicitor's office with the dossier he had promised. This set out his recollections of life at Rockcliffe School and his own allegations on top of those which had been levelled against him. As a solicitor, if still a young solicitor, Rashid Ali had not led an exactly sheltered life. As a member of the Outcasts it did not take long to become extremely broad-minded. Nevertheless the contents of the Danby dossier were definitely not for readers of a sensitive disposition. Rashid Ali came to an early conclusion: if he was to make anything of the trip to Rockcliffe, he could not afford to be tied up on the field of play.

Alan Birch agreed. They were once again in the Morose Macaw. For professional reasons Rashid Ali had been able to do no more than hint at the delicacy of his mission. The best cover was to go as twelfth man, not as captain. Someone needed to be press-ganged into the eleven and that someone needed to be able to bat. They each decided to work on two of their colleagues, but it was clear when they next spoke that the lure of Rockcliffe ales by itself was not strong enough to overcome other engagements or the aversion to playing a warm-up game and especially a warm-up game against a school or, as Phil Cole more graphically put it, 'a load of poxy kids'.

It always pays to be well-briefed. For a second time and more thoroughly, Rashid Ali went through the papers which Neil Danby had left with him. And there it was: a reference to the organ loft. But it was not so much the dark deeds described as taking place there which grabbed Rashid Ali's attention. It was the fact of there being an organ loft. This in turn presupposed an organ. That triggered an interesting thought. Yes, he was told in a further conversation with the school, there was an organ in the hall (it had once been a chapel, but the decline of Christianity at Rockcliffe had been ahead of the field) and it was one of which they were particularly proud. There were across Europe only three examples of this make of organ which remained in working condition. Had he not cut short the flow of enthusiastic words which his inquiry had prompted, Rashid Ali might have become an expert in organ technology. But, he thought to himself as he replaced the receiver, there was no need. He knew all he needed to know to bait the hook.

Having a position of responsibility with the Monumental Metallurg Company required a readiness to travel anywhere at the drop of a hat. There were also regular management conferences. Too many times Dean Faulds, a promising technical engineer, had been deprived of his cricket by corporate demands. He had put aside any thought of making the trip to Rockcliffe because he was down to make the trip to Broadmarsh-in-the-Vale for a seminar in ethical business systems. The only redeeming feature of this gathering was its venue. Leeburn Manor was on the upside of luxurious, the downside being the absence of any kind of real ale. Otherwise Leeburn Manor was to the jaded executive what the zest of lime is to a gin and tonic at the end of a long and stressful day. So Dean Faulds did not altogether mourn the loss of early season cricket practice. Lean of frame, he did not think it would take much to slot back into the groove when the time came. This approach was not unique amongst the Outcasts.

Mentioned to him in passing conversation, the name of Multiglobal Strategies Inc would have meant nothing to Dean Faulds. Suddenly it was to mean a lot. Over a weekend the Monumental Metallurg Company was swallowed by Multiglobal Strategies Inc. From Monday morning life was different for Dean Faulds. The earliest manifestation of this difference was the cancellation of the seminar in ethical business systems. There was more than one reason for this.

J Lazio Durt, the Chief Operating Officer of Multiglobal Strategies Inc, had not wasted much of his life attending seminars about ethical business systems. Ethics had played little part in his rise to power and fortune. Multiglobal Strategies Inc were already the owners of a chain of high-class resorts which included Leeburn Manor. Expenditure at such establishments, J Lazio Durt decreed, was for the employees of other companies, not his own. So it was a momentous Monday morning at the Monumental Metallurg Company as Dean Faulds and his colleagues braced themselves for more changes to their workstyle. The phone call from Rashid Ali came as light relief.

It would have been easy for Dean Faulds, had he thought quickly enough, to take advantage of the call, declare his availability for the practice match against Rockcliffe School and leave it at that. And it would have been equally easy for Rashid Ali to have left it at that. Many complications would have been avoided. But the conversation proved not to be quite so straightforward and, too late, Dean Faulds found himself trapped in a web which had been three years or so in the making. It was actually true that he played the organ; it was also true that he knew something about the instrument. That, however, was the limit of the truth. Over time and many, many pints of real ale, the limit had been stretched. At first Dean Faulds had failed to recognise where his nods, knowing smiles and throwaway lines had taken him in the minds of his friends. Later he had found it more difficult to disabuse them of the belief that he was nothing if not a virtuoso and historical expert. Eventually he had relaxed, reckoning that his sporting life would never actually interact with his supposed musical life. Not until now. Dean Faulds tried to sound interested in the organ at Rockcliffe School whilst realising he had said far too much to change his mind again about playing in the match. When he had put the phone down, he made a mental note to give the chapel or whatever a wide berth.

There remained one team point to settle. This required another meeting at the Morose Macaw. If Rashid Ali had relegated himself to twelfth man, it followed that he could not captain the side. The customary Outcasts' arrangement was for club members to take it in turns to act as match manager and captain. So far Rashid Ali had performed most of the first role, but was ruled out from completion of the job. It took a while (three rounds in fact) for a name to emerge. Ray Burrill was still the newest and youngest member of the club. He had not yet been captain. For a first timer, he would be getting a head start in view of what Rash had already done. It was after all only a school side. At his age, twenty-three, Ray would have more empathy with the players on the opposing team. The trend of the thinking was remorseless – but it still took three rounds, and then a fourth, to confirm it.

Ray Burrill received the news of his nomination with satisfaction. It was a moment for which he had been preparing. As the newest and youngest of the Outcasts he could not shake off the feeling of being a probationer. This feeling was reinforced by his status as a trainee in his chosen profession, veterinary medicine. In the few games he had played for the Outcasts, his feats had marked him as a genuine all-rounder – on the field. In the bars and clubhouses he had sometimes been found off the pace. Before getting embroiled with the Outcasts he had been too much a lager man and was still being schooled in proper drinking. After a carefully arranged programme of close-season pub tours he was confident that the embarrassments of his first season could be avoided. He took it as a sign of recognition that he was being asked to take charge. He was determined to make it a match to remember. And it would be.

Ray Burrill might not have been the most seasoned member of the Outcasts, but he had been with them long enough to realise that he was not being presented with the strongest bunch of players for the game against Rockcliffe School. In vain did he try to persuade Rashid Ali to do more than be twelfth man. Rashid Ali did not share with him his special reason for wanting to be on the Rockcliffe campus. So, faced with the realisation that the names he had been given were the team, the whole team and nothing but the team, Ray Burrill turned his energies towards completion of the administrative arrangements for the match. There were several matters to be resolved, not least the shortest distance from the school's cricket ground to the pumps dispensing Rockcliffe Ales.

With such notable beer at their destination, it was obviously foolish to have any of his team reliant on their cars. It was in respect of transport that Ray Burrill encountered his first snag (or benefit depending on how it was viewed). The Outcasts' regular purveyor of mass transit facilities announced, in response to Ray's inquiry, that all his coaches were off the road for their annual overhaul. In truth the regulatory authorities had finally caught up with Bill Blimp and Executive Sporting Coachways. Some of his vehicles would never again travel the highways and byways of Britain with their traditional cargo of ill-behaved sportsmen and women. In the pride of his fleet the last puke had sounded. Bill Blimp was in the process of scouring the market to find some (just) serviceable vehicles which he could afford to run and which his usual clientele could afford to hire. For the moment he was off the road. Although the Roads Minister was unaware of this, it was the biggest single contribution to road safety which had so far distinguished his period in office.

Meanwhile another minister from the Department of Transport was in the news. Ray Burrill had been a railway buff since as a nine year-old he had been given a model train set. Complete with an oval track this comprised a diesel locomotive, an open wagon, a petrol tank wagon (advertising a brand of petrol no longer available as a result of a particularly acrimonious take-over battle), a brake van (the toy manufacturer having failed to anticipate a change in railway practice in this regard) and, what Ray remembered most, a yellow goods van bearing the logo of *Wisden Cricketers' Almanack*. When reading the papers, Ray's eye was usually arrested by any headline mentioning railways, although only after he had read the cricket reports. That was how he learned that the Minister for Rail Transport and Public Safety had officially opened a new station: Rockcliffe Parkway.

Verifying the information was no easy task. After all, Ray Burrill had reckoned, there could easily be more than one Rockcliffe. Nevertheless, working on the assumption that the new station might lie on one of the lines from Liverpool Street, Ray began his inquiries. There was no reply to his repeated calls to his local station. He then tried a national rail inquiry number. Having held the line for half an hour and having become more familiar with the music of Johann Strauss the Younger than in his life to date, he was very firmly told that no such station as Rockcliffe Parkway existed on the network. His protests were swept aside by another wave of 'The Blue Danube'. Nothing if not persistent, Ray took himself off to Liverpool Street Station where it was relayed to him by no less a person than the Ticket Office Manager that this was information which could not be revealed to a member of the public. Determined to get to the source, Ray Burrill rang the Private Office of the Minister for Rail Transport and Public Safety. A cautious and half-incoherent assistant private secretary confirmed that the Minister had opened a new rail station somewhere in England, but its exact whereabouts could not be made known for security reasons. At which point Ray Burrill was inclined to give up and consider other options, but the next day his eye was taken by a bold advertisement in his morning paper announcing that it was 'easier by rail' and bearing a Railtrack telephone number. One last try.

A pleasant, clear voice almost instantly answered the phone. It was his habit to commence calls with the words, 'Hello, my name is Burrill.' On this occasion he was taken aback to get the response, 'Is that you, Ray?' It turned out that they had been at college together. With half a mind trying to recapture her image and calculating whether he should suggest meeting for a drink, Ray described his interest in Rockcliffe Parkway. Then he got the truth. The station was where he hoped and it had been opened by the Minister for Rail Transport and Public Safety. However, that had been an official opening designed to get press publicity before local council elections. The actual opening in an operational sense would not be for another two weeks, too late to catch the pre-election local weekly papers, but early enough for Ray's purposes.

Realising there were several supplementary questions he needed to pose and recognising his contact at Railtrack as up to now his only productive source, Ray Burrill, without a clear recollection of Rachel Ross, decided that he would invite her 'for a quick drink'. It was hard to say which of them was the more disappointed by the encounter. Away from the telephone it was apparent that Rachel's voice lost its pleasantness and clarity. After a while Ray became uncomfortable with its harsh edge. There were no harsh edges to Rachel's figure. It was very full and very rounded. If she had been that big at college, Ray thought to himself, he would have been bound to remember. But then as a student neither Rachel nor her friends would have been able to afford

the large gin and tonics which Ray now found himself supplying. If Rachel had thought that Ray's interest in meeting her again was socially motivated, she was badly let down. Thoughts of dinner, theatre and natural progression were cruelly eliminated when, what seemed half a bottle of gin later, Ray, who had rigidly stuck to orange juice, claimed (wholly fictitiously) that he had an indoor net to attend. After the

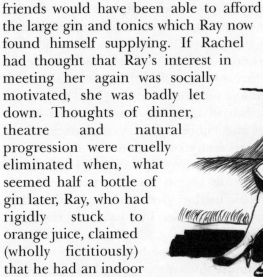
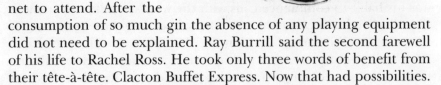

consumption of so much gin the absence of any playing equipment did not need to be explained. Ray Burrill said the second farewell of his life to Rachel Ross. He took only three words of benefit from their tête-à-tête. Clacton Buffet Express. Now that had possibilities.

It would have been far far better if Rashid Ali, having passed managerial responsibility for the Rockcliffe match to Ray Burrill, had had no more direct dealings with the school. However, with his client's needs uppermost, he thought he could see a way of exploiting his capture (as he saw it) of Dean Faulds for the fixture. He was therefore tempted into one more phone call to Rockcliffe School. He let it be known to the headmaster's office that in the Outcasts' team there would be a celebrated organist who would be only too pleased to see and perhaps play their notable instrument. This, thought Rashid Ali, would give Dean Faulds, with himself in tow, a perfect additional cover to prowl round the school premises.

The available Outcasts received with some incredulity the instruction that they were to travel to Rockcliffe by the Clacton Buffet Express departing from Liverpool Street Station at 11.55 am. The message was in the nature of an instruction by reason of having a cheap-day return ticket stapled to it. Surprisingly there was no argument. Amazingly there were no defaulters. Basil Smith was almost a defaulter, but this was entirely involuntary. His wife offered to give him a lift to the station. Claiming certainty in this and in so many other things, Jane Smith insisted that the departure point for Rockcliffe was King's Cross. By this time Basil had only his ticket which stated no more than 'London Terminal' and so his wife's contention could not be contested. Basil was deposited at King's Cross where any falsely created doubt was quickly removed. He took to the Circle Line, which, compared with the previous car ride, provided (unusually) a stress-free journey.

Five minutes before the departure of the Clacton Buffet Express, two men wearing the uniform of a famous London store hurried towards the barrier with a large hamper. This was quickly hailed and signed for by Alan Birch and lifted into a section of the train thoughtfully reserved by Ray Burrill (the thought being for other passengers). There had been no way that Alan Birch would stomach school food. He had had to make his own culinary arrangements. Even with his known penchant for gastronomic fare these seemed extravagant lengths – as his friends continued to tease him when they were not otherwise engaged in chastising Ray Burrill.

Tom Culpinshaw took seriously his role as steward on the Clacton Buffet Express. He was of the old school of buffet car attendants. He had worked on the Manchester Pullman when it was a real Pullman.

When Tom Culpinshaw had served your porridge it came from a tureen and the double cream and the syrup were poured from silver jugs. It was a dying art. Tom Culpinshaw had fretted over the decline in standards until finally leaving British Rail in disgust. But he had missed the railway. After a succession of unsatisfactory appointments in catering, he had found an opportunity to return.

One of the consequences of rail privatisation had been the gradual introduction of competition. This had led to a number of entrepreneurs looking for opportunities to run trains. Operating the Clacton Buffet Express was the first speculative venture for Expresso Trains Ltd, the brainchild of Dinky Dawson and Nigel Fossington-Carr who had achieved rapid riches in city trading. One of their innovative ideas had been the introduction of a buffet service and one of their inspirations had been to hire Tom Culpinshaw to run it. Given an extraordinary degree of discretion by two young men whose only knowledge of running a railway came from table-top games many years ago, Tom Culpinshaw behaved with responsibility, but not without flair. Microwaved meals were not strictly his style, but real coffee and real ale were. His idiosyncratic choice of Tittlebury's Turbo Bitter proved a real hit. His buffet car, decorated with pictures of Duckworth and Tyldesley, was regularly a heaving throng of happy travellers. Expresso Trains Ltd gained significant market share between London and Clacton. Regular passengers had even petitioned the train operating company, Railtrack and the Minister for Rail Transport and Public Safety for the service to be slowed down to avoid consumption having to be rushed.

But Expresso Trains Ltd were operating their service to Clacton with a single train set, painted lime green and purple, and, more to the point, a single steward. The former was more resilient than the latter. Tom Culpinshaw had not missed many working days in his life. He was generally a fit and healthy man. Although advancing in years, Tom still turned out as wicket-keeper for an Old Lancastrians side in the capital. On the previous Sunday (in keeping with most trains, the Clacton Buffet Express did not run on Sunday), Tom Culpinshaw's side had played their first match in bitterly cold conditions. Whether the cause was exposure to the elements or his habit of appealing loud and often, Tom Culpinshaw gradually succumbed to tonsillitis. Early on Saturday morning, with what remained of his voice, he had had to call in sick.

If this was no more than a minor inconvenience to Expresso Trains Ltd and a disappointment to the travelling public for whom closed buffet cars were not an unusual experience, it was a terrible shock to Ray Burrill. He had been sure that the scepticism of his colleagues over the rail mode of transport would have been triumphantly overcome on sight of Tittlebury's Turbo Bitter. Instead the only sight was a rolled-down shutter, hiding from view even cans of lager which in any case most Outcasts would have regarded as unfit for human consumption. The only sound for Ray Burrill's acute discomfort was some well maintained banter targeting his organisational abilities. Ray felt it was going to be a desperate day and at that stage he did not know the half.

So there they were: twelve Outcasts with their regular umpire, former policeman Syd Breakwell, marooned on a train without a drink in reach. There were, of course, the contents of Alan Birch's outsize hamper on which eyes lingered, but knowledge of its contents was resolutely denied them. There would have been no break at all in the verbal taking-apart alternately of Ray Burrill and Alan Birch had not, fifteen minutes into the journey, a trolley appeared, propelled by an unprepossessing youth with a twitch.

Although given insufficient notice to organise a substitute steward for their buffet car, the management of Expresso Trains Ltd had not been altogether devoid of initiative. The seventeen-year-old son of their marketing manager was undergoing a period of work experience with the company. His father saw how this might usefully be extended. Accordingly Harry Northwood had been prised from his bed at what for him was an unearthly hour on a Saturday morning. He was not in good shape and listened aghast to what was expected of him. He might not have been old enough to dispense alcoholic drinks, but he was plenty old enough to consume them. On the previous night he had had a skinful. The idea of pushing a trolley loaded with food and beverages up and down a moving train seemed to Harry Northwood in his condition a special kind of purgatory. It was only when his father mentioned the two words 'wage' and 'tips' that Harry brightened. Last night there had been not only excessive consumption, but also excessive expenditure.

Harry's finances were in desperate need of replenishment and so a truly desperate means had to be grasped.

Thus it was that a half-awake Harry Northwood struggled into that part of the Clacton Buffet Express which had become the Outcasts' den. It was as well Tom Culpinshaw was not there. His sense of smartness in service would have been seriously assaulted by the sight of his deputy. There had been no ready-made uniform for Harry to wear. His dress consisted of a pair of black chinos which looked as though they had been slept in (they had), a white shirt which had somehow evaded his mother's weekly wash (more than once), a pair of black trainers which were plainly not new and an untied black bow tie (in his hurry Harry's hand had missed the made-up one). On to his uninviting form was diverted the exasperation which the Outcasts had until then reserved for Ray Burrill and Alan Birch.

When it was realised that the trolley did not carry even the inadequate substitute of canned beer (Ray in his own defence had explained what he had expected to find on the train), the exasperation heightened and, with it, Harry Northwood's twitch rate. Coffee and biscuits were a poor substitute for the Outcasts' usual match preparation. Not without education and some sense of responsibility (he told himself he was son of management) Harry gamely battled back at the tide of banter and jibes as he served these comestibles. His twitch had almost subsided and he was about to move on when he noticed the profusion of cricket bat handles in the luggage of this group of passengers. His innocent question yielded by way of answer not only their destination, but also their opponents. The trolley stopped. The twitch restarted.

The Outcasts were treated to a de-brief, the like of which they had never previously heard. Harry Northwood's school, Kingsutton, had played Rockcliffe ten days ago. They had lost – and not just the match. Their opening batsman was without two teeth and his partner the nail on his left thumb. Three players had experienced various fractures. One was still in hospital. Most of them had lost their nerve. In Harry's case a spell of work experience had proved timely therapy. Now he visibly shook as he told of individuals in the Rockcliffe side. Scorn and criticism drained from the Outcasts as they appreciated what it was costing Harry Northwood to relive the nightmare match. Yet in the end it seemed to do him good as the sympathy of his audience grew and enveloped him. In a heart-warming gesture, Syd Breakwell was even moved to lean across and tie the young man's bow tie.

'Piss-artists.' That was the view Rockcliffe's cricket coach took of his side's up-coming opponents. From Terry Lilgate this was an outrageous assertion. Not wholly inaccurate, of course, from anyone who had half-heard of the Outcasts, but, if awards were issued, Terry Lilgate would have been a grand master of the genre. His cricket had been learnt chiefly at club level. He had had trials for a first-class county, but had not been taken on the staff. He had been – at least for a while – a good professional in a competitive league. His drinking too had been learnt in a competitive league and his prowess in this direction was more easily sustained than his command over bat and ball. It had become necessary to apply his cricket knowledge in another sphere. There had been an unfortunate engagement at one school where, following a dinner party at the headmaster's house, he had left a trail of vomit from the lounge to the upstairs bathroom and had then collapsed unconscious into the bed of the headmaster's wife's aged mother, who was already occupying it. Her screams would be remembered with a chill by some of the other dinner guests downstairs for the rest of their lives. Such a blip on his curriculum vitae was no obstacle to his securing appointment at Rockcliffe. Terry Lilgate looked to be absolutely what they wanted.

He had already fashioned Rockcliffe School's cricket team into a formidable fighting force. The current year's side was already looking largely settled. There was a core of seven players who had been in last year's eleven. Terry Lilgate thought he had identified half a dozen others with the potential to complete the team. An outing against a bunch of joke cricketers from London gave him the opportunity to try out a couple of the younger lads who he thought might have the killer instinct. Jack Dolland was a rangy fifteen year-old who had a bit of pace and could make the ball rear awkwardly from short of a length – increasingly from well short of a length as Terry Lilgate took grip of the situation. Then there was the Yank.

Cooperbatch T Gulfstrode or even Gulfstrode Minor (there was an elder Gulfstrode at Rockcliffe) were both several syllables too long for Terry Lilgate even when sober. So in the cricketing arena

Cooperbatch T Gulfstrode was the Yank. Young Cooperbatch (he was fourteen and in his first year) did not have a complete grasp of cricket. Before coming to the United Kingdom, he had played only baseball. He could honestly say that he had never known that a game called cricket existed until he was shown the brochure of the school his brother and he were to attend as a consequence of their father's posting to Europe. But when it came to the point it looked perfectly straightforward. There was a ball and a stick and the idea was to knock hell out of the ball with the stick. Cooperbatch T Gulfstrode was a well-built (an unkind person would say overweight) youngster and he found that the greater width of the cricket bat when compared with its baseball equivalent enabled him to knock quite a lot of hell out of a cricket ball. The style would not have pleased a purist, but Terry Lilgate was no purist. The effect was impressive. When Cooperbatch T Gulfstrode was at the wicket, there was less need to keep a look-out for the sharp single, because the young boy's swinging bat was often enough finding the boundary. In any case Cooperbatch was not designed for the sharp single. Nor was fielding the strongest part of his game. The fleetlessness of his foot was to some extent compensated for by a powerful and accurate throwing arm.

Against the approaching 'piss-artists' Terry Lilgate was convinced that he was fielding a well-equipped team. His batsmen included big hitters and careful stroke-makers; his bowlers a quartet of mostly raw and entirely ferocious quickies. The Outcasts would not know what had hit them and, in Terry Lilgate's vocabulary, the operative word was 'hit'. In his turn, Terry Lilgate could not know how much by this time the Outcasts did in fact know. Leaving his team warming up in the nets – with strict instructions not to damage each other – Terry Lilgate reckoned it was time for a drink and headed for the Brewery Tavern. Fortunately for his own sake he never made it.

When the Clacton Buffet Express pulled into Rockcliffe Parkway, the Outcasts were sadder but wiser men. Soon they were to be sadder still, but for the moment their eyes were not focused on the billowing black smoke in the middle distance. The hunt was on for the station exit. Those familiar with the 'parkway' style of station would know that they are built in a plain and simple style, being essentially adjuncts to giant car parks. Florian Tripperwood, the architect commissioned to design the new station near Rockcliffe, had taken the basic design concept beyond simplicity and into severity. There was virtually nothing to complicate the strips of platform except, Ray Burrill noted, a solitary sausage over which he had to step as he left the train. He wondered about its provenance as he took in his immediate surroundings. Waiting room was too misleading a description to apply to the small shelters which had been allowed either side of the tracks. These were not for standing, more for crouching. The waiting was intended to take place below. All of the comfortable and convenient adjuncts of a rail halt were below platform level. The task of the first-time visitor to Rockcliffe Parkway was to discover how to go below. Florian Tripperwood was against signs. The station name and the lighting were incorporated into the platform surface, but when it came to the ramp exiting from platform level, the passenger had to have an appetite for discovery. Come winter Rockcliffe Parkway would be dubbed Ice Station Zebra. At the official opening the Minister for Rail Transport and Public Safety had been overheard calling it something much less flattering.

Once the Outcasts had worked out the direction to take, their eyes gained an uninterrupted view of the inferno which was raging no great distance away. It was not until they had reached the lower level of the station and been greeted by the school handyman cum minibus driver, Fred Minns, that they became aware of its significance. 'Bad business about the brewery,' Fred Minns announced. 'I reckon the school's lucky to 'ave escaped.' In case the visitors had still not made the connection, he went on, 'Brewery's gone and taken the Tavern with it.' There was silence in the minibus, a numbing silence. What had already taken on the character of a disagreeable day had now become exceptionally awful. Ray Burrill averted his eyes from his colleagues' gaze. He knew or thought he knew where blame was being cast. Rashid Ali's face was inscrutable. Encouraged by the impact which his words had obviously had, Fred Minns chatted on. The Outcasts were treated to sensational (and much exaggerated) detail of the drama in the village. Ray was beginning to wish that the school had gone up in flames with the brewery if only to save him further embarrassment.

When the minibus ground to a halt, Ray Burrill was forced to acknowledge that the school was still there. As they descended they were greeted by a young man dressed in what appeared to be school uniform and yet not a member of the cricket team. It was not in the nature of a formal greeting. Rather he moved among them inquiring whether any of them were interested in purchasing any 'gear'. Maybe they were still suffering the shock of arrival, but the full impact of this communication did not at first sink in.

A somewhat more recognisable welcome was provided by the master in charge of cricket. Terry Lilgate lurched towards the visitors, conveying by his appearance the clear message that a source of alcohol, notwithstanding the demise of the brewery, must exist somewhere in the locality. The source was in fact the senior common room. Whilst many of the boys in the school could easily have been persuaded otherwise, the bar in the senior common room was not open at all times. However, it had not taken Terry Lilgate long after his arrival at Rockcliffe to obtain a duplicate key which gave him an access denied to others. After his narrow escape from the brewery and tavern inferno, he had felt amply justified in recourse to this alternative. Perhaps the shock had caused him to misjudge the amount of restorative he needed. Unaware of this mitigating circumstance and bearing a slight disposition towards envy, the Outcasts had no difficulty in making an instant judgement about their host. He was drunk.

Directed towards their changing-room, the Outcasts were surprised to be greeted by Stewart Thorogood. He had declared himself unavailable for the game and so he was put under some pressure to explain his presence. Stewart Thorogood's love-life had flourished over the close season following his amazing reunion in Gigton the previous year with a former, but fleeting girlfriend. There had been nothing fleeting about their second coupling. Before the turn of the year Amanda had moved into his flat. Going steady had become living together. There were some doubts on the part of his friends whether Stewart would be as available for cricket in the coming season as he had been hitherto. His tendered apologies for absence from the team to visit Rockcliffe could have had more than one explanation, but his friends were suspicious. Amanda, it now transpired, had had a last-minute call to duty by her employers and Stewart had found himself, at least until the evening, at a loose end. On a whim he had motored to Rockcliffe. It proved to be an inspiration.

At this point they were joined by their scorer, Simon Crossley, and his wife, Sophie. This was not a surprise. On any reasonable length of journey out of London, Simon and Sophie would travel independently, by tandem. That this arrangement would apply to the Rockcliffe visit had been confirmed to Ray Burrill as match organiser. In fact it had not applied. Simon and Sophie, for personal reasons, had not wanted to cycle all the way to Rockcliffe. They had booked themselves in for a self-catering farmhouse weekend just a few miles from Rockcliffe whither they and their tandem had come the previous day in a hired estate car. Their hideaway proved to be a fortuitous asset.

With everyone gathered in the changing-room, a plan had to be made. Although this was threatening to be the driest match in which the Outcasts had ever taken part, for once the priority was to find a way of measuring up to this alarming schoolboy team. As yet the discussion was confined to cricketing considerations. Pressure was immediately put on both Stewart Thorogood and Rashid Ali to play on the basis that the Outcasts were going to need maximum fire-power. Stewart was unmoved. For one thing, he had brought no kit and for another he could not stay all afternoon. Whilst he was less specific as to the latter, the cause for his eagerness to be back was that he had reservations for himself and Amanda at one of the hottest new restaurants in town.

Rashid Ali was torn. He could see that the Outcasts' batting line-up was not their strongest. His skills might be useful against these schoolboy tyros. On the other hand he had come to Rockcliffe with a job to do and he did not want to be tied down most of the day on the field. It was Greg Roberts who had the idea. He was sitting across the room from the twins, Nigel and Tom Redman, musing whether strangers could tell them apart. Then he glanced at Basil Smith. Basil and his wife had just returned from a fortnight in Malaga. Basil's complexion tended towards sallow, but now he was extremely brown. His hair was black, thinning on top, but uncharacteristically long and curling at the sides and back. Despite the protests of Mrs Smith, Basil had not found time to visit a hairdresser in weeks and was secretly rather pleased with the results. A little more hair round the sides and back comforted him for what was disappearing on top. He felt it gave him a slightly bohemian appearance. What struck Greg Roberts was that, together with his current suntan, it gave Basil a distinctly Indian appearance. Jam a cap down firmly on his head and who could tell the difference?

Would the Rockcliffe team realise? Could they get away with it? How would they get away with it? These were the questions which reverberated around the changing-room. Rashid Ali's name would need to be on the team sheet. The real Rashid Ali would bat, but Basil Smith, 'the Nawab of Wandsworth', as he was instantly named, would field. It would make life easier if Rockcliffe batted first, because then Basil could be consigned to the relative anonymity of the deep field. His bowling would have to be sacrificed as that might bring him under too close scrutiny. Rashid Ali would hopefully have done all he had to do before he was needed to bat. The plan had holes in it, but no other way could be found of engaging Rashid Ali's batting prowess. However, as events proved, this subterfuge alone would be insufficient to tilt the advantage to the Outcasts.

Terry Lilgate appeared at the entrance to the Outcasts' changing-room in a coat the whiteness of which was akin to a one-day international ball which had been used for thirty overs. It was the Outcasts' first intimation that the school's coach was also to be their umpire. In the short period he had spent away from their company since he had welcomed them, it was clear that he had made time to procure additional refreshment. He leant against the door of the changing-room as he announced that it was time to toss.

Ordinarily the conduct of the toss is one of the more pleasant and undemanding features of the game of cricket. It did not seem so to Ray Burrill. Not being used to the captaincy role he had imagined that in the absence of television cameras and international cricket luminaries, the only people present at the ceremony would be himself and the opposing captain. He was in fact confronted by a semi-circle made up of the whole of the Rockcliffe team who wore, frankly, menacing looks and some extremely smart shell suits. From a logo on the front which featured a figure in a balaclava, it seemed that the kit was sponsored, but it was not a logo which Ray Burrill instantly recognised. As he took in the appearance of the Rockcliffe School XI, he found himself wondering who on earth would be prepared to sponsor such a repellent crowd of youngsters unless it was an armaments' manufacturer.

The Rockcliffe captain detached himself from the crowd with the words 'Tom Barnes' and a hand outstretched. Ray Burrill took it in good faith and wondered seconds later whether that had been wholly necessary. Ray regarded himself as physically fit, but was unprepared for the ferocity of the school captain's grip. He hoped his bowling hand would recover. Tom Barnes towered a good four inches above him and uttered his next words in the clear expectation of receiving a negative answer. 'Got a coin? No, well I've got my lucky crown piece.' But Ray did have a coin with him. That was one of the administrative details which he had covered in his match preparation.

Disdainfully Tom Barnes took the proffered ten pence coin, spun it into the air and invited Ray to call. 'Heads,' he said and heads it looked as though it might have been until a large boot came down upon it. The large boot belonged to Rockcliffe's opening bowler, Jack Dolland. He smartly bent down, retrieved the coin and announced, 'Tails.' So tails it was. Same difference, thought Ray Burrill, as Tom Barnes said that Rockcliffe would bat. He also thought that it had been quite unnecessary on the part of the rest of the Rockcliffe team to cheer the decision.

Ray Burrill had a moment to take in his team's opponents. They were mostly big lads, several of them with metal protrusions and adornments. Clearly the school had a liberal attitude towards the appearance of its pupils. Some of the haircuts could fairly be described as aggressive and only just failed to reflect all colours of the rainbow. It occurred to Ray Burrill to ask whether they were playing a limited overs match. Tom Barnes quickly dismissed any such idea. 'We'll bat till tea,' he said, winking at the other members of his team who sniggered. 'We'll see if we can give you a total to chase.' More sniggers. At which point they went their separate ways.

FIRST INNINGS

As he prepared to lead the Outcasts on to the field, Ray Burrill observed the umpires on their way to the middle. He remained surprised that Syd Breakwell's companion was Terry Lilgate, who when last seen had not appeared to be in full control of his faculties. As he stared at their retreating backs, Ray began to wonder whether they shared the same destination. Syd Breakwell's path was straight enough, but Terry Lilgate appeared to have difficulty staying by his side. His route to the pitch was oddly circuitous. In the end he arrived at the same place as Syd Breakwell, having taken twice as long to get there. And that was then the trouble. He seemed to want to take up station at the end which Syd had innocently chosen. The latter eventually shrugged his shoulders and walked to the other end, known for years as the brewery end, but now presumably to be rechristened.

There was no indication to Ray Burrill as to the end from which the first over was to be bowled. Both umpires were standing over the stumps at their respective ends with neither showing any disposition to move to square leg. Another shrug of the shoulders and Syd Breakwell finally conceded. The opening batsmen for the school were Tom Barnes, their captain, and Douglas Hamerskill. Both looked as though they meant business. Their whites were very white, very clean and pressed. Their kit looked new and expensive. They bristled with pugnacious professionalism. Helmets, thought Ray, were a touch too far in light of the bowling resources at his disposal. It had every appearance of being a hard day. He could not believe his luck when, with the game barely started, Rockcliffe's score stood at 0–2.

Too late Tom Barnes and Philip Bond arrived at the same conclusion as Ray Burrill that Terry Lilgate and his faculties had by this time only a loose connection. The more culpable was Philip Bond because he had had slightly longer to think about it. Tom Barnes asked for a middle stump guard. He perhaps should have been alerted by the alacrity with which the umpire confirmed his first inquiry. Ray Burrill had asked Charlie Colson to open the bowling for the Outcasts from the school hall end. Charlie Colson did not usually have the privilege of opening the bowling. Even first change would amount to promotion. The field he set in consultation with his captain reflected this estimation. It was essentially defensive with fielders distributed as opposed to being strategically placed.

So far as the Outcasts were concerned this was pre-season. For Charlie Colson it was a stage prior to that. He had not turned an arm (as opposed to a leg) over in months. He had had a game of squash in February from which his muscles had barely stopped aching in March. The visit of some long-lost friends from overseas a week ago had led to a succession of prodigious drinking bouts in which the hangover potential of real ale as opposed to lager had been put very deliberately to the test. Charlie was in no doubt that he had won, but it had been a phyrric victory. The recovery of even minimal physical prowess had been put off sine die. But a day and a contest had now presented themselves. Charlie was not feeling up to it. But an Outcast had to go through the motions.

And it was no more than through the motions he was going when Charlie ran in to bowl the first ball of the match. The ball he delivered was not very fast and not very tricky. He did not let go a no-ball; nor did he bowl a wide. It was straight and ordinary, a ball of no particular distinction. Bowled in the nets to a set of stumps it would have hit middle and this is precisely what it did at Rockcliffe. Tom Barnes's bat came down in a perfectly respectable arc with classic style, but just an inch adrift of the trajectory of the ball. He looked at the mess of his wicket with disbelief and took himself off in an ugly, blaspheming mood which might (or then again might not) have put him in trouble with an international match referee had one been officiating.

Whether at that stage Tom Barnes was too angry or too uncomprehending was not clear, but there was no meaningful exchange of confidences between him and the incoming batsman, Philip Bond. It is doubtful in any case whether instruction would have been accepted. Bond the blond, so known for his predilection for the peroxide bottle, had a high regard for his cricket skills. His self-esteem was heightened for a number of reasons. Undoubtedly successive bottles of peroxide had enhanced his natural good looks and augmented his circle of female admirers. He knew he was talented in all sports and radiated confidence. He possessed the easy charm of someone to whom all gifts effortlessly came, not least if they relied on the wealth of his doting parents.

Charlie Colson, surrounded by his applauding team-mates, was torn between saying it had just been a practice ball or the diabolical one which went on straight. Remembering that too many of his supposed in-swingers went on straight and that his loosener had pitched in a straight line from wicket to wicket, unlike many of his usual deliveries, Charlie contented himself with an enigmatic smile. This soon gave way to a frown as he realised from his team's reaction that he had raised expectations about his next ball. He need not have worried.

Like his predecessor, Philip Bond had chosen a middle-stump guard. What he had been given in the clouded judgment of Umpire Lilgate was not the same as that received by Tom Barnes, but nor, alas, was it middle stump. It could not be expected that Charlie Colson so early in the match and so early in the season would bowl two straight balls in succession. The expectation was fulfilled and Charlie's second ball drifted towards leg stump. As it turned out there was nothing to impede the ball's progress and it reached its destination neatly dislodging the bail. Too late the batsman had sensed danger. Looking to glide the ball to the boundary behind square, he had straightened himself and tried to execute the stroke. All he achieved was his own execution. He had positioned himself with the umpire's aid too far towards the off side. The ball passed nearer his backside than his blade and the Outcasts had their second wicket.

Bond the blond was the second Rockcliffe batsman to drag himself away from the wicket in disbelief. His disbelief was shared by the Outcasts. Charlie Colson, they knew, was a useful second or third change, but no-one classified him as a strike bowler. It had to be a record, they reckoned, for one of their number to take two wickets in two balls at the start of an innings. Charlie himself was nonplussed and unsure how to play it as he was once again besieged. Hat-trick ball was coming up. He began to realise that more was expected of him. Ray Burrill was encouraging him to have an attacking field. For all that there was pleasure in the moment, Charlie Colson could not quite make himself believe that the best was yet to come.

William Briggs was no fool. His father was Professor of English Social Studies at a Far Eastern University and his mother, a first-class honours graduate from Oxford, wrote occasional literary treatises under her own name, and frequent racy detective novels under the pseudonym, Cyril Carpenter. Neither of them had visited the United Kingdom in several years and the placing of their son in Rockcliffe School owed everything to the recommendation of a friend, who had been best man at their wedding. He was also a close friend of the headmaster of Rockcliffe School and there was an understanding between them regarding the introduction of new pupils.

William Briggs would have done creditably at any of England's finest schools. At Rockcliffe he was an intellectual giant. Having spent most of his life abroad, William, or Billy as he had quickly become known, assumed Rockcliffe to be typical of the English boarding school and had settled down to make the best of it. In a school of low scholastic attainment his obvious intelligence might have marked him down for mockery, but the fact that he quickly showed himself to be a natural games player enabled him to fit in quite amicably with his fellow pupils. The acquisition of a gold ring in his left ear had sealed their approval. Billy had proved to be quite a kid.

Spectators would have assumed that the incoming batsman's resort to the bowler's end was to consult his partner. Not so. William Briggs did no more than wink at Douglas Hamerskill and concentrated his attention instead on Terry Lilgate. His assessment did not take long before he was off to take up position at the striker's end. He took his own guard, ignoring the umpire who, for good measure, appeared to be ignoring him. William Briggs studied the field placings which had now assumed a more hostile pattern. Anticipation was high among the Outcasts as the hat-trick ball was delivered.

Anticipation was also high in the bursar's office where two men met. They were the bursar and his accountant or, to be more precise, his turf accountant. The bursar's knowledge of horses and racing had been derived from his sister who had been a successful trainer up to the point of being trampled to death in the winner's enclosure by her much fancied favourite, Cilla the Chilla. Apart from mourning his sister's passing, the bursar mourned the abrupt end to the flow of information which had come his way from her stables. Whether by this time he was possessed of a deep love of racing or in the grip of a gambling bug, he had maintained his investments. The returns at first diminished and later disappeared. Not even stealing a couple of hours each morning from his attention to the school's accounts to read the racing press made any difference. Sadly he was driven into stealing more than time. Confronted eventually by crisis he had summoned his bookmaker with the idea of persuading him to accept a rescheduling of his debts. Sammy (the Satchel) Smith had kept the appointment in the belief that he would at last be getting some cash. It would be hard to say who would be the more disappointed.

It was equally hard to say whether Charlie Colson or the rest of the fielding side was the more disappointed as the first over unravelled as unravel it surely did, albeit slowly and painfully. To do justice to the hat-trick ball, it was straight and of good length. William Briggs was better placed than his predecessors to pick its line and he played it patiently back to the bowler. If Charlie was regretful that he had not been able to produce a wicket-taking ball, the feeling quickly passed, for there was much more to worry about. Perhaps he tried too hard with the fourth ball, because he slammed it in far too short. William Briggs could spot a gift and pounced. The ball cleared the white boundary line at deep mid-wicket with feet to spare. There was no signal from the umpire apart from a gentle swaying. Syd Breakwell at square leg looked disapproving. The scorers needed no clarification.

Four balls and sixteen runs later no-one could be in any doubt that a legitimate over had been completed, except that is for the umpire who had not yet brought it formally to a finish. Informally, however, a halt came. Responding at last to the realisation that boundaries needed action by the umpire, Terry Lilgate greeted

William Briggs's most recent shot with a waving of the arm so vigorous that he lost his balance and fell forward completely demolishing the stumps. The Outcasts stood around showing concern. They were pushed aside by two men advancing from the pavilion, who, without any thought for a stretcher, dragged Terry Lilgate from the scene by his legs. It was not a first aid technique from the manual of St John Ambulance. With Terry Lilgate's departure, the first over came to an end. It had yielded twenty-two runs and two wickets.

Syd Breakwell's sense of what was proper had been offended by proceedings so far. It was amid much tut-tutting that he took up position over the stumps at the brewery end. Once he took in what he could see of the features of the batsman facing him at the crease, the tut-tutting might have continued, but he suppressed it. The earrings he could not see, but the ring through each eyebrow he could. He inwardly winced and then he stared. There was something familiar about that face. If the years could be rolled back, he was sure he had seen those features staring at him defiantly from the dock. Douglas Hamerskill (born Hamer) stared up the pitch and brusquely asked for his guard. Having obliged with his usual flourish, Syd Breakwell continued to gaze thoughtfully at the batsman, who seemed irritated by the attention. Recognising that it was foolish to provoke umpires, he kept to himself the vulgar comment which came too easily to his mind.

One of the two men who had pulled Terry Lilgate off the field of play had also pulled the white coat from him. Thus attired, he returned to the middle to take over as umpire. From the Outcasts' point-of-view, his replacement of Terry Lilgate could not be counted as a gain. Barry Papwell, the physical training instructor at

Rockcliffe School, was an utterly partisan character who brought to the spirit of cricket the qualities which Radovan Karadzic contributed to multi-ethnicity.

'Left arm over,' announced Syd Breakwell, still with an appraising eye on the batsman. This indicated that the Outcasts' other opening bowler was Nigel Redman. In his relatively short career with the Outcasts, Ray Burrill had never actually played in the same side as Nigel Redman and so he did not know what to expect. It even came as news to him that Nigel was a left-arm bowler and he was caught in the middle of setting a field which presumed otherwise. He made some subtle adjustments to cover for his error before discovering that Douglas Hamerskill was a left-hander and the placement had to be wholly revised. Ray Burrill felt embarrassed. It was a feeling which would take a long time to go away.

It had been such a long time since Nigel Redman had last bowled for the Outcasts that Ray Burrill was not the only one unsure what to expect. The twins' mother's wavering hold on good health limited their appearances for the Outcasts. When it came to a choice between the two of them, Tom's leg-spin usually got the vote. Nigel would be at best sixth choice as an opening bowler. Ray Burrill did not have to wait long to discover why, but at first appearances were deceptive.

Douglas Hamerskill, defiant as he felt, was nevertheless slightly unnerved by the umpire's attention. The guilt complex of someone who instinctively disliked authority of any kind jostled with his basic technique of batting and led him to play out a very ordinary over with three immaculate defensive strokes to the balls he had to play. Syd Breakwell walked to square leg on completion of the game's first six-ball over. Charlie Colson found himself in consultation with his captain before bowling his next over. The exact fruits of the conversation were hard to assess.

'Things seem to be settling down.' This was Simon Crossley's opening gambit with his fellow scorer, an acne-ridden adolescent whose thoughts were tied up, not in cricket, but in the lusts and imaginings to which adolescents were prone. This was quickly confirmed by his response. The words, 'I don't give a f.....g rap for this poxy game,' left little room for ambiguity. It seemed that Gary

Pocke was not on duty as an act of selfless devotion to cricket. That was a pity, thought Simon, and not just because good company would have enhanced his own day. It took the merest sideways glance to see that the school's scorebook would not be enhanced by the scribblings of Gary Pocke. A double pity, because Rockcliffe boasted an excellent mobile scoreboard inside which the scorers sat. It was not always, Simon reckoned, that he was rewarded with such superior facilities. Enclosed maybe, but extremely functional. And then Gary Pocke removed his trainers.

Simon Crossley's attention was wrenched from Gary Pocke's feet by the cry of 'Scorer!' William Briggs had resumed his assault on Charlie Colson's bowling, punching the second ball, which was short, one bounce over the mid-wicket boundary. Another followed before the end of the over. Impatience was building up in Douglas Hamerskill as he still had no run to his name whilst his partner had reached thirty. Putting aside other thoughts, he resolved that Nigel Redman's bowling would go for plenty. He was not expecting the obstacles which appeared in his path. Buoyed by a maiden over, Nigel Redman produced a beauty for the first ball of his second over. It was a devastating yorker which deserved more than it got. Douglas Hamerskill was hit on a tender part of his right foot from where it rebounded past first slip, whose appeal was louder than that of his brother the bowler. Umpire Breakwell's booming 'not out' was even louder (with Syd Breakwell, volume was often in inverse proportion to certainty). This cacophony of shouts was perhaps why William Briggs had difficulty making himself heard. Looking up from a session of foot-rubbing, Douglas Hamerskill was horrified to see his partner charging towards him. With an obscenity frozen on his lips, he belatedly set off. Despite the handicap of his aching foot, he made his ground. So enthused had he been by his appeal that Tom Redman was late in attempting to retrieve the ball, and his eventual throw was awry. Having narrowly escaped being run out by his partner, Douglas Hamerskill was obliged to watch in frustration as William Briggs dealt with the remainder of Nigel Redman's over on its merits, his personal score advancing by twelve.

A sore and disgruntled Douglas Hamerskill turned his attention to Charlie Colson, sure that he could equal his partner's stroke-making. The bowler, fired up by anxious words from his captain, was now trying to inject some energy into his bowling The opening ball of his third over was quick, too quick for Douglas Hamerskill and too quick for Kevin Newton behind the stumps. Four byes resulted. The next ball had slightly less pace, but there was a hint of swing. The batsman, deeply committed to aggression, played a loose shot and was lucky not to nick the ball to first slip where Tom Redman might (or might not) have caught it. Douglas Hamerskill decided that the delivery (not his stroke) was a flash in the pan and was not deterred. Umpire Papwell was more cautious. 'No-ball,' he yelled as Charlie Colson came past him again.

Both bowler and batsman were taken aback. Douglas Hamerskill checked his stroke and pushed the ball back up the pitch. Charlie Colson, with an entirely justifiable glare at the umpire, repaced his run-up and came in once more. The ball was short and marginally down the leg side. The batsman had scarcely moved into position to mow it to the square leg boundary when the cry 'wide ball' reached him. The ball was distinctly hittable, but Douglas Hamerskill was distinctly distracted and he almost fell over with the momentum of his vain waft at it. Not now sure what to expect from the umpire (he would have a discreet word when opportunity arose), Douglas Hamerskill missed out on a straight full toss. He thought he saw a grin on the face of William Briggs. Aggression gave way to rage.

The next four shots attempted by Douglas Hamerskill would not have been admired by his coach had he witnessed them. Fortunately for Douglas, his coach lay comatose on the pavilion floor and was spared the spectacle. The wilder Douglas's blows became, the better Charlie Colson bowled. The psychological pendulum swung from batsman to bowler. Douglas Hamerskill was left smarting, but his wicket remained intact and he had time to recover his composure. It was a pity he did not make good use of it.

Charlie Colson may have felt better in his mind, but his body was protesting after another extended over. His head throbbed and his limbs ached. He retreated slowly and vaguely in the direction of third man doubting whether the span of Nigel Redman's next over would be sufficient to put him in shape to bowl another over himself. Third man proved to be no recovery area. Nigel Redman commendably found a consistent line on and just outside off stump. His length was less consistent. William Briggs angled his bat and nudged the first ball wide of slip. It travelled quickly in Charlie

Colson's direction. The batsman stayed in his ground before realising that Charlie was moving rather more slowly towards the ball. He could have had runs. Presented with the opportunity twice more during the over, William Briggs did not make the same mistake. Charlie Colson was sent first in one direction and then the other. Off the last ball of the over he again targeted third man, dabbing the ball towards Charlie for a gentle single. It was run by Douglas Hamerskill with some reluctance.

It was with similar reluctance that Charlie Colson presented himself at the wicket, hoping not to bowl the next over. He found Ray Burrill unsympathetic. 'Need at least one more over, Charlie,' Ray breezily announced. 'Liked the last one.' He might not like the next one, Charlie Colson thought as his protestations of modesty and lack of capacity fell on deaf ears. At least, he told himself, he would have to slow things down if he was to get through another over. His first ball fortuitously pitching in line, took William Briggs by surprise and almost took his wicket. He played too soon and the ball lobbed back over the bowler's head. A fitter man than Charlie Colson would surely have stretched and caught it, but Charlie by now was just relieved not to have conceded a run. For the rest of the over he was not so fortunate. Three balls fell woefully short and were cut or pulled by William Briggs with relish. The first of these boundaries brought him his fifty which was greeted with enthusiasm from those gathered round the ground, but with distinct half-heartedness from his partner. Douglas Hamerskill's lack of appreciation was intensified when William Briggs called him for a sharp single off the last ball of the over.

If Ray Burrill, worried by a scoring rate already in excess of nine an over, felt he needed to be in more control of the situation, a similar thought was going through the mind of the headmaster of Rockcliffe School. Herbert Banston had barely finished congratulating himself on overcoming one crisis when a second suddenly materialised. The headmaster resented regulations in general and school inspections in particular. In his view, the paying public was the best judge of whether his school was any good. And the public continued to pay. It was a major irritant therefore that the public had to be second-guessed from time to time by independent school inspectors. These people with their professional eye were bound to see things which Herbert Banston had successfully concealed from parents and potential parents. It had been an enormous stroke of luck to be informed that the inspection team would be headed by Mr Frederick Fulstock. 'Fruity Fulstock,' the headmaster had yelled in a voice of near triumph to his secretary.

They went back a long way. At university they had come together with the foundation of Studentaid, an organisation which sounded faintly charitable and worthy, but which had a distinctly different way of satisfying student needs. This wholly uncharitable and unworthy enterprise had netted Bertie Banston and Fruity Fulstock a modest profit and an undying mutual obligation. Although their individual careers had separated, albeit in a common profession, they had found various ways of obliging each other in subsequent years, not always without pecuniary advantage. By now each knew sufficient about the other to make the stakes very high. A clandestine pre-inspection meeting between them had arranged what the inspection team would see and it was duly arranged. Rockcliffe had received a glowing report.

That was why Herbert Banston gazed with resentment at the letter which lay on the blotter of his desk. An inspection into educational standards, however unwelcome, was one thing, but prying by Social Services was a monstrous intrusion. Picking up the County Council letter as if it was an explosive device, he noted again the name of the Director of Social Services who had signed it. Aneurin Singh. (The director's parents had greatly admired a prominent member of Mr Attlee's Government.) Complaining that inadequate attention had been given to his previous letters (they had been binned), Mr Singh announced that there would now be a unilateral inspection. The headmaster reflected grimly that County Councillor Percy Harport had been put on the board of governors to ward off this kind of thing. As he picked up the telephone, he glanced out from his first-floor office window. It was at this moment that Rashid Ali chose to walk furtively past. The telephone fell abruptly from Herbert Banston's suddenly enfeebled hands.

The telephone's experience was being shared on the field of play by the match ball. Nigel Redman was beginning to turn in a worthy performance. His next over was a testing examination of William

Briggs's technique. Douglas Hamerskill, in uncomradely spirit, found himself enjoying his partner's discomfiture. Just when he saw his opportunity beckoning in the next over, Nigel Redman's last ball was dropped short and swung hard and high by William Briggs in the direction of deep fine leg. Had this been a deliberate trap it is doubtful whether either bowler or captain would have had Basil Smith fielding in that area. He was in the deep because of the overriding need to keep him as inconspicuous as possible. Basil believed he was further adding to the illusion that he was Rashid Ali by donning a pair of sunglasses. These were not the light-enhancing sunglasses sported by first-class cricketers, but an old pair he had fished out of a drawer before leaving home. As he searched skywards for the ball, he realised that they enhanced nothing. What should have been a straightforward catch, Basil Smith failed by several feet to take. The batsmen ran three, the third by Douglas Hamerskill with marked lack of enthusiasm.

Charlie Colson did not have to plead to be relieved at the school hall end. His bowling in his last over had done the talking. In any case, Ray Burrill was of a mind to try his own particular mixture of off-cutters and off-breaks. Charlie Colson wanted to leave the field for half an hour for a kip, but there was no sign of a twelfth man, or even Stewart Thorogood. He was reduced to manoeuvring himself into a quiet corner where he hoped the ball would not find him too often. Ray Burrill took account of his needs whilst applying rather more science to setting the field for his own bowling than he had done for either Charlie or Nigel Redman. In asking Kevin Newton to stand up to the wicket, Ray abandoned science in favour of a huge gamble.

Since last season the greatest single contribution which Kevin Newton had made to his wicket-keeping was to have his hair cut. His (genuinely) fair hair had been worn long. It had cascaded around his head and, most observers would have said, over his eyes. Kevin had always denied that his sight was in any way impeded. The byes total was only one strand of evidence which persuaded his team-mates otherwise. Kevin was deputy to Rashid Ali as the Outcasts' wicket-keeper by a very wide margin indeed. Kevin's decision to cut (more accurately crop) his hair was in no way a concession to the team view. During the winter he had seen a film in which one of the lesser actors had borne, he thought, a striking resemblance to himself. In scenes taken on location in sun-drenched Hawaii, the actor with the short, blond hair had looked good. It was a relatively harmless piece of vanity which had therefore propelled Kevin to his hairdresser for what the latter insisted was a restyle, not a cut (£25 as opposed to £10).

Out of a total score of seventy, the presence of only four byes was ample confirmation to the rest of the side that Kevin's new hair style/cut was favouring the Outcasts as much as himself. Standing up to the brisk pace of Ray Burrill risked the theory. However, there were surprises all round. William Briggs barely laid bat on ball during Ray Burrill's first over. Kevin Newton succeeded in laying glove on all the deliveries which went past the bat. Douglas Hamerskill gaped as his partner's progress seemed to be interrupted. After the recent passage of play, it came almost as a shock to him that he was to have the opportunity of facing again.

At the start of the tenth over, Nigel Redman maintained his acquaintance with line and length. This did not bother Douglas Hamerskill who reckoned he needed to get used to the feel of bat on ball. The line of Nigel's third ball wavered towards leg stump and Douglas Hamerskill saw his chance. He aimed to clip it firmly towards mid-wicket. His eagerness betrayed him. Instead of a clean hit, he nicked it on to his pad. Instead of speeding to the boundary square or just behind square of the wicket, the ball rolled unconvincingly towards fine leg. 'One,' shouted William Briggs and they ran. Douglas Hamerskill overcame his disappointment with the thought that he was at last off the mark. The thought was short-lived. As he came level with Umpire Breakwell he found him pirouetting on one leg, slapping his raised knee and signalling a leg-bye. Douglas was outraged. He took off his helmet, the better to make his protest. Syd Breakwell easily dismissed his complaint ('Look in the scorebook afterwards, young man, I fancy you'll see it was a leg-bye'), but he could not so easily dismiss the face. He knew now where he had seen it before. In the meantime Nigel Redman recovered his line and conceded no more than a single – off the last ball of the over – allowing William Briggs to retain strike.

Len Hamer, known to his associates and the Metropolitan Police alike as the Hammer, was the face Syd Breakwell had just seen. Rockcliffe's opening batsman had to be his son. The likeness was uncanny. If so, that was very interesting. Syd Breakwell began to rack his brains. Where was the Hammer? Inside or on the loose? Whatever, there was certainly money coming from somewhere to finance the son's education. Syd Breakwell's usually sunny brow furrowed.

First match of the season or not, Ray Burrill was quite pleased with how he felt. The six sessions he had spent in the indoor cricket school had paid off. True, he had been bowling to schoolchildren and primary schoolchildren at that (something he was not anxious to mention), but it had helped him to loosen up and get his action into some sort of shape. The over he bowled to William Briggs was a model of its kind. He achieved bounce and some turn. When he threw in his arm ball it completely baffled the batsman and missed the off stump by the veritable lick of varnish. It missed the wicket-keeper's gloves by a wider margin, proving that Kevin Newton's performance was not wholly transformed. Four byes accrued.

One more over, Ray Burrill signalled to Nigel Redman, believing that it might now be worth trying spin at both ends. This time, Douglas Hamerskill was determined to tuck into Nigel Redman, but it proved to be his partner's appetite which was satisfied. With a rest beckoning, Nigel Redman decided to put extra effort into his last over. The result was a first ball which was appreciably faster than anything he had previously bowled. Douglas Hamerskill was unprepared and swished in vain. The ball cannoned off his pads and appeared to be making good progress to the boundary. Douglas Hamerskill was content that it should get there. He would be prepared for Nigel Redman's next delivery. With this thought in his mind, he took his eye off the ball. His partner was watching more intently and calculated that Greg Roberts would intercept it. He made a late decision to run with a roar at his partner. Douglas Hamerskill was too taken aback to protest and once again found himself robbed of the action. Salt was rubbed into the wound when Nigel Redman, striving for pace, over-pitched and was twice driven sweetly either side of the wicket. On the whole he was relieved to take his sweater.

At the start of the thirteenth over, both bowler and batsman fancied their chances. Ray Burrill thought that the runless, luckless left-hander was ripe for the taking and Douglas Hamerskill thought much the same about the bowler. After the first two deliveries, the batsman understood why his prolific partner had treated this bowler with a degree of respect. He was accurate and could vary his pace well. Douglas Hamerskill remembered the arm ball which had nearly removed William Briggs. He was prepared for it. What he was not prepared for was a beautifully disguised slower ball (which Ray Burrill talked about for weeks afterwards whilst being unable to reproduce it). Douglas Hamerskill thought he was going to hit it high over the school hall. Forward he came, lunging. Hitting over the ball and toppling over, the batsman was well out of his ground when the ball reached Kevin Newton behind the stumps, who was also not prepared for it. He nevertheless broke the stumps with a triumphant cry whilst surreptitiously retrieving the ball from its resting place behind the flap of his pad. Had Kevin Newton's kit extended to the modern, streamlined keepers' pads, the uncertainty might not have arisen. The ball would have fallen to ground for all to see. The batsman had been well and truly beaten and Kevin Newton persuaded himself that he had been in possession of the ball albeit not in the strict sense that the laws of cricket required. An umpire concentrating on the situation would have been able to make the right distinction. However, Syd Breakwell's mind was more on the father and his murky past than the son and his fruitless present. All he saw was a batsman clearly out of his ground, and a shattered wicket. He also saw a fielding side in enthusiastic celebration, believing that the ball had travelled cleanly into the glove which now held it aloft. 'That's out, I'm afraid, young man,' came the verdict.

An incredulous Douglas Hamerskill had to go. His return to the pavilion took him past Syd Breakwell, who had chosen to stand at point. Barely coming to terms with his dismissal, he was in an ugly mood which would have been ten times uglier had he known the truth. He unwisely muttered as he passed Syd Breakwell. His anger gave way to a different emotion when the umpire rebuked him with the words 'Have a care, young man, I know about your dad.' From what he could see of the reaction on the face beneath the helmet, Syd Breakwell knew he had not been wrong about his man even if he had been wrong about his removal. He had to get to a telephone.

There was then a fortuitous pause. Billy the Kid signalled to the pavilion that he would like a drink. There was also no immediate sign of an incoming batsman. There was equally no sign of the Outcasts' official twelfth man. Stewart Thorogood felt obliged to step into the breach and take out some drinks even though he did not think he was dressed for the part. In white shellsuit pants and a cream T-shirt bearing an uncomplimentary slogan about Australian cricket, which he would not have been advised to wear in the southern hemisphere, Stewart, complete with two days' growth, looked more the part of a modern cricketer than he was prepared to acknowledge.

Mentioning to his fellow umpire and to Ray Burrill that he must make a call, Syd Breakwell excused himself. Ray Burrill thought he meant 'pay a call' and found himself wondering whether Syd had reached the age when he was being affected by bladder problems. With dark humour, Ray reckoned this might have rather a drastic effect on his umpiring career, but turned his mind back to the job in hand. He told David Pelham to loosen up and be ready to bowl the next over from the brewery end. In anticipation they discussed field placements. Discussion turned out to be quite extended. Drink bottles and their bearers had gone, but neither a batsman nor an umpire had appeared.

It had taken Syd Breakwell, with the use of the Crossleys' mobile phone, longer than he had thought to track down his one-time junior and now Superintendent, Derek Byfleet. He was not at Divisional Headquarters, nor at home. It was from his wife rather than his office that he learnt that the superintendent was out on an urgent case. She was able to give him a mobile number which was answered. Syd Breakwell put across his message and his suspicions as briefly as he could and was duly thanked. There had not been time for the usual pleasantries between old colleagues, but as he walked back on to the field, Syd was doing his best to equate the background noise he had heard with urgent police work. He was sure he had heard the sound of bat on ball. Derek Byfleet was an avid cricket lover and there was a big match taking place at Lord's.

There was not yet any renewed sound of bat on ball at Rockcliffe. The game was back up to establishment in the umpiring department, but lacking the necessary second batsman. Cooperbatch T Gulfstrode, the Yank, had disappeared. The Rockcliffe captain, Tom Barnes, belatedly recognised the absence and was forced to reorganise his batting order. He sent in Wayne

Tibbins with the instruction to 'Give 'em hell.' He set himself the task of a wider search for Cooperbatch T Gulfstrode and looked forward to the pleasure of giving him some hell as well. It was a pleasure perforce deferred.

Wayne Tibbins was well equipped to give bowlers hell. He was a large seventeen year-old from Birmingham to which city his grandparents had migrated from Jamaica. He weighed a stone for every year of his life, but it was flatteringly distributed. He looked an athlete. Foreswearing a helmet, he strode to the wicket with gold necklace and diamond ear studs which flashed in the sun. His bat would soon be flashing with them. He had watched from the pavilion with impatience mounting in step with Douglas Hamerskill's frustration. He was more than ready for action.

Ray Burrill had so far bowled fifteen balls without conceding a run. He was enjoying figures of one for nought. His enjoyment was to be short-lived. To get the pace of the wicket Wayne Tibbins played the first ball with studious defence. To the second he opened his massive shoulders. It was the arm ball. It went like a rocket between wicket-keeper and first slip for four. Wayne Tibbins chided himself and took careful guard. Ray's next ball was short of a length – too short. It was pulled hard and high clearing the boundary at deep mid-wicket. Wayne Tibbins had announced himself.

Simon Crossley in the mobile scorebox had tried to keep his gaze resolutely on the cricket, not just because a competent scorer had to concentrate at all times on what was happening in the middle, but also to keep his attention off Gary Pocke's feet. When his trainers had been removed, Simon had at first imagined Gary was wearing socks. He was wrong, but his mistake had been understandable. The feet were almost indistinguishable in colour from the trainers which had previously covered them. After a while their odour began to make its existence felt. Simon found himself having to lean forward every few minutes to get a gulp of fresh air from outside. He would have preferred to move outside altogether, but knew he could not rely on Gary Pocke to operate the board.

After the unpromising start, conversation between the scorers had been minimal. Simon had tried several times to break the ice, but had been rewarded with little more than grunts. Not interested in doing the job in any case, it seemed that Gary Pocke could see no point in embellishing the task with polite conversation. He split his time between the scorebook and a pile of lurid comics. The split was far from even. And then Gary had suddenly spoken. 'Got a fag, mate?' Simon's negative response earned him a scowl and a half-suppressed curse. Simon was truly sorry. He was a non-smoker, but at that moment and in those circumstances, a cabin full of cigarette smoke would have had positively therapeutic qualities. It was a relief when Stewart Thorogood dropped by for a chat.

To Ray Burrill's disappointment, David Pelham bowled an indifferent first over which did nothing to quell the school side's scoring rate. David had obviously not spent any of the previous weeks bowling, even at toddlers. He was rusty and was lucky not to concede more than nine runs, all of them to William Briggs. The school had a hundred on the board with only fourteen overs gone. After the initial mauling by Wayne Tibbins, Ray Burrill felt restored in confidence bowling to William Briggs. This was borne out as the over progressed. The bowler teased the batsman – and the 'keeper too – with a clever mixture of flight and pace. After four balls, no more than two byes had been added to the total. William Briggs now became infected with the impatience bug which had blighted Douglas Hamerskill. Instead of his confidence being bolstered by the plight of his partner at the other end, he began to see himself as inferior to the new arrival. It must have been this sudden onset of doubt which influenced the next shot he played. To a delivery he judged to be going down the leg side, he launched an ugly smear. The ball straightened on him, took a leading edge and ascended vertically.

Ray Burrill knew it should be left to the wicket-keeper, but he hesitated. The sight of Kevin Newton running forward even without flopping hair unnerved him. With the ball still on high, the batsmen were about their business. One run was completed. As Wayne Tibbins turned and commenced the second, Ray finally made up his mind. 'Mine,' he yelled. It was not the only sound which escaped him, for in the next second he was shoulder-barged (his version) by Wayne ('he stepped into my path') Tibbins. Ray was spun round. The ball struck his right shoulder a painful blow and ricocheted into a gloved hand shoved out by Kevin Newton whose momentum had carried him alongside his captain. Whatever the recriminations, a wicket had fallen.

Since his own dismissal, Tom Barnes, the Rockcliffe skipper, had immersed himself in the more general responsibilities associated with the job. This made him all the more cross that he had not noticed the disappearance of Cooperbatch T Gulfstrode. He had quite definitely been with the rest of the team when the match began. He had been in his whites and Tom was willing to swear that he had seen him with his pads on. So where on earth had he gone? Inquiries initiated by the captain had been made in all the likely places around the school, but there were no sightings to report. It did not occur to him that the young boy might have come to harm. He could only think of the harm the Yank would come to when he clapped eyes on him again.

Next to the crease was Angus Flabert, the Rockcliffe wicket-keeper. He was neat and diminutive in appearance, but his nearly shaven head, an eagle tattoo on his neck and gold rings dangling from his ears, on which it would have been possible to hang curtains, contributed to an air of menace. Nicknamed Gorgeous Gus, he was Terry Lilgate's favourite – 'a right little belter'. True to type he belted the first ball he received straight past the bowler for two. Reacting to his painful shoulder, Ray Burrill found it hard to recapture his rhythm.

Rustiness had not deserted David Pelham. His second over was not one of which he was proud. He did occasionally stray towards an off-stump line, but his stock ball had an attachment to the leg-side and consequently an attachment to the middle of Wayne Tibbins's bat. Two handsome on-drives, a pull over deep long-on and a leg glide which the Nawab of Wandsworth just got to progressed the school's score to 124. It was an alarming scoring rate and Ray Burrill's troubles did not end there. His shoulder was still very sore and he found he could not turn his arm over without acute discomfort. With Basil Smith sidelined on grounds of subterfuge, the only one of his regular bowlers so far untried was Tom Redman, but Ray Burrill did not think that this was quite the right moment for leg spin or at least Tom Redman's standard of leg spin.

Greg Roberts was surprised to be summoned. It was either an inspired piece of captaincy or pure lunacy. Greg Roberts was such an occasional bowler for the Outcasts that this was another whom Ray Burrill had not actually seen bowl. Greg was asked if he could try to keep an end tight for a couple of overs. Privately Greg doubted it, but he was always willing to have a go when the rare opportunity came up. A very defensive field was set and to some extent his captain's hopes were fulfilled. Discounting a wide and a no-ball, the over was of such variety that the batsman could rarely locate the right line to play. A single off the last ball was the only run off the bat.

With concern and deep thought, Ray Burrill watched another David Pelham over. In fairness to the bowler, he showed improvement, but still had difficulty with his line. Following the concession of a leg-bye he actually beat the mighty Wayne Tibbins with one which bit and turned. Yet every other ball seemed to slant to leg and the batsman helped himself. Ten more runs were added. It was then the turn of Greg Roberts again. The first ball was a wide and the second a long-hop which Gus Flabert was not fast enough to recognise. He scooped it away towards the square-leg umpire and took a single. Greg Roberts was now up against Wayne Tibbins, but he was still without a compass. The ball went first one side of the wicket and then the other. When he pitched leg stump or outside he was driven and pulled. He pitched leg stump or outside three times. It was hardly containment.

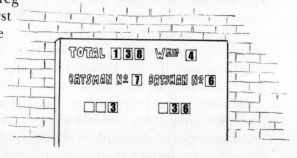

The mighty Tibbins. Ray Burrill pondered. He was trying to recall exactly what had been said to them by acting steward Harry Northwood on the Clacton Buffet Express. With a stammer and a twitch he had referred to 'that terrifying b...black b...b...b...', but Ray Burrill had got the impression he meant a bowler. His impression was correct. The 'terrifying b...black b...b...b...' of Harry Northwood's experience was Charlie Burns with whom the Outcasts had yet to make official acquaintance. The reason for Harry Northwood's lack of evidence was that Wayne Tibbins had not played in the match against Harry's school. He had obtained leave of absence in order to collect a special consignment from his uncle who was arriving at Stansted Airport having been on holiday in Colombia.

By his fourth over, David Pelham was getting nearer to respectability. He was aided by the fact that he was bowling to Gus Flabert rather than Wayne Tibbins. Pugnacious though he was by instinct, Gus Flabert found himself having to exercise maximum care to keep David Pelham at bay. To some extent David Pelham redeemed himself by bowling a maiden. At which point Ray Burrill thanked Greg Roberts for his services and recalled Nigel Redman. A glimmer of an idea was taking shape in his mind.

If Nigel Redman had supposed that the change of line and direction provided by a left-arm bowler was what Ray Burrill was seeking, he would have been wrong. His first ball, a loosener, pitched outside leg stump and was lifted effortlessly to the square-leg boundary by Wayne Tibbins. Within the space of eight overs he had reached a thunderous fifty. There were cheers from the boundary, some of admiration, some of respect and a few from younger boys out of fear. Nigel Redman corrected his line and three times passed Wayne Tibbins's bat outside off-stump. When he pitched middle he was pushed for a single and he kept Gus Flabert quiet with his last ball which was of near-yorker length.

Before commencing his next over, David Pelham went into close consultation with his captain. Field placings were changed. David Pelham, now feeling more in command of himself, bowled three balls of decent length which Wayne Tibbins met with a flourish without getting a run. The field was changed. The bowler adjusted his line. Wayne Tibbins got two runs and a boundary during the rest of the over.

Discussion followed with Nigel Redman. Gus Flabert was allowed an easy single and then the field was changed. The next two deliveries were driven and carved for four by Wayne Tibbins. A further field change. Apart from a wide, there were no further runs scored.

Charlie Colson, who had been trying to avoid the captain's eye, looked up to find Ray Burrill beckoning to him. 'One over, Charlie, that's all I want,' and Ray Burrill explained why. Charlie Colson, who had recovered to the extent that he felt he could murder a pint, reckoned his state of health would not be set back too severely by one over at this stage. His only worry was whether he had the necessary control. With field set back, Gus Flabert took the single he was offered. The field closed in. Charlie Colson swallowed.

Concentration. He managed four balls in a row around six inches outside off-stump. The length varied, but the width was what his captain had requested. Another change in the field. And then Charlie Colson tried a bouncer.

Rashid Ali's familiarisation tour was almost complete. He had identified the administration block from which he had been observed by the headmaster. In the furthest corner of the site was the school sanatorium. It was understandably separated by some distance from the boarding accommodation and the rest of the school. Rashid Ali nevertheless decided on a close-up inspection. It seemed to be a centre of activity. Rashid wondered whether there was some sort of epidemic in the school. He could count several – very pretty – nurses. One or two males emerged. Too old to be pupils. Doctors or teachers, Rash concluded. As he took in the scene, a lady appeared on the doorstep who was obviously matron. She was plump, pink-cheeked, bespectacled and in her forties, wearing a starched apron over a green tunic, which, depending on opinion, toned or clashed with a curled mop of orange hair.

'How may we be of service to you?' seemed to Rashid Ali an unusual opening. 'A sporting gentleman, I'll be bound,' matron continued. 'Well, I'm sure we can cope with everything here. We haven't had the pleasure' (the word was accompanied by a slight flutter of the eyes behind her large red-framed glasses) 'of your company before, I don't think.' Rashid Ali at first had some difficulty getting the drift of the matron's approach. It was only when she made to grab his arm that the penny began to float downwards. When matron called into the building, 'Dulcie, I have a guest for you,' the penny's descent accelerated. Without coming face-to-face with Dulcie, Rashid Ali began his retreat. 'Later, later,' he muttered. Matron was unabashed. 'Oh, I can see you're a shy one. Waiting till dark, are you?' Rashid Ali hid his realisation behind a sickly smile, thanked matron profusely and tried to cover his backward strides with a nonchalant air. As he made his way back towards the main concentration of school buildings, he marvelled at the way in which the school's assets were being worked. Or was the sanatorium a separate profit centre?

Wayne Tibbins was undone by the sucker punch. Having been restricted by a steady stream of balls outside his off-stump, he fastened greedily on the juicy offering of a short-pitched ball and swung at it with all his considerable might. Carelessly and carried away by his sense of impregnability he had not checked the latest adjustments to the field. Ray Burrill had directed no fewer than three of his players into what he thought would be the target zone. As the ball soared backward of square it seemed all that the captain had to do was nominate the fielder to take the catch. He selected Alan Birch on the grounds that he was the safest pair of hands. Fortuitously he was also the tallest of the three converging Outcasts. Ray's carefuly crafted plan was almost wrecked at the last moment when it looked as though Wayne Tibbins's hook was going to clear the boundary. A frantic leap by Alan Birch just parried the ball and it fell forward into the hands of John Furness. Wayne Tibbins might have completed two lengths of the pitch, but he was out. And he was not pleased.

By contrast Ray Burrill was extremely pleased. It was true he had bought the wicket. It was true that the price had not been cheap. Yet it was his reading of the situation which gave him special satisfaction. Terry Lilgate was still trying to coach Wayne Tibbins into being a complete batsman. Short of this goal, Wayne Tibbins could nevertheless be a formidable contributor with his restricted range of shots. So far he could not co-ordinate eye and feet to make any productive off-side strokes. To his credit Ray Burrill had spotted this restriction in Wayne Tibbins's play.

Another person who was not pleased was the headmaster. Herbert Banston had ventured out of his office with a view to tailing the person he had convinced himself was Aneurin Singh of the Social Services. Everything about Rashid Ali's demeanour and behaviour reinforced the headmaster's conviction that the Social Services' inspection was upon him. His mood blackened when he saw Rashid Ali heading towards the sanatorium. He could not believe it when he saw matron engaging him in conversation. Even from a distance he could see that her body language could not have been more unhelpful to the school's extreme predicament. As Rashid Ali turned away from his encounter with matron, so Herbert Banston retreated to his quarters to work out his next move.

The scorebox was a further place where displeasure was manifesting itself. Simon Crossley was already struggling for breath in the malodorous atmosphere, but it was Gary Pocke who announced that he could take no more. He needed a smoke. Thrusting his scorebook in Simon's direction, he exited the box muttering that he would be back 'in a mo'. Simon's joy at his departure was almost immediately cancelled out by the thought of his return. The fall of a wicket gave him a moment to examine the state of the home team's scorebook. His first thought was to tidy up the mess, but this was quickly overtaken by the realisation that Gary Pocke had somehow managed to advance Rockcliffe's score by twenty runs. Simon made rapid amendments, but left the smudges and thumb marks in place. For a while he was able to breathe fresher air.

Fresh air, the bursar decided, was what he needed. He had spent two hours poring over the school's finances more with a view to his own interests rather than those of the school. His position, he decided, was grim and getting grimmer by the minute. Speech Day was approaching. This was the day when the school's silverware had to be on display. Cups and bowls would be handed over (strictly temporarily) to spotty-faced prize-winners. At the moment this would be difficult, because the cups and bowls were resting in the vault of the pawnbrokers in nearby Chipping Rockcliffe. Messrs Ryporf and Glote preferred to be known as financial facilitators to the gentry. Their criteria had proved just flexible enough to include the bursar. There was no similar flexibility when it came to the return of objects deposited. Hard cash was a *sine qua non*. Between Messrs Ryporf and Glote on the one hand and Sammy (the Satchel) Smith on the other, the bursar was being squeezed. He needed more than fresh air.

Gus Flabert's new partner was Derek Orman. Although coming in as low as eight (seven as it happened on this occasion), Derek Orman was in the side purely for his batting. He was a young prospect being tried out by Terry Lilgate, who liked the boy's style and what he recognised to be his Yorkshire grit. It was not so much the Yorkshire grit which Ray Burrill recognised, but the accent. He immediately made a bowling change. Word was that Yorkshire batsmen could not cope with leg-spin. It was up to Tom Redman to prove the point.

The headmaster was by now back on the telephone. His quarry was County Councillor Percy Harport, but the chase took longer than he could easily tolerate. The county councillor's number was engaged. A disembodied voice asked him whether he would like the redial service. He pressed the indicated button only to be told that the service was not available on this occasion. After several manual redials, Herbert Banston eventually got a ringing tone. After what he regarded as too long a pause, an answer came: 'The Harport residence.' It was a smooth, impervious voice. No, the county councillor was not at home. No, he was not at liberty to say where he was. No, madam was at a bridge party. The monotony and fruitlessness of those responses stoked Herbert Banston's anger until he roared down the phone that this was a matter of the utmost urgency, vital to the security of Percy Harport's county council seat. As the respondent at the Harport residence still had work to do, including the placing of several bets on the afternoon's races and was therefore anxious to resume control of the telephone, he decided to volunteer the information that Mr Harport was at his golf club. He genuinely believed this to be true for otherwise he and his 'assistant' would not have dared to be in the house.

Tom Redman was as rusty as the other bowlers in his team. When a leg spinner is rusty, the product can be extremely variable. The amount of spin which Tom Redman could impart was not immediately apparent as neither of his first two deliveries pitched and the third was not allowed to by a batsman taking the opportunity, as he saw it, to help himself. Even Ray Burrill had to admire the way in which someone of Gus Flabert's stature despatched the waist-high full-toss which had been Tom Redman's initial offering. The fourth ball pitched, but was far too short. It was pulled by the batsman towards deep mid-wicket, but fortunately for the Outcasts it was retrieved first bounce and the batsmen were able to run only two. Gus Flabert then got a ball which surprised him by virtue of being just about on a length. He played a late defensive shot. The final ball of the over was a wide full-toss and only an athletic piece of fielding by Dean Faulds restricted Gus Flabert to a single. The score had leapt by fifteen and was now 189–5. Ray Burrill's theory remained untested.

Gary Pocke had returned to the scorebox, retrieving his scorebook with a grunt which Simon Crossley hoped was meant to represent undying gratitude. Gary's mission had obviously been accomplished, for he was soon lighting a cigarette. Off came the filthy trainers to lay bare once again the filthy feet. Simon braced himself for the offensive odour, but found that it was neutralised by the smell of cigarette smoke, but not ordinary cigarette smoke. Gary turned to see Simon staring at him. His face broke into an ugly leer. 'Fancy a puff, mate? You look as though you could do wiv a bit o' livening up.' Simon declined, but Gary persisted. 'There's more where this came from. I can fix you up if you've got the dosh.' Simon declined again, but this time his refusal was supplemented by a gesture with the twelve-inch ruler which was a part of his scoring equipment. It was not a gesture known to the laws of cricket, but it obviously struck the necessary chord with Gary Pocke. He swore and then contented himself with silence – and inhalation.

Ray Burrill kept his promise and put Charlie Colson out to pasture once again. David Pelham was called back into the attack. He managed to bowl a tidy over to Gus Flabert which cost no more than one scoring stroke for two runs. The captain persisted with Tom Redman, who rewarded him by finding his length. The first ball turned, but was wide of off-stump. Derek Orman poked unconvincingly in its direction and got an edge which went wide of slip for a single. This gave the strike to Gus Flabert, who positively salivated at the prospect. But the ball he received was also on a good length. It was not threatening, however, and was eased away for a single. With his next delivery to Derek Orman, Tom Redman got his direction right and some turn. There was a scuffle of feet and bat. The ball squeezed between wicket-keeper and first slip and was signalled by Umpire Papwell as a leg-bye as if to emphasise he would not have upheld an appeal for a catch had the ball gone to hand (as it should have done). As if three balls on a length had been too much, Tom Redman lapsed with his fourth and was put away by Gus Flabert, but only for three. Basil Smith in his distant empire had stuck out a fortuitous boot and projected the ball into the hands of John Furness who had been approaching fast (for him) from the opposite direction. Now it was Tom Redman versus Derek Orman once again. Dare he?

A similar question was tantalising the bursar now re-installed in his office. The school's investment portfolio was ample. Some parents had been amazingly generous benefactors. Funds had been further boosted by loans of some very large sums. The school was allowed to benefit from the interest whilst the capital remained secure (and hidden). The bursar wondered whether there was any way in which he could invoke the same modus operandi. He would need the money for only a short period whilst he redeemed the school's silver. The problem, however, was gaining access. Certain special codes were needed. The bursar alternately pressed keys and clicked the mouse, but made no progress. Literally he could not hack it. And then suddenly he remembered a discussion in the common room and thought of someone who might.

Tom Redman had begun experimenting with a flipper towards the end of the previous season. It was a little early in the new season to try to advance the experiment. At this stage he was struggling for line and length. Yet he had seen the look of uncertainty on Derek Orman's face. Perhaps it would be worth a try. Spectacularly, it was. Bravely the batsman came forward, but he was deceived for pace and flight. He played over the ball and was bowled neck and crop. 'Bad luck,' said his partner as Derek Orman departed, but whilst speaking, Gus Flabert was making a mental note of the flipper in case it was repeated. He did not know exactly how experimental a weapon in the bowler's armoury it truly was.

Last seen being dragged unceremoniously from the pitch, Terry Lilgate had begun to recover. For the moment there was no question of the hair of the dog. The previously handy Brewery Tavern was gone. The next pub was only in driving distance and not even Terry Lilgate was prepared to risk that. Nor could he risk invading the common room because he knew that the usual staff poker school would be in session. He was not supposed to know about it, but after a heavy night in the Brewery Tavern one of the participants, bemoaning his luck, had let it slip. Terry Lilgate had taken him in hand. In return for some coaching in the finer arts of the game, he took ten per cent of his confidant's winnings. For the moment Terry Lilgate's reviving mind was obliged to concentrate as best it could on cricket.

The school's score did not look too bad, but the coach was disturbed to see that so many wickets had fallen. He was also puzzled to see David Simms about to enter the field of play in place of Derek Orman. It was strange that with only six wickets down batsman number nine was going in. Pausing only to instruct David Simms to 'play steady, there's all the time in the world', Terry Lilgate stumbled in search of the captain. The complete disappearance of the Yank had then to be admitted by Tom Barnes. All his searches in the school had yielded no sign. Fury and fear welled up in Terry Lilgate in equal measure. He tore a strip off Tom Barnes for failing to look after the boy whilst being all too well aware whom the headmaster would blame. This could even be a matter for the police, Terry Lilgate thought with a shiver of distaste, but first he would have to organise another search. Before raising the alarm with the headmaster, he had to be sure. Manpower was required and he knew where to find it. He headed towards the prefects' room. Too bad he would have to interrupt their Saturday viewing of hard-porn videos. As he was their supplier, they would be in no position to complain. The preoccupation with the whereabouts of Cooperbatch T Gulfstrode was the understandable cause of both Terry Lilgate and Tom Barnes failing to notice the absence of another member of the team.

As is so often the case, triumph was followed by disaster. Carried away by the (fortuitous) perfection of his flipper, Tom Redman presented the new batsman with an appalling, short-pitched and wide delivery. Discarding the advice so recently imparted to him by Terry Lilgate, David Simms struck it for four. There was applause as the school's total passed two hundred. Ray Burrill (wrongly) was unworried. He felt that the Outcasts might have broken the back of Rockcliffe's batting. What he had overlooked was Harry Northwood's lack of information about the batting capability of the school's lower order. When they had played Harry's school, not all their batsmen had been required to perform. The last three in the order were all fast bowlers. Just as Terry Lilgate had injected hostility into their bowling, so he had instilled resistance into their batting. And there was still Gus Flabert, his mentor's little belter, who was about to do some belting. Ray Burrill's decision to have a more aggressive field was untimely.

Philip Bond's way of getting over his unlucky dismissal had been very different from that of his captain. Stewart Thorogood had come across him with his arms entwined around a young girl attired in one of the skimpiest dresses which it had been Stewart's good fortune to see. The two were so absorbed in each other that at first they failed to notice Stewart's presence. When they finally broke apart, Stewart quickly assessed that their combined frustration was caused less by his intrusion and more by the curbs imposed by being on the school campus. Ever ready to smooth the path of young love, Stewart thought he might be able to help. After a brief consultation with Simon and Sophie Crossley and a few words with Bond the blond and his blonde companion, a departure was arranged.

His previous over having been fairly tight, David Pelham fell in with his captain's suggestion of a commensurately tight field. The first person to disagree was Greg Roberts who had been stationed at forward short-leg. As the ball struck his shin, Greg swore instantly and loudly. There were several targets for his cursing: the bowler for sending down a loose ball, the captain for having stationed him so close to the bat, himself for failing to equip himself with protection and finally and not least, the batsman who he was sure had aimed to hit him. A smile had lingered on Gus Flabert's face too long before giving way to an expression of concern as Greg writhed on the ground. It was several minutes before Greg felt able to continue and then a few more minutes whilst he retrieved from the pavilion several defensive items. As he could do no more than hobble, Greg thought it was cruel logic on Ray Burrill's part to keep him in the same fielding position. It was no comfort for Ray to have added that Greg had prevented a run being taken.

For the remainder of the over David Pelham maintained a tidy line. It did not prevent Gus Flabert shaping for shots which made Greg Roberts cringe. His gymnastic display was watched by his team-mates with a mixture of amusement and sympathy. One almighty leap allowed the ball to pass safely beneath him and almost reach the boundary. Gus Flabert had to be content with three whilst the last two balls of the over were blocked by David Simms.

With Charlie Colson's head and his own shoulder still aching, Ray Burrill decided to persevere with Tom Redman's leg-spin. Not wishing to be entirely on the defensive at this stage of the innings, Ray wanted to keep a number of close to the wicket fielders. He allowed Greg Roberts to move to slip and put John Furness at silly mid-off. A titter rose from some of the younger spectators as helmet, shin pads and box were transferred from one fielder to the other. It did not take John Furness long to realise that he was now the one in the danger zone. Gus Flabert appeared to transfer his interest to the off-side. At Tom Redman's third ball he played a fierce drive towards cover. It struck John Furness on the boot and rose into what media commentators would describe as the top of the thigh. The player had not felt so winded since the morning after he had consumed seventeen pints of Waddlecombe's West Country Bitter following a charity (cricket) match. A glass of water was called for and the game suffered another interruption, though John Furness's suffering was the greater. However, others too could claim to be suffering, in mind if not in body.

With what seemed a social services vendetta being waged against him, the headmaster was in mental anguish. When he most needed help from County Councillor Percy Harport he could not reach him. This was intolerable. He paced the length and breadth of his office while he combed the length and breadth of his mind. And then he thought of something. On one occasion when the County Councillor had been in his office he had left a business card and Herbert Banston seemed to remember him saying that he had written his mobile number on it. The fifth drawer yielded the craved item by which time the contents of four others were strewn across the floor.

Picking up his own mobile (Herbert Banston had no wish for this call to go through the school switchboard) he punched in the numbers. A female voice answered. The voice did not strike the headmaster as belonging to the receptionist of the golf club. His doubts were reinforced by the noises off. There was the sound of heavy breathing as though someone had been running, and then a male voice could be heard. The words were not entirely distinct, but they sounded like, 'Put that bloody phone down, you stupid girl.' This was followed by a gasp (probably male), a giggle (definitely female) and a click. The headmaster tried again.

The ringing tone must have continued for more than a minute before connection was made. 'Harport here,' came a firm voice. Herbert Banston asked for confirmation that he was speaking to County Councillor Harport. 'Yes, yes,' he was told somewhat impatiently, 'what is it, man?' The headmaster told him what it was. The county councillor expressed extreme surprise that an inspection, official or otherwise, could be taking place without the approval of the committee. He assured Herbert Banston that he would make inquiries and 'get things moving right away'. It was an assurance with which the headmaster for the moment had to be content. He ended on a conciliatory note apologising for troubling the county councillor at his golf club. 'Oh, yes, my golf club. You were lucky to catch me – just off for another nine holes.' Herbert Banston agreed he had been lucky to catch up with him, especially in view of his failed first attempt. 'Must have been a wrong number, old boy,' Percy Harport retorted, 'but good guess knowing I was at the club.' The headmaster explained why it was not a guess. 'Manservant,' the distraught respondee wailed, 'I don't have a manservant. Oh, good God!' Click. Suddenly Percy Harport had something more important than Aneurin Singh and his Saturday afternoon activities on his mind.

Herbert Banston was unaware of this changed priority. He nursed the half-hope that the hounds could be called off. Thank goodness he had been able to reach his ally on the County Council. Odd about that wrong number. Then he smiled as he remembered. He had used the memory button on his phone. It had been the right number after all. His smile broadened as he committed the incident to his own memory.

Back on the cricket ground there were few smiles. John Furness had managed a slow recovery and was given compassionate leave at third man. There was no rush of volunteers to go in his place at silly mid-off. In any case John Furness had indicated his wish to hang on to helmet, shin pads and box even though he was to field in the deep. There also appeared to be a change of tactic on the part of the school team. Once the prefects had been pressed into a dragnet of the school, Terry Lilgate told Tom Barnes to concentrate on the cricket and issued further instructions. The captain took the opportunity of John Furness's indisposition to convey them to the batsmen at the crease and the two still to come. When Tom Redman resumed his over, Gus Flabert curbed his instincts and he and his partner helped themselves to just a couple of easy singles. There followed eight more overs of sedate spin and studied batting. The only merit of this passage of play was that it allowed time for the injuries sustained by the fielding side to abate. But not their black mood.

By contrast, the mood of Philip Bond and his companion had brightened. Escorted by Stewart Thorogood and Sophie Crossley they were whisked away to a rural idyll, a dreamy farmhouse seemingly no distance from the school yet in a completely isolated setting. Bond the blond had taken no account of the direction they had taken or the actual distance they had travelled. He was too wrapped up in his partner and thoughts of what lay ahead. Sophie showed the couple through the door into this earthly paradise with a cheery 'make yourself at home'. Philip Bond could think of nothing more certain. With a wink, Stewart Thorogood left them. 'I'll give you an hour,' he said. It was at least partially true.

'The Yank's been snatched.' Had he been half-way sober and calmly collected, Terry Lilgate might have announced himself differently when he hurled himself into the headmaster's office. The fevered state of his mind made him all too vulnerable to wild suggestions. As it was he certainly commanded the headmaster's attention. Herbert Banston hurriedly closed the safe in the corner and spun round to assimilate the new crisis. Staff at the school knew that Cooperbatch T Gulfstrode was the son of a mega-rich man. They were also aware that mega-rich men in the United States had often acquired enemies along the road to becoming mega-rich men. Cooperbatch T Gulfstrode was supposed to be safe in their care. The elder brother, Marvin G Gulfstrode III, had been located (in circumstances which Terry Lilgate thought it wise to withhold from the headmaster), but a fifty per cent success rate was hardly likely to be acceptable to Marvin G Gulfstrode II and the formidable Marileen Gulfstrode. Without so much as one drop of alcohol to fuel it, the headmaster's mind quickly became as inflamed as Terry Lilgate's. To have to cope with a kidnapping was traumatic enough, but to be doing so with no less a person than the local director of social services on the prowl was a disaster. The headmaster could see no alternative to calling the police and their arrival would almost inevitably be spotted by the snooping bureaucrat. Unless. Herbert Banston's mind began to whirr again. A diversion might be arranged. He looked at his watch and before summoning the police he put in a call to the school's director of music.

Ray Burrill began to feel that the game was drifting and it was not drifting in the Outcasts' direction. His depleted resources did not allow much room for manoeuvre, but he decided to recall Nigel Redman in place of David Pelham, who, he thought, could be tried at the school hall end. Nigel went through some elaborate exercises of which certain Test match bowlers might have been proud. They would also have been proud of the first ball he delivered in his new spell. Described by the bowler in the immediate aftermath as 'just a loosener,' it emphatically loosened the bails. Nigel Redman might not have intended it, but he produced a sizzling leg-stump yorker. It totally surprised David Simms and Umpire Papwell too, because he lacked the presence of mind to claim (falsely) that it was a no-ball. David Simms had to depart and Rockcliffe were 228-7.

The bursar arrived breathless at the cricket field perimeter in time to see Charlie Burns marching out to bat. This was a severe disappointment. He had nothing against Charlie Burns the cricketer nor against cricket in general. In ordinary circumstances the bursar would have been happy to while away a couple of hours watching a match unfold. But these were far from ordinary circumstances. And as the afternoon wore on, they were deteriorating. His interest in the cricket on this occasion was not to observe the beauty of a leg glance or to marvel at the grace and pace of a young fast bowler. He was exclusively concerned with Charlie Burns the computer wizard and not Charlie Burns the cricket tyro. Had he arrived in time he would have attempted to forestall his innings, but he had been delayed by a phone call, and what could only be termed a threatening phone call. Sammy (the Satchel) Smith had had time to reflect on their earlier conversation and the passage of time had served only to harden his heart. Monday. That was the deadline. Failure would mean a visit from two of Sammy's collectors. If they did not collect, they delivered. The bursar shuddered at the prospect of a beating. He knew Sammy's collectors. One of them, after all, was a parent.

To avoid losing sight of his man, the bursar felt he had no alternative but to watch the match. He prayed for his early dismissal. Here again he was to be disappointed. Charlie Burns had had his instructions and so, instead of the crash, bang, wallop which Charlie thought was the fitting characteristic of Rockcliffe's fastest bowler when batting, he set out to build an innings. He got through Nigel Redman's over without any sign of difficulty. He was helped by the bowler. Having accidentally produced an absolute purler to get rid of David Simms, Nigel Redman's more applied efforts proved to be very wayward. Charlie Burns only had to play one ball and this he did with exaggerated defence. The final ball of the over was as fast as the first, but not so well directed. Four byes resulted.

Meanwhile at the headmaster's office, an inspector had called. Herbert Banston thought this was a remarkably rapid response to his call only to discover that Detective Inspector Horrocks had arrived on other business. The two men took an instant dislike to one another. It was hard to say which of them was in the blacker mood. It had been the detective inspector's day off. Having taken a tongue-lashing from his wife for the last two weeks, he had determined that today he must cut the grass. The consequence of once again postponing the task was going to mean a frosty evening at home, always supposing that he would get home. However, the call from Superintendent Byfleet had to be obeyed and Paul Horrocks could see its potential importance. However, he could also see that his superior had no intention of having his own afternoon disturbed. And Paul Horrocks knew exactly where the superintendent was and in whose hospitality box.

This inspector, the headmaster quickly discovered, had not arrived with a view to getting a boy back, but rather to take one away. Herbert Banston's first instinct, that of a dutiful headteacher, was to resist. He had the duty of care. He could not accept one of his boys being carted away from the school premises. It was not a case of like father like son as far as the school was concerned. Here Herbert Banston found himself venturing on to thin ice. He had never liked to think about the source of Douglas Hamerskill's school fees. The detective inspector, distrustful of private schools and antipathetic to this greasy-looking headmaster, turned up the heat. 'I'm afraid, sir, I shall have to insist. I'm sure it'll be better interviewing the lad away from prying eyes.' The reference to prying eyes jolted the headmaster. His first instinct quickly gave way to his second: self-preservation. This ghastly new mess needed to be shunted out of the way as soon as possible.

Even with his new-found urge to distance himself from this latest embarrassment, Herbert Banston realised that Douglas Hamerskill could not be abandoned into the hands of the police without some chaperon from the school. It should properly be a woman. It could not be matron, Herbert Banston quickly prompted himself. The director of music he had assigned to another task. That left his wife. Letitia Banston was not ideally cast for the role to which she was now summoned by her husband. She loathed the children in the school. She tolerated her position as headmaster's wife only because it gave her a degree of social status and allowed her at the same time to keep a check on her wayward husband. Her background as a trained accountant enabled her to watch over the school's finances and guarantee the income to live up to the position in society she craved. She was so alien to the concept of pastoral care that she could have trained warders in prisoner-of-war camps. Whilst awaiting her arrival, Herbert Banston surveyed the creased polo shirt and stained cotton trousers worn by Paul Horrocks (who had got as close to cutting the lawn as changing into his gardening clothes) and uttered a silent prayer over the absence of police uniform. Even the woman police constable accompanying him was in jeans and a T-shirt. Maybe, just maybe, no-one would pay attention to them.

The pace of activity to be observed in various parts of the school premises was unmatched on the cricket field. The reappearance of

Terry Lilgate persuaded Gus Flabert into an elaborate display of defence to show he was following instructions. Charlie Burns looked to be docility itself – an image far removed from the 'terrifying b...black b...b...b...' of Harry Northwood's excited memory. The overs ticked by. The bursar ground his teeth with mounting impatience. Otherwise tranquillity reigned. Then, all at once, commotion.

The string of spectators around the ground was briefly augmented by three. A procession of Detective Inspector Paul Horrocks, WPC Jane Flatlock and Mrs Letitia Banston moved purposely towards the pavilion. Douglas Hamerskill saw them coming. He was not fooled. It was in his blood. Coppers, he could tell. It was nevertheless a minute or two before curiosity gave way to alarm. A sixth sense brought him out into the open. At fifty yards an expression on Letitia Banston's face instilled movement into his feet. As he began to slide away, the processional trio broke into a trot. Within seconds the race was on. Attention drifted from the cricket. The stirring on the boundary's edge caused David Pelham to pause as he was about to bowl his next over to Gus Flabert. For a moment play was suspended.

But only for a moment. The chase was short-lived. It was not won by one of the professionals. Adding substance to the notion that no-one would have escaped from any prison which she might have run, Letitia Banston swiftly made up ground on Douglas Hamerskill and took him out with a tackle which any rugby union full-back would have admired. Perhaps Douglas Hamerskill was slowed down by his unlaced boots or by his forty-a-day habit. It would never be known. What was known was that he was bundled into an unmarked car and driven away at speed. He took no further part in the match. Terry Lilgate and Tom Barnes had been stunned witnesses of this episode. Recovering, Tom Barnes thought to console his coach by remarking that at least their bowling strength was intact. They would have been well advised to count.

Spectators with a trace of reluctance transferred their attention back to the match. They were not rewarded with much by way of spectacle. The keen observer of the niceties of cricket can be relied on to find some point of interest in any contest between bat and ball. But this was David Pelham of the Outcasts CC bowling to Gus

Flabert of Rockcliffe School. It was not in the class of Jim Laker against Colin MacDonald in a grim test of endurance at Old Trafford. If the bowling was not of the highest class, it was getting better, but the batsman was not giving it a particularly critical examination. David Pelham achieved a second successive maiden over. After Nigel Redman had added another, marred only by two byes carelessly conceded by Kevin Newton, David Pelham made it three in a row.

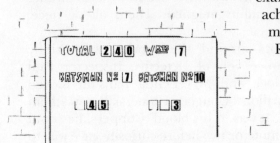

At which point Molly Parkin walked out. This was a sensation. Her team of four ladies in the tea room could not believe it. Molly Parkin had been on the staff of the school for thirty years. She was thought of as a maid of all work. She would turn her hand to anything. She could always be counted upon to be there at school events. For the last ten years she had supervised tea at all of the school's sporting fixtures. When it came to cricket she knew that tea was taken without fail between 4 and 4.30 pm. Now it was getting on for 5 pm. and there was not a sign of the innings coming to an end. What was coming to an end was Molly Parkin's tether. 'Out we go, ladies,' she commanded, 'they can fend for themselves.' After a few seconds of incredulity, her helpers followed, wondering what on earth could have produced this sudden show of militancy in someone whom they had always thought to be a most conservative lady. It was not until the next day that they saw the report of Chris de Burgh's concert in Colchester.

In her tactical appreciation of the state of the game, Molly Parkin had been ahead of the Outcasts, although not by much. She and her squad were barely out of sight before Alan Birch sidled up to Ray Burrill to observe, 'The swine are going to bat us out of this.' Concurrence with this assessment persuaded Ray Burrill to attempt a dangerous ploy. He beckoned Greg Roberts. He had bought one wicket. He was now prepared to pay more for another. The big spender got it right again.

Ray Burrill had sensed that Charlie Burns, in playing a defensive role, had been competing against his natural instincts. Prompted by Alan Birch, he thought he would now present him with what could fairly be described as overwhelming temptation. After four balls of Greg's over it was Ray Burrill who was beginning to feel overwhelmed. The initial delivery, whilst costing nothing, gave a hint of what might be to come. It was an appalling long-hop at which Charlie Burns attempted an almighty swing. Perhaps his previous passivity had dulled his eye or perhaps his feet had become leaden. Missing the bat, the ball struck in between. Coming from his stomach the ball was still rising when it reached Kevin Newton. The 'keeper flung out a protective hand and succeeded in deflecting the ball towards the slip fielder somewhat optimistically posted by Ray Burrill. Whether in excitement or in need of his tea, Greg Roberts appealed. Unsighted and confused, but not wishing to appear either, Syd Breakwell gave a magisterial 'not out'.

There was no scope for confusion (on either side) with the next two balls. They went far and high over bowler and umpire. Very occasional bowler he might be, but Greg Roberts had his pride. He was determined not to be hit for three sixes in a row. He succeeded. It was a quicker ball, slightly short of a length. Charlie Burns stepped back and with powerful forearms and a wicked gleam in his eye, punched it head high straight back down the wicket. Greg Roberts dived to his left and Syd Breakwell to his right. Lives were saved even if another four runs were lost to the fielding side.

A by now chastened Greg Roberts held back his fifth ball and pitched it fuller in length. Charlie Burns was coming forward with violence aforethought when he checked, took a step back and was hit on the pad. It was relief as much as anything which prompted Greg's appeal. There was a pause. That in itself was unusual. Syd Breakwell normally never hesitated. The great umpires – and Syd Breakwell had spent many hours watching them on television – were decisive, and the ex-policeman admired their certainty. On this occasion Syd Breakwell was less than his immediate self as a succession of thoughts raced through his mind. First, it looked out; secondly, Greg Roberts was the bowler and Syd knew that he bowled rubbish; thirdly, the batsman was evidently homicidal and deserved to perish; fourthly, he must not be biased; fifthly, it could have been going down the leg side; sixthly, he had damned near been decapitated; seventhly, the batsman had played back; eighthly, he was not sure; ninthly, he was sure that Rockcliffe were not playing the game; tenthly, he felt sorry for the bowler; eleventhly, he knew the batsman should have the benefit of the doubt; finally, he looked up. 'Out,' he said, gingerly raising a finger bruised by impact with the ground as he had hurled himself out of the way of the previous delivery. If Charlie Burns had not smirked when Syd Breakwell met his eyes, he might after all have got away with it. As it was, Rockcliffe had lost their eighth wicket. Their last and only available batsman, Jack Dolland, set off for the crease.

Whilst Greg Roberts was receiving slightly doubting congratulations from his comrades, Gus Flabert was busy asserting himself with his new partner. Gus might have been shorter (by some inches) than Jack Dolland, but he was his senior in the school and very much his senior in the cricket team. It was not a meeting of equal partners. Gus Flabert knew that the tactic was to continue to stretch the innings and in any case he fancied getting to his fifty. The initial advice to Jack Dolland was simply 'Block it.' And to a harmless full toss from Greg Roberts that is precisely what he did.

Charlie Burns was alone in the school's changing-room when the bursar pounced. Charlie had just shed his protection and his sweaty clothes. He was naked and searching for his bowling trousers when the bursar said, 'I need you and I need you now.' There could have been a most unfortunate misunderstanding. The risk of an unfortunate misunderstanding increased when the bursar added, 'I'll make it worth your while.' In increased desperation, Charlie Burns searched for his kit. It was as well that he did not mishear the next part of the bursar's overture: 'I hear that you're a very good hacker.' Charlie Burns finally felt able to face him and he began to understand the proposition being put to him. Five hundred quid would get him that stacking system he fancied. He would be back by the end of the tea interval. No problem. He followed the bursar, but at a discreet distance. As they left, Stewart Thorogood entered.

In the tea room, David Simms was also alone. From what he could see, the team tea was a tea of two halves, two very unequal halves. Laid out on two parallel sets of trestle tables were plates of sandwiches, some of which were curling at the edges, sausage rolls which were more roll than sausage, cakes mainly sponge and heavy rather than light and an assortment of – judging by their appearance – windfall apples. But on a side table, things looked very different. Laid out according to Alan Birch's strict instructions were the contents of his hamper. Scooped from a tin was a quantity of Beluga Caviar. Its neighbour was a triangular section of foie gras from Strasbourg. To follow these delicacies were two wonderfully thin slices of smoked salmon. The discerning palate could then experience a portion of pigeon in port jelly and thus fortified would be ready for a portion of filet de boeuf en croûte. Breast of goose and grouse stuffed with artichokes presented themselves as alternatives. As supplementaries there were quails' eggs, beef tomatoes filled with tuna, anchovies and brandy, an avocado pear with prawns and peppers, fresh asparagus and a range of salads. Crème brulée, trifle, coconut cheesecake and kiwi fruit syllabub were available as desserts. A plate of cheeses varying in source by animal and country was intended to round off the repast. The accompanying wines were half bottles of a Chassagne-Montrachet Grand Cru and a prize-winning Pommard. David Simms scoffed the lot.

David Pelham, bowling better and better, reeled off another over. Gus Flabert took a single off the fifth ball and Jack Dolland blocked the sixth. Ray Burrill felt he had no more need of Greg Roberts and recalled Tom Redman. The leg-spinner got away with two loose balls which Gus Flabert failed to punish, but the batsman strolled a single off the fourth ball and Jack Dolland blocked out the rest of the over. There was a brief exchange between captain and bowler which led to the batsmen's tactics being thwarted. David Pelham succeeded in bowling a maiden to Gus Flabert and put Jack Dolland on strike. Rockcliffe's last man proved equal to the challenge. Apart from overcoming a highly speculative appeal for leg before wicket and/or a catch off bat and pad, Jack Dolland kept his wicket intact. In the fifty-first over, Gus Flabert scrambled a single. Apart from Kevin Newton opening his legs to allow two more byes, there was no addition to the score during the next four overs as the batsmen refused to be tempted by bowling which steadily became more accurate. Gus Flabert and Jack Dolland were enjoying themselves. Ray Burrill was not. He was forced to think again.

Feeling with some justification that the end of the innings was overdue, Rashid Ali and Stewart Thorogood converged on a strangely quiet tea room. The scene they encountered gave rise successively to anger, amusement and inspiration. The sandwiches, sausage rolls, sponge cakes and bruised apples lay in unappetising, undisturbed order. For the rest it was chaos. Scraps of food, smeared plates, dirty dishes and empty bottles were strewn over the floor. In their midst squatted a drooping figure hardly to be recognised as one of Rockcliffe's demon quartet of fast bowlers. Stomach cramp, the head spins and fatigue were claiming David Simms whose head was slumped on his chest. A slow dribble dripped towards the mess which was his cricket shirt. A miniature of port, which had come with the plate of cheeses, lay half-consumed in his hand. It was not a pretty sight and Stewart Thorogood, with an eye for detail, could not help thinking, a waste of rather a good port. It was the nearest any of the Outcasts had come to a drink all day.

Why did he do it? What drove David Simms to devour the rich contents of a food hamper from one of London's premier stores? Was it a deprived home background? Was it the relentless stodgy diet of the Rockcliffe school kitchen which triggered a reaction? Was it devilment? Or was it just greed? Sociologists and child psychologists might endlessly have discussed the behavioural theories. Stewart Thorogood and Rashid Ali had neither the time nor the inclination. Annoyance gave way to a burst of merriment as they wondered how Alan Birch would respond to the usurping of his gourmet experience. As the chuckling faded, it was Stewart Thorogood who first saw the nature of the opportunity presented. He it was who suggested a convenient resting place for the now prone body of David Simms. But it was Rashid Ali who recognised the need to tidy up the scene to avoid giving a clue to anyone on the Rockcliffe side as to what had happened. They tossed a coin to decide who would break the news to Alan Birch when he came off the field.

On the field, Ray Burrill gave a speculative twirl of his arm and winced. He could not bring himself back into the attack. He was reluctant to do further damage to his drinking arm, and anyway he would have to save himself for batting. Charlie Colson was beckoned from the deep where he had been skulking relatively quietly for more than an hour. In truth, Charlie was feeling better, but he was also feeling like a drink. Ray Burrill told him brusquely that he would have to earn it. Getting the last wicket was paramount. Pace was what Ray Burrill asked for as he sought to get back to basics. What got number eleven batsmen out was usually pace. As it turned out, it was neither the captain's perception nor the bowler's prowess which gained the result.

Rosie Banston, the headmaster's elder daughter, had faced the prospect of an afternoon imprisoned in her parents' house. Letitia Banston had put her foot down. Rosie was going nowhere until she had spring-cleaned her room and washed and ironed a mounting pile of dirty clothes. Rose had to learn sometime to look after herself and her mother was determined that the burden of chores had to be shared. With glowering sullenness, Rosie was steeling herself for this disagreeable drudgery whilst putting off as long as possible the commencement. Following a telephone call, her mother's announcement that 'Your father wants me' was greeted by Rosie with a combination of relief and hilarity (she was sure her father had not wanted her mother for years).

Her mother's exit was followed very shortly by Rosie's, chores neglected. Rosie had far better things to do. She had a rendezvous with a couple of sixth-formers who in turn were keeping company with a couple of bottles of Polish vodka. Rosie made up for a late start as the bottles made their round. What persuaded them outside no-one could afterwards remember. The jigging, giggling trio took up station behind the sight screen with the remaining vodka. Inhibitions were shed and, with them, other things.

Charlie Colson agreed with Ray Burrill that a fastish yorker was what was required to dispose of Jack Dolland. Theory is one thing, practice another. His first ball (accidentally) was an outswinger pitched full but wide. It was not clear which shot Jack Dolland had intended to play. He appeared to stretch forward in defence, but it was not the face of his bat which met the ball. There was a thick outside edge and the ball went to third slip at comfortable catching height. However, there was not actually a fielder at third slip and the ball was too quick for third man. Jack Dolland had at last achieved his first scoring shot. It was also to be his last.

The only merit in Charlie Colson's second delivery was that it was straight. But it would not have taken a wicket if the batsman had used his bat. As it was, Jack Dolland froze in his backlift and stared down the wicket transfixed. Secretly the adolescent had nursed a crush for the headmaster's elder daughter. Her emergence from behind the sight screen with her long blond hair barely covering what she was barely exhibiting took all the batsman's attention. In the absence of Cooperbatch T Gulfstrode, the innings ended well ahead of the commotion caused by Rosie Banston's appearance. Anxious as they had been five minutes earlier to leave the field as quickly as possible, some of the Outcasts were now noticeably slow to move.

TEA INTERVAL

Tea was a depressing interlude. The building in which tea was set to take place was far from inviting. Now called the tea room, it was originally a nineteenth-century fire shed which had stood on this site before the construction of the school. Since ceasing to be used for its created purpose, it had performed a variety of roles for which it had been progressively rejected as being either too hot, too cold, too small, too large or too dangerous. Just when the school was on the point of seeking its demolition with a view to building extra changing rooms, some organ of local government officialdom decided it should be listed. The school managed to reach a compromise deal with the local authority whereby with minimal repair and adaptation the basic structure of the building was retained in all its nastiness. As the serving of teas to games players and spectators alike was a very low priority in the Rockcliffe scheme of things, duty could be done at low cost and least disturbance. Only the likes of Molly Parkin, her predecessors and successors had to be squared to forsake the cosiness of the main school kitchen for this utterly unappealing outpost.

The fare provided was equally unappealing to the Outcasts although the speed with which members of the home team fell on it suggested that, for them, it was the norm or better. Sophie Crossley took charge of the tea urn which had been abandoned by Molly Parkin and her team. She could not do much about the quality of the beverage which emerged. It was tea with an antiseptic taste. Alan Birch was spared this discovery. The news of the despoliation of his picnic had been broken to him by Stewart Thorogood with as straight a face as he could manage. Not even the fate of the culprit abated his fury. With one look at the bare trestle which had once supported his gourmet fare, Alan Birch stamped out of the tea room. He cursed the amount he had lashed out and lost on this extravagance, not least the ten pound note he had given Molly Parkin to set it out for him.

It was a depressing tea interval for Terry Lilgate. At first he had thought nothing of the spare places, but as the minutes passed alarm bells began ringing alongside the other noises in his still clearing head. He counted. Six. Only six plus Glyn Appold, whose appropriate title in the circumstances was seventh man. A wave of panic gripped Terry Lilgate. Tom Barnes was plucked from his seat. The captain went into this hastily-summoned conference clutching two spam sandwiches. (It was a mistake to miss out when meat in any form made its appearance on the school menu.) They knew they were missing the Yank and Douglas Hamerskill, but in neither tea room, pavilion nor visible surrounding area could they catch any glimpse of Philip Bond, David Simms or Charlie Burns. For the second time the prefects would have to be prised from their porn for a search of the school estate. Terry Lilgate dared not think of having to make another missing persons' report to the headmaster.

It was a depressing tea interval for Cooperbatch T Gulfstrode. He was sitting, as instructed, on the third bench on the left in St James's Park. He had been there half an hour and was beginning to wonder whether he was on a fool's errand. It had certainly not been a fool who had organised it. The school secretary had taken the call just before she had left the office, Saturday being her half-day off. Realising that Cooperbatch would be playing cricket and the cricket ground was on her way home, she decided to deliver the message personally. Told to ring his Uncle Jay urgently, Cooperbatch wasted no time. He did not recognise the number (he should have known it was a mobile) nor the voice of his uncle's PA who spoke with him. He was told to travel to London immediately (there was a convenient train if he moved fast). His uncle had big news for him. Cooperbatch was to tell no-one, especially not his brother. Phoning for a taxi, he had found the number engaged. Forgetting about changing out of his whites, Cooperbatch had made for the school entrance with a view to thumbing a lift. He was in luck. The only car in sight, an estate driven by a lady, had obligingly pulled up and he was on his way.

It had all seemed so simple to the grasping and covetous mind of Cooperbatch T Gulfstrode. With his elder brother earmarked to inherit the family business and the bulk of the family wealth, Cooperbatch had carved out for himself a place in the affections of Uncle Jay. His mother's brother was every bit as substantial a businessman as Marvin G Gulfstrode II and, more relevantly, had another enormous asset. He was childless. Uncle Jay had taken a shine to young Cooperbatch and had dropped hints that he could see a future for him in his corporation. A call from Uncle Jay was one which Cooperbatch could not possibly afford to ignore.

Unease began to grip Cooperbatch T Gulfstrode as he sat on his own in the park in his cricket clothes. He could not remember the number of his uncle's PA. In any case there was not a telephone box in sight and he was reluctant to move away from the appointed meeting place. He was a lonely figure in white (except for a brown stain on the upper part of his trousers). On the southbound Clacton Buffet Express, trolley steward Harry Northwood had recognised Cooperbatch as a member of the cricket team from hell. He had exacted a modicum of revenge by deftly spilling a plastic mug of coffee into Cooperbatch's lap.

'Lost your bat, sonny?' inquired a passing London policeman. Cooperbatch T Gulfstrode failed to note the light inflection in the officer's voice. Had he done so and had he been less absolutely fed up, he might have engaged in polite repartee. Sadly he lapsed all too quickly into the vernacular of Queens (the district of New York from which he hailed) which by now was reinforced by his daily exposure to the lingua franca of Rockcliffe School. Cooperbatch's snarled answer was, 'Why don't you go ...' and the suggestion ended with the word 'yourself?'. The police officer, although up to that point feeling at peace with the world, did not regard this as repartee and that is why fifteen minutes later Cooperbatch T Gulfstrode was sitting in Vine Street police station. His companion and guardian, whilst details were being taken, was a WPC who could have bested Letitia Banston in her dislike of teenagers in general and precocious American teenagers in particular.

It was a depressing tea interval for Philip Bond. With his inhibitions removed by the privacy and comfort of their rural nest, his relationship with his girlfriend entered an energetic and physically demanding phase. After a while he felt as drained as when he had completed one of Terry Lilgate's pre-match workouts in the school gymnasium – although they were not as much fun. They must have dozed. Philip Bond had lost all sense of time. Neither he nor his girlfriend were wearing watches; his was in the pocket of his trousers hanging in the changing-room. There did not appear to be a clock in the house. Nor a telephone. Nor was their friendly chauffeur outside with the car as he had said he would be. It dawned on Philip Bond that he was not so much in a nest as a trap. Not knowing exactly where they were (he had opted for history rather than geography at GCSE) he was unsure how to escape. He would, he gloomily reckoned, never be able to talk himself out of his absence from school and from the bowling attack. He finally poured out his troubles to his companion and she tried to comfort him. 'Don't worry,' she said. 'I'll find a way of squaring Daddy.' She was Serena, Herbert Banston's younger daughter and the apple of his eye. Unlike Bond the blond, she did not seem to be in any hurry to leave the farmhouse. And she could be very persuasive.

It was a depressing tea interval for the bursar. He had his man, Charlie Burns, with him in the accounts office and there had not been the early breakthrough for which the bursar had been hoping. He had, he thought, been reliably informed that Charlie Burns was capable, at a pinch, of breaking into the Pentagon's computer systems and so he had hoped that this infinitely simpler task would be routine to such a palpable wizard. However, as the palpable wizard well recognised, what the bursar wanted required time as well as intelligence. Charlie Burns had sufficient intelligence to see what the bursar was about. There could be more in this than a stacking system. Equally he realised that he might not actually be able to break into the account which the bursar was targeting if it was guarded by the latest security procedures. Before this point was reached, he decided he must up his price. The bursar could see that he had little option because the boy could be awkward if he got suspicious. He protested when Charlie Burns said he wanted an initial down-payment of half the newly agreed fee in readies. The petty cash box yielded only £145 and Charlie Burns had to settle for that. With his eye on still greater riches, he resumed his tapping of the keyboard. The bursar was left to sweat, unable to resist thoughts of the bookmaker's associates entering his mind. Thoughts of cricket were nowhere in Charlie Burns's mind.

It was a depressing tea interval which beckoned for Rockcliffe's director of music. Fawn Felucca was in her twenties and strikingly good-looking. Born in Doncaster of a Yorkshire mother and an Italian father, she had acquired musical talent from the former (a piano teacher) and diplomas from the latter (a forger). It had not crossed Herbert Banston's mind that the Carlozzi Academy of Music did not exist. In any case he spent little time on the impressive-looking certificates and much more on the impressive-looking Miss Felucca. Her appointment had been a formality and the headmaster had lusted after her from the moment she took up residence. Sadly for him, his ardour had not been reciprocated. Fawn Felucca preferred to find her pleasures with the younger teachers and the older boys. If this encouraged them to greater musical heights, she felt thoroughly justified (and thoroughly satisfied).

The headmaster's call had disrupted her afternoon. She had an early evening concert to supervise and there were last minute arrangements to be made. It was a charity event and she expected a large attendance from the surrounding community. 'Italian Prisoners of Conscience' was the nominated charity. Registered in Doncaster, it was not one of the more familiar good causes, but it was very much a family good cause in Fawn Felucca's eyes. Her father languished in prison in Milan and his incarceration was on her conscience. She desperately needed money to pay the Italian lawyers who were handling his appeal. She did not mind roping in a visitor to swell the audience, but having to go out and search the school for him was an exercise she would have wished to avoid. More urgent from her point of view was the need to locate the French horn without which performance of the third item in the programme would be considerably impeded. The Indian – and the headmaster – would have to wait.

It remained a depressing tea interval for the cricket coach. No sighting of his missing fast bowlers had been reported. Terry Lilgate was left with two duties. He needed to acquaint the headmaster with the latest disappearances and he needed substitutes. He saw it as his priority to address the cricket problem first. With the second eleven and the colts playing away, the only resource left to him was the Under-15s. Terry Lilgate marched across to their pitch and instructed six of the boys to collect their kit and follow him to the main pavilion. This was to the astonishment of the teacher in charge as Rockcliffe were fielding at the time. The visitors, struggling at 32–7 in reply to Rockcliffe's 108, subsequently made an easy job of knocking off the runs.

It was a depressing tea interval for the headmaster. If he had thought that things were bad enough and it would be difficult for them to get worse, he was mistaken. Things got worse with ease. He had received no report back from Fawn Felucca. He did not know whether she had been able to track down the supposed director of social services and lure him towards the delights offered by the school's music department and by the director of music herself. No police officer had yet arrived to take particulars of the missing boy. There was no word from his wife (possibly a mixed blessing), but he felt he ought to know the fate of the Hamerskill boy. He had waited so far in vain for something more from his tame county councillor. His mood descended abruptly from depression to misery when his daughter Rosie, restored to her clothes, was hauled before him. (For safety's sake, her erstwhile companions were kept away from him). Herbert Banston's fury knew no bounds. He assumed his daughter's escapade would have been witnessed by the county council official and, with half the school at the match, anonymity would not be long preserved. He had cursed the girl and cursed her mother before remembering that it was he who had caused supervision to be removed. Rosie Banston was helped to a couch in the secretary's office where she promptly fell into a drunken and noisy sleep.

The headmaster had scarcely recovered from this shock when Terry Lilgate reappeared. Three more boys gone. It was unbelievable. Herbert Banston began to think that he and the school were victims of some kind of sinister plot. He knew that the school took pupils whose parents did not all belong to the professional and executive classes. Had he given offence? Was revenge being taken for poor exam results? Had it been a mistake to expel the boy who had tried to poison his science teacher? Perhaps he had let too much sarcasm creep into his end of term reports. His increasingly wild imaginings were forestalled by the arrival of his next visitor. Detective Sergeant Jolliface was about to be on the case.

When news came through to the Regional Crime Centre that a Rockcliffe schoolboy had been apprehended by the Met, the Superintendent in charge saw a way of killing two birds with one stone. By despatching Det Sgt Jolliface to the school with this message of good cheer, the Superintendent thought he could strike a blow for police efficiency and community relations. He could also get George Jolliface out of his hair. It was after all a fairly passive duty, but as an afterthought he decided to give the detective sergeant a minder. For this purpose he selected one of his latest recruits, a bright young detective constable, Christopher Wormhurst, known inevitably but unfairly to his colleagues as Wormy. Having given his order, the superintendent felt able to put aside for a while the questions which so frequently exercised him. Why on earth had George Jolliface been transferred from Traffic and why to his patch? The question would only too soon re-emerge.

George Jolliface could not believe his luck. What had started out as a dogsbody errand looked as though it was turning into a major criminal investigation. After first being embraced by Herbert Banston, whose pleasure that Cooperbatch T Gulfstrode had been located stemmed less from his concern for the boy's welfare and more from relief that the prospect of being sued for billions of dollars had receded, the detective sergeant was confronted with the news of three more missing pupils. This was the real stuff of policing and he was the man on the spot. He recognised that the investigation called for perception, tact and sensitivity. What he did not recognise was that he possessed none of these qualities. He brushed aside his young colleague's suggestion that they should ring through to headquarters, if only because the search might have to cover a wider area. After all, Christopher Wormhurst reasoned, the first missing boy had been found in London. But George Jolliface was already fuelled by a mixture of instinct and excitement. It had a higher octane than reason. The detective sergeant ordered the junior officer in the direction of the cricket ground to 'ask some questions'. The detective constable set off on what he was sure was a misguided mission, but there was the consolation of cricket in the background. Thus, by the wildest of chances, the case was cracked.

On balance, the Outcasts came through the tea interval in cheerful mood. From Stewart Thorogood's conspiratorial account they believed they had control of the situation. No beer, Ray Burrill was once again reminded, but probably control. As he retook the umpire's coat, Terry Lilgate thought otherwise.

SECOND INNINGS

'Six o'clock and then twenty overs.' Terry Lilgate said it in such a way as to make clear the terms were not negotiable. As if to emphasise the point, he abruptly stalked towards the pitch leaving Syd Breakwell to trail along resignedly in his wake. Tom Barnes followed with a Rockcliffe team radically altered in its composition. As he watched them troop on to the field, Ray Burrill reckoned the earring and stud count was about the same. He had not been given the option to approve the substitution of so many players. In all conscience, he could hardly have refused. Yet twenty-four overs (at most he calculated) was a tall order to get 266 runs even against schoolboy opposition and even against reduced schoolboy opposition. There was still Jack Dolland. As Ray Burrill contemplated the remarkably long run-up the boy was pacing out, he glanced at Stewart Thorogood, who nodded.

The Outcasts' makeshift opening pair were Alan Birch and David Pelham. Alan Birch was a volunteer, David Pelham a pressed man. The latter's doubts were reinforced as he too watched Jack Dolland mark out his run. He was thankful that Alan Birch was due to take the first ball. His relief was not long-lasting. The field settings had to take account of the changed composition of the side. Tom Barnes put his older and more experienced players in close catching positions behind the wicket, leaving the youngsters for the most part to do the running.

There was no doubting that Jack Dolland was quick, astonishingly quick for a fifteen year-old. His opening delivery was short of a length and wide of off stump. Alan Birch played, missed and swore (all in silence as he chastised himself). Gus Flabert behind the stumps audibly swore as he dived for the ball, missed and conceded a bye as third man was brought into play. All too soon David Pelham found himself at the receiving end. It was a short, not always dignified, but in its way, useful innings. Having seen Jack Dolland's pace, David Pelham had no real desire to hang around. It was to be death or glory. He reminded himself that he was judged more on his bowling than his batting.

Despite hearing the whispered instruction 'shorter' which passed between Terry Lilgate and the bowler, David Pelham got a ball of fuller length at which he swung and swung magnificently. It took off well above the catching height of the slip cordon and was still rising when it cleared the rope. Terry Lilgate reluctantly raised his arms to signal the six. There was an acknowledgment from the scorebox. The coach's instruction to Jack Dolland was this time more audible and more expressive. The bowler ran in. Shorter the ball proved to be, but wide of leg stump. David Pelham, by no means a complete duffer with the bat, sensed a free hit and flung his bat more in hope than expectation of connecting. But connect he did and the ball soared over deep fine-leg for another six.

As angry by now as his coach, Jack Dolland tore in and delivered a brute of a ball which was short, fast, lifting and pitched on middle stump. David Pelham bent his body, but negligently left his bat in the air. When the ball struck the bat it might have gone anywhere, but as it was only a thin edge, its general sense of direction was undisturbed and it went all the way to the boundary. In disbelief, Terry Lilgate signalled a third time. The fifth ball was not quite so short and was directed more towards off. The adrenaline was flowing. David Pelham decided and decided quickly. He rocked back and struck. It was a brilliantly executed shot. The ball went like a tracer bullet between two hapless young fielders, both relieved they had not been obstructing its route to the rope. Terry Lilgate blinked. He had now been forced to stare in the direction of the scorebox four times. There could not be any doubt: it was undermanned. Blast that Gary Pocke. And then Terry Lilgate suddenly realised where the boy would have gone late on a Saturday afternoon. He would see that young Gary would be in deep trouble if he did not get his cut.

Simon Crossley had indeed returned to an empty scorebox. He and Sophie had skipped tea and pedalled away towards Chipping Rockcliffe in search of lovers' lane and an off-licence. Back on duty with both missions accomplished, Simon found only a scorebook, not a scorer. He checked whether Gary Pocke's total tallied with his, but any relevant figures which might have been on the page had been obscured by what appeared to be psychedelic drawings. It was only on staring at them a second time that he saw a pattern which would have made a slattern blush. The only compensation for having to man the scorebox by himself was that the aroma of funny fags and filthy feet had gone.

There was no evidence that Terry Lilgate had any understanding of the convention whereby an umpire does not coach. A three-way conversation took place between bowler, captain and umpire before another ball was bowled. It was Tom Barnes's advice which prevailed. Jack Dolland, having been told to calm down, came in off a short run, delivered a half-pace ball which pitched outside leg stump and struck David Pelham's back foot which was also outside leg stump. It was good enough for Terry Lilgate, who answered a concerted appeal with a pointing finger. A stupefied David Pelham had to retire, albeit with mixed feelings. The Outcasts were 23-1 after only one over.

If Ray Burrill was in charge of the team, Stewart Thorogood had assumed control of overall strategy. The sense of challenge he felt was very much tugging against his evening social arrangements. It was almost with relief that he received a call from Amanda on his mobile to say that she would be late back. Dinner at Le Hot Spot would have to be postponed with an immediate saving, Stewart reckoned, of £200. So, instead of departing after the tea interval, Stewart continued to plot and plan. One of the problems was Basil Smith, the Nawab of Wandsworth.

The neatly-turned out figure of Dean Faulds, red hair hidden under a red helmet, had joined Alan Birch. For the moment he was at the non-striker's end. In the absence of no fewer than three of his fast bowlers, Tom Barnes was forced to plug the gap himself. He was no more than a change bowler. As Rockcliffe's fast men usually carried out the destruction of their opponents' batting, the role of change bowler was redundant. Tom Barnes was therefore a very unpractised performer with the ball. As an opening bowler he was a complete rookie. And it showed. What he bowled was on the slow side of medium and he was not instantly accurate. Alan Birch played two balls in contemplative fashion and then sent the junior substitute fielders running in all directions as he relieved his feelings over the plundered hamper by finding the boundary four times.

Struggling round that boundary was the diminutive figure of Rockcliffe's substitute twelfth man. He had been put in charge of distributing at strategic points along the boundary containers of an energy-giving drink. The containers emblazoned in Rockcliffe colours and stamped with the school's name were placed in a plastic-coated metal basket such as milkmen used. The burden was obviously proving troublesome for a small boy, who had already spent half an afternoon fielding. Stewart Thorogood in a show of sympathy volunteered to ease his task by sharing the duty.

Basil Smith had been denied tea with his team-mates (a favour as it turned out), because at that point Rashid Ali had to resume his identity. Stewart Thorogood had lent him his car to go off and find a burger or kebab. He had dutifully returned assuming that Stewart would be departing. Not so. It was Basil's disappearance which Stewart seemed to have on his mind. Becoming Rashid Ali had not been terribly difficult. Un-becoming Rashid Ali was not so easy. Greg Roberts had been acute in observing how Indian in appearance Basil had seemed in the wake of his holiday. Three hours later he was hardly less Indian in his looks. The trick which had so far successfully been pulled needed to be sustained. Stewart recommended that Basil went walk-about with the cricket ground firmly off the itinerary.

Dean Faulds took guard. Jack Dolland had resumed his full run. The first ball of his new over was certainly short-pitched. It leapt above the batsman's head. It overshot the wicket-keeper and four byes resulted. The second ball was less short, but Dean Faulds, his eye unadjusted, took a painful blow to the chest. There was a pause before he felt able to resume. Ray Burrill paced assiduously in front of the pavilion, concerned as much about the loss of time as Dean

Faulds's well-being. Had he been in any doubt before, Dean Faulds was now sure. If it was short, he would hook. It was short and he did hook – cleanly and well over the boundary. The bowler gave him a vicious look and another bouncer. Dean Faulds pivoted and the ball flew over the mid-wicket boundary. The next ball was fuller and outside the off stump. The batsman played it on to his pads. The fielding side erupted. 'Out,' yelled Terry Lilgate. Dean Faulds stared, but left.

They met. She was heading towards the cricket, having looked around fruitlessly elsewhere. He was keeping out of the way of it. She had remembered that her virtuoso organist was to be found amongst the cricketers. He was wondering how he had ever agreed to take part in this dreadful outing. Fawn Felucca turned the corner and stared at him. The Indian. Basil Smith stared at her. The beauty. If he had not been committed (totally, completely, absolutely) to the formidable Jane, Basil Smith might have been carried away on a marvellous, transcendental whim. She appeared to be attracted to him; at least it was the inference he drew from her straightaway taking his arm. He did not resist and within five minutes he was in the school hall with a concert programme in his hand, and there was £5 in her hand for (she had smiled so sweetly) the Italian Prisoners of Conscience.

Alan Birch's advice to his new partner, Charlie Colson, was as simple as his analysis of what was going on: 'Whatever happens, don't let it hit your pads.' Charlie Colson felt more concerned about the ball hitting his chest and certain other parts of his anatomy. He had tried to achieve a makeshift chest protector by stuffing a folded newspaper inside his shirt. Alan Birch could make out a part headline '...ician in sex sca...' and turned over the possibilities in his mind as he watched Charlie Colson prepare himself to face the last ball of the over. It failed to hit his pads or his bat, being too full and too wide. Similarly it missed the gloves and for that matter the pads of Gus Flabert standing back. Terry Lilgate was forced to signal four more byes. Jack Dolland retired to the boundary to slake his thirst from the plastic bottle which had been placed for his convenience.

Before starting his second over, Tom Barnes changed tactics. With only one strike bowler at his disposal, he himself would have to aim for containment. He took out the slips and close-to-the-wicket fielders and deployed an entirely defensive field. The theory was probably right in the circumstances, but Tom Barnes had to be able to bowl to it. For three balls he managed and gave away only singles. Then he dropped short and Charlie Colson put him away for three. A full toss gave Alan Birch a straight driven boundary to which he added a clipped single off the last. It had been the cheapest over of the innings so far, but it had still cost eleven runs.

Alan Birch had not faced the pace of Jack Dolland since the first ball of the Outcasts' reply, but he had kept him under close observation. An impartial close observer would have said that the bowler overstepped the mark in sending down the first ball of his new over. By a foot at least. From Terry Lilgate there was no call even supposing he had noticed. Alan Birch had been prepared for a short ball and short it certainly was. He swayed out of its line and it harmlessly passed both him and the wicket-keeper. This time it was rescued before reaching the boundary, but the batsmen ran two byes. Despite not being called for a no-ball, Jack Dolland made an elaborate fuss of repacing his run-up. To no good effect, because his next ball, whilst legitimate, was short, pullable and was duly pulled over the head of deep mid-wicket for four. This time, detected Alan Birch, it was the bowler who swayed as he made his way back to the end of his run. The next delivery was less fast, on target and solidly blocked. Jack Dolland repeated this feat with the fourth ball of the over. There was an audible 'shorter, damn it' from Terry Lilgate as the bowler marched back. Shorter it proved, but down the leg side and Alan Birch pulled it again. It was hard to say who was the more agitated, bowler or umpire. The sixth ball was an anodyne affair and it led to an anodyne single. The Outcasts were an astonishing 81-2 after only five overs.

No-one had said anything to Fawn Felucca about two Indians. However, she was not disposed to argue as a second Indian propelled into her presence the virtuoso organist for whom she had been hoping. When it had come to the point, Rashid Ali had struggled to get Dean Faulds to co-operate. In common with many batsmen Dean Faulds was not easily approached after dismissal, particularly so when there was no good bitter around as a palliative. But Rashid Ali, having persuaded Ray Burrill that he would bat no higher than seven, was anxious to be on the move again to see what else he could discover about the school. Having already seen notices advertising the school concert, he also felt some obligation to 'deliver' Dean Faulds. The latter was most reluctant to move anywhere, but realised that he would risk total exposure in the eyes of his friends if he did not make some kind of effort. Removing his whites, it was a choice of blue tracksuit bottoms or black jeans. He chose blue with a white fleecy top. It might not have been the correct dress for a concert recital, but with his red hair, he at least looked patriotic. He felt a complete coward.

As he prepared to bowl again to Alan Birch, Tom Barnes was idly wondering what Clive Lloyd and Viv Richards would have felt if, mid-match, they had been robbed of their battery of fast bowlers. He lessened his pace in striving for greater accuracy and restricted Alan Birch to three scoring strokes which each yielded two runs. Fortified by another dose of the energy drink, Jack Dolland tore in like a man possessed. If anything, he was becoming dispossessed of common sense and equilibrium. The ball pitched approximately half-way between the batting crease and Syd Breakwell standing at square leg. An alert deep fine leg rescued it before it reached the boundary. The batsmen were too bemused to run. Even Terry Lilgate was obliged to signal a wide – although he needed a reminder from his opposite number. Charlie Colson tentatively took up position again, speculating about the trajectory of the next delivery. It proved to be conventionally straight. Unconventionally it pitched in the bowler's half of the strip and took off steeply. Charlie Colson had time to get out of the way and it should have been caught in the raised hands of the wicket-keeper standing deep. At the critical moment, however, one of Gus Flabert's hands unaccountably descended to groin level for an adjustment to his protection. The hand remaining aloft did no more than grab unsuccessfully at the ball and it sped to the rope ahead of a despairing dive from the deep fine-leg rescuer of the previous ball. Profanities were exchanged between bowler and wicket-keeper before Jack Dolland stalked back to the end of his run. At this point a mischievous thought entered Charlie Colson's mind.

Jack Dolland charged forward. He accelerated fast. It was clear he was bent on unleashing the super lethal delivery. He was no more than a stride or two behind the umpire when Charlie Colson stepped aside with a gesture intended to give the impression that he had been disturbed by a movement behind the bowler's arm. This was pure theatre on Charlie Colson's part. What followed was real drama. Without releasing the ball, Jack Dolland kept on running until he was eyeball to eyeball with the batsman. Some heated unpleasantries ensued, entirely from one source. Charlie Colson, no stranger to foul language, admirably kept his cool and felt that he had had a points victory. It was his only victory, although that was not apparent from the next ball bowled. A ruffled Jack Dolland produced a beamer which Charlie avoided and Gus Flabert missed. There was a further addition to the byes total. A fast ebbing technique allied to raw fury then produced a demon of a delivery. A too complacent Charlie Colson had lulled himself into no longer expecting it. His bat and his feet were all over the place. In a trice so were his stumps. Charlie did not delay his departure and was fortunate not to see the insulting gesture with which Jack Dolland wished him on his way.

Detective Sergeant George Jolliface had so far progressed barrenly in his search of the central school buildings, photographs of the missing pupils to hand. Had he been a school teacher he might have been suspicious of the lingering smell of tobacco smoke in the library or of the dishevelled appearance of two boys in the chemistry lab, but George Jolliface was concerned about none of these things. He was on the track of real crime and he was convinced it was hovering close. When he eventually came up against the closed door of the accounts office with the clear sound of voices beyond it, he was sure he had hit the jackpot.

Inside the accounts office the bursar and Charlie Burns were both aware that the jackpot, far from being hit, had not yet been sighted. This was not the moment for interruption. Progress had been made. Charlie Burns had bid up his fee from the bursar to a level of £1500. He had hopes of going higher. He realised that he was not going to get any more cash in hand and so he had slyly suggested that his fee, suitably disguised, could be invoiced to the school by his father's wholesale grocery firm. His father would play ball. Charlie Burns should have noticed the alacrity with which the bursar had accepted the suggestion. It was, after all, a technique he had been practising for some years with a number of suppliers, not all fictitious. Nevertheless Charlie thought he was getting nearer to cracking the system and the bursar shared the hope. The sudden pounding on the office door was a totally unwelcome distraction. The bursar could not have begun to guess who was on the outside, but he wanted no-one through the door who could possibly begin to guess the nature of the exercise on which he was engaged. 'Go away,' he eventually said, but not in those exact words.

George Jolliface's suspicions were immediately augmented, and his voice amplified. 'This is the police. Have you got a boy in that room?' When the answer, again none too politely worded, was undeniably affirmative, George Jolliface positively glowed with triumph. He did not know to whom he was speaking and he gave himself no chance to consider that there might be a reasonable (albeit non-admissible) explanation. What George Jolliface did know was that funny things went on at public schools. Putting the worst possible construction on what lay beyond, George Jolliface put his shoulder to the door.

There were three balls left in the over. Jack Dolland had not dallied long in the congratulations, preferring to wander off and slake his thirst. He needed to be reminded after a few minutes that a new batsman required his attention. Ray Burrill had taken his time over his guard (wisely double-checking Terry Lilgate's guidance) and his examination of the field. His eye dwelt, in particular, on the bowler. Jack Dolland's approach to the wicket appeared to have dropped a gear. It also seemed that his radar had been disturbed. Ray Burrill was a mere spectator as three times the ball was sprayed around either side of him. Three times Terry Lilgate could find no official fault with the width, but by the end of the over it was clear that he was finding fault with Jack Dolland.

It is an observable fact that young players ape the sports stars they see on television, trying hard to learn all facets of their behaviour and technique so that one day they too might be leading professionals. Rockcliffe's cricketers certainly knew how to spit. Gus Flabert appeared to have acquired the habit of adjusting his box. The only difference was that where batsmen went through this procedure between deliveries, the school's wicket-keeper was allowing his hand to stray in that direction as the ball was being bowled. This led to an unfortunate lapse when Tom Barnes got a ball to move away late from Alan Birch and take the edge. What should have been a routine catch was spilled. In anticipation, Terry Lilgate had already raised his finger. Disbelievingly, he let his arm fall to his side. 'You pillock,' he muttered in Gus Flabert's direction. And that was indeed closely related to the problem from which Gus Flabert was suffering. As he was standing in direct line between umpire and wicket-keeper, Alan Birch thought that the taunt was intended for him. He took his revenge, if not on the umpire. Tom Barnes, whose over did not live up to its opening, was driven, square cut and glanced for three elegant, uncompromising boundaries, the last of which took him to his fifty. The Outcasts' score passed the hundred mark.

George Jolliface was a powerfully built man. He was also a single-(colleagues would say simple) minded man. He was determined to get inside the office where he was increasingly sure he was going to find one or more of the missing boys. The door had other ideas. The result of three body charges came nearer to a splintered shoulder than splintered woodwork. Charlie Burns, having had time to switch the computer to some innocuous programme, nodded to the bursar, who thought it was safe to open the door. Safe for him maybe, but not for the detective sergeant who was beginning his fourth charge. His momentum carried him across the office and into collision with a metal filing

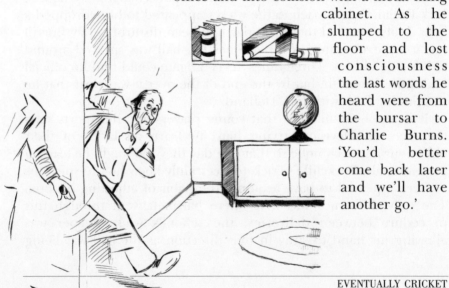

cabinet. As he slumped to the floor and lost consciousness the last words he heard were from the bursar to Charlie Burns. 'You'd better come back later and we'll have another go.'

As swiftly as George Jolliface lost consciousness, Charlie Burns suddenly realised that he should be at a cricket match. Although his absence had caused Terry Lilgate fury, his return was better received than he had dared to expect. Timing is always of the essence. Jack Dolland's run-up at the start of his next over had lost all rhythm. He bowled a full toss outside leg stump and Ray Burrill eased himself off the mark with a firm clip behind square and no more than a slight twinge from his injured shoulder. The next ball was half-speed and very short. Ray Burrill had time to consider and reject a hook shot (too early in his innings, he decided). The ball rose over his shoulder and was not pouched by the wicket-keeper, because the wicket-keeper was once again attending to his anatomy. Two byes were added.

The third ball never arrived. Jack Dolland looked to have difficulty in getting back to the end of his run and equal difficulty recognising that he had reached it. One of the younger fielders intercepted him. He was swivelled around to face the distant batsman. He set off swaying from side to side. He stumbled and then he fell. Like George Jolliface in another place it was plain that he would not immediately rise again. As he was carried off, Charlie Burns hove into view. In the circumstances Terry Lilgate was in a forgiving mood (the questions would come later). Charlie Burns was ordered to complete the over. The 'terrifying b...black b...b...b...' of Harry Northwood's scarred memory had arrived.

Regarding the musical output of the school, Fawn Felucca was a generalist. She contributed flair, colour, creativity, inspiration, but as little actual teaching as possible. Nor, when it came to a concert, did she conduct. This task fell to her deputy, who had also been her predecessor. In retirement, conducting the orchestra was something he told himself he still enjoyed although his sad, lined face probably betrayed a greater truth about the effect of thirty years of trying to drum musical appreciation and instrumental competence into successive waves of increasingly apathetic youngsters. Fawn Felucca had devised the concert programme, but at the concert itself she reserved for herself the combined role of administrative supervisor, mistress of ceremonies and cheerleader.

Cheer was an ingredient which concerts at Rockcliffe School badly needed. Few, barring the innocent, attended in pursuit of a musical treat. Not all the charm of Fawn Felucca nor the diligence of the teaching staff could lift the performance of the pupils much above pedestrian level. Only a handful of parents came. Many had no love of music and in some cases precious little love for their children. Some local tradespeople were in the audience out of a show of loyalty to the school and with an eye to the income they received from their proximity to it. Younger pupils not engaged in playing games were under orders to attend, but a significant proportion had learnt wonderfully imaginative reasons for excusing themselves. Yet the hall was full.

It had been a simple idea. In the vicinity of Chipping Rockcliffe there was a plethora of homes for the elderly – flats, residential properties, warden-controlled bungalows and sheltered accommodation. Fawn Felucca was a modern young lady. She knew that this represented more than bums on seats. Many of these elderly people might not be able to spend extravagantly, but nor were they paupers. Free entry to the concerts was good for the public image of the school and usually led to quite generous contributions to the collection which Fawn Felucca had the wit to organise on behalf of her inventive causes. It was a bonus that most of these same elderly people had reached a point in life when they had encountered hearing difficulties. Thus the inadequacies of the music performed by the school did not prevent them attending again and again.

Charlie Burns was stiff, distracted and uneasy. He had missed a warm-up session during the tea interval which would normally have preceded his opening spell. His mind was on money and how close he felt he was to it. He was confident he could put the squeeze on the bursar whether or not his hacking was ultimately successful. By contrast he was less confident about his relationship with Terry Lilgate. He felt it was a case of the calm before the storm. So the four balls he bowled in place of Jack Dolland were an ordinary assortment which would have brought fewer runs had they not caused more difficulty for the wicket-keeper than for the batsman. Ray Burrill collected two and Gus Flabert conceded six.

Fawn Felucca had taken Dean Faulds to her heart – and bosom. He was clasped closely to her as she kissed him on both cheeks in the warmest of welcomes. She was pleased to have an organist of supposed high repute to add lustre to the concert and extra money to her collection. She had not expected such a good-looking young man. Red hair did something for her. True, Dean Faulds did not appear exactly suitably dressed for an organ recital, but in other respects she thought he was very suitably dressed. Having acquainted herself with him, she led him up the stairs to acquaint him with the organ. Dean Faulds followed with anticipation, the organ not being at the forefront of his mind. As she disappeared from view, Fawn Felucca gave the signal for the concert to begin. Rashid Ali took it as the signal for him to disappear as well. Basil Smith thought that he had better stay.

The headmaster should have been at the concert. However, as he liked good music he was pleased that he was not. The only disappointment was the missed opportunity to curry favour with his director of music. But, he told himself, he had to stay at his post to await reports. He hoped that for the moment the director of social services was neutralised. He had been led by George Jolliface to expect an early result in the case of the missing pupils. Cooperbatch T Gulfstrode was on his way back under police escort. Douglas Hamerskill was receiving the combined attention of the police and Mrs Banston (he reflected momentarily on which was the worse fate). Possibly this horrendous afternoon would get better; within minutes it got appallingly worse.

At the end of the ninth over with the Outcasts 122-3, Tom Barnes was reviewing his options. They were few. He had been going for around eleven an over. The only other regular bowler left in the side was William Briggs. Coming in off two paces, he bowled off-spinners which could not always be relied on to spin very much. His advantage was accuracy; his disadvantage was the speed with which he completed his overs. Time was a factor. If Rockcliffe were unable to blast out their opponents in their accustomed fashion, the only alternative was to deny them time to win. With the reappearance of Charlie Burns, Tom Barnes was unsure which course would be the more productive. Indecision led him to bowl himself one more over. Like the balls he bowled, he erred.

In some ways it was fortunate that none of them passed the bat, because Gus Flabert's attention did not seem to be completely on the game. He seemed to be in the grip of the adjustment-of-box habit and the ball was consequently less in the grip of his gloves. A sharply run single off Tom Barnes's first ball became five when Gus Flabert failed to gather an over-enthusiastic return from one of the substitute fielders. The wicket-keeper was spared examination from the second delivery as Ray Burrill slashed it square on the off-side for four. Then he on-drove for two and followed this shot with a single in the same direction. Alan Birch was presented with a short ball which he square cut and they ran three. Ray Burrill cover drove the final delivery which was also rescued before it reached the boundary. Tom Barnes realised he was now costing over twelve an over. He needed something special from Charlie Burns.

Although they were not yet aware of it, the people in the school hall were shortly to get something special themselves. After the first three items of the concert it was needed. Basil Smith thought to himself it was a miracle that the Overture 'Dr Miracle' by Bizet was completed without someone walking out. The audience stayed intact during the second movement of Haydn's Trumpet Concerto out of sympathy for the soloist, a boy of thirteen who fought a brave battle with the instrument. By the end of Handel's Sonata for Two Violins which had set even false teeth on edge, there was a distinct air of restlessness in the hall. At this point Fawn Felucca appeared. She had bad news. For Mrs Florence Trumpington of Roseleigh Residential Home for the widows of officers and gentlemen, it was too much. She expired, but, as she had lived her life, she did it quietly and decently and no-one noticed until the concert was over.

Had she lived to hear it, Florence Trumpington might not have found the news too distressing. The French horn had not been found and so Bradley Bingham would be unable to perform Jerome Kern's 'All the things you are'. Those who on other occasions had heard Bradley Bingham's rendition of this piece had been given cause to wonder about all the things it might have been. However, Fawn Felucca announced, with exaggeration stemming from her personal enthusiasm, she could now introduce the world-famous classical organist, Dino Faulds. With that she shot back up the organ loft stairs. Basil Smith suppressed a chuckle. The audience wondered whether it would be worth the wait. But soon every foot, except the two attached to Florence Trumpington, was tapping as the unmistakable strains of 'I do like to be beside the seaside' rolled through the hall.

'You've sent him where?' shrieked the headmaster at a bemused bursar. 'The san? Oh good God!' The bursar was disappointed with this reaction to what he thought had been a sensible move on his part. He had not been made privy to the arrangement by which on occasions the so-called Community Leisure Service operated out of the sanatorium building. The bursar had equally not been made a director of Rockcliffe Community Leisure Services Ltd. The headmaster realised that he had to make an urgent call to matron, but was reluctant to do so in the presence of his colleague. Trying hard to appear calm, he soothed the bursar's ruffled feelings and ushered him from the room. He was about to pick up the phone when his wife appeared.

Charlie Burns knew what was needed of him. He tried to put himself in an aggressive frame of mind. As he turned at the end of his intimidatingly long run, he was sure he could hear the sound of the red, red robin bob bob bobbin' along. This was the wrong mood music and it affected his approach. He delivered the ball from about twenty-four yards. It exploded off the pitch, cleared both batsman and 'keeper and was over the boundary before anyone had scarcely moved. Charlie Burns chastised himself, tried to shut his ears to extraneous sounds and ran in again with maximum menace. It was a brute of a ball which had it been straight would have lodged between Ray Burrill's ribs. Gus Flabert did not seem to see it and first slip was not risking his fingers. Four more byes were added to the Outcasts' score. The next ball was straighter and shorter. Ray Burrill leapt, but not far enough (away) and he was hit on the shoulder. He let out a yell, dropped his bat and fell to the ground. Stewart Thorogood was galvanised into action. He shot round the ground and re-filled the drink bottle.

On arrival at the police station with Douglas Hamerskill, Letitia Banston had but one thought: how to get away as quickly as possible. She was a welfare minimalist. She doubted whether the odious boy would be beaten up by the police or would be found hanging in his cell in the morning (either of which extremities she could have contemplated with equanimity). She believed that once the boy had a lawyer by his side she had fulfilled her obligation. This took two cups of stewed tea longer than she would have wished, but then she demanded that she be driven back to the school. A harassed desk sergeant succumbed to her demand.

When she arrived back in her husband's outer office, her mood was not improved by the sight of her sleeping daughter. Details of what had led to this situation triggered a furious exchange as each parent sought to pin responsibility on the other. Criticism extended to 'that slut of a mother of yours' and 'your idle, drunken father'. The Banstons were going at full throttle when one of them made a reference to the whereabouts of their other daughter. 'She's at home,' said Letitia Banston. A phone call suggested otherwise. The anger of the parents subsided into concern. Not another missing person, groaned Herbert Banston. He gazed out of his office window in despair and caught sight of the one person who seemingly refused to go missing – his supposed Aneurin Singh.

Rashid Ali was en route for the cricket ground. Meticulous as ever about his cricket, he thought he should check on the Outcasts' progress. He arrived to find it had been halted. As he hurriedly prepared for action, Stewart Thorogood brought him up-to-date. Ray Burrill had retired hurt with a severely bruised shoulder. John Furness had lasted two balls. The first hit nothing and was stopped by the 'keeper only because it was heading for his groin where his gloves happened to be at the time. The second hit John Furness's pad which was doubly unfortunate. The pad covered the leg which had been struck while he was fielding. His hopping around did not deter Umpire Lilgate from giving a favourable response to an lbw shout. Kevin Newton was now at the crease with a look of impermanence about him. In the background an organ could be heard playing 'Run, rabbit, run'. Yes, indeedy, thought Charlie Burns.

Having rid himself of his wife, who had taken the protesting Rosie with her, Herbert Banston at last got the opportunity to ring matron. In standard medical speak he was assured that the patient was comfortable. It was probably just as well for his peace of mind that he did not know how comfortable.

Dean Faulds had disposed of two Al Jolson favourites and was moving towards the end of his repertoire. As he swung into a selection from 'The Desert Song' he whispered to Fawn Felucca that he would shortly be signing off, to coin a phrase his father had used. Demand for theatre organists had fallen by these times, but Dean Faulds had picked up what he knew when he had been allowed to clamber aboard the mighty organ after the cinema audience had left. Fawn Felucca put her hand on his knee and squeezed. Dean Faulds assumed assent and smiled.

The director of music had to admit that the recital had not been quite what she had expected. However, there were two compensations. The tunes had loosened up the audience (except, alas, one of its members) and this might in turn loosen their purse strings in due course. The second compensation was the organist himself, who in manner and appearance had exceeded her expectations. After the last note of the reprise of 'I do like to be beside the seaside' had faded, there was a generous round of applause. Fawn Felucca's head appeared over the balcony to invite another round after a vote of thanks to her guest. Dean Faulds's head also appeared over the balcony. It was then Bizet's turn again. Fawn Felucca made the announcement. The orchestra embarked on the suite: 'L'Arlésienne'. The two heads disappeared.

The Rockcliffe cricket captain cursed his luck. Had he one more fast bowler he was sure he could cause the Outcasts to collapse in a manner worthy of an England Test team in the Nineties. Collapse, Tom Barnes, reflected bitterly, might be the operative word. But he had no David Simms, he had no Philip Bond and he no longer had Jack Dolland. In front of younger members of the school he did not relish the prospect of another caning at the hands of Alan Birch. Perhaps after all it was time for Billy the Kid.

William Briggs had not expected to bowl. With Rockcliffe's usual battery of fast bowlers there was on most occasions little cause for spin. He had been asked to bowl in the nets since the start of term and so he was not completely out of practice. However, this would be his first competitive over of the season. He was given a defensive field. Apart from a backward short-leg only the wicket-keeper was close to the bat. Alan Birch looked around him, paying particular attention to the 'keeper who could not seem to keep entirely still.

Time was slipping away and so Alan Birch resolved that boldness had to be his friend.

The off-spinner's first delivery was a full toss which Alan Birch placed between mid-off and cover for two. William Briggs thought he had flighted his next ball rather well. Alan Birch treated it as a fuller full toss. With two steps down the wicket he lofted it over the sight screen. Syd Breakwell pivoted towards the score-box and gave a magnificently theatrical signal. The bowler took a risk and once again gave the ball air. So too did Alan Birch. William Briggs got the message. As Alan Birch advanced a third time, the bowler maintained a high trajectory, but pushed it through with a flourish. The batsman was deceived and should have been easily stumped. Unfortunately Gus Flabert was in no position to gather the ball. To his horror, William Briggs saw that at the critical moment, the 'keeper actually had his glove off and was scratching his inside leg. The ball was collected by the fielder from backward short-leg, but not before two byes had been collected by the batsmen. William Briggs tried to repeat the formula, but this time Alan Birch was not deceived. He held back and then took one step before crashing the ball to the extra-cover boundary. Off the last ball Alan Birch intended a single, but this battle was won by the bowler, who directed it down the leg side. Syd Breakwell could well have called it a wide, but felt that William Briggs had taken sufficient punishment.

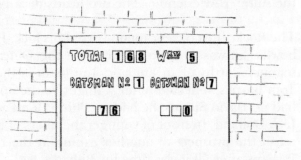

Detective Constable Christopher Wormhurst had taken his time. As instructed, he had asked questions, but he had allowed his attention to wander to the match, which seemed to be of a spectacular if not dramatic nature. He had confined his questioning to those who appeared to be school-related amongst the spectators. After a while he had found someone who remembered seeing a black player leaving the ground with a man. The same helpful spectator said that he thought the man was the bursar. Christopher Wormhurst would have taken action on this information had not, at that moment, the black player returned. In respect of the other two missing boys, he was still inclined to cling to his original theory. He proceeded slowly round the boundary towards the pavilion where he bumped into an old friend.

In the school hall, the orchestra's battle with Bizet had reached the Minuetto stage. There were no longer any feet tapping. People were checking their programmes to establish how far they were away from the interval, when wine and biscuits would be served. (Fawn Felucca worked on the basis that an alcoholic glow boosted takings in the collection.) Suddenly, Basil Smith became aware of a strange background noise. There was nothing remotely musical about it although perhaps it had a certain rhythm. It seemed to emanate from the organ loft. Basil Smith's first thought was that someone might be pumping up the organ, but it was surely not that kind of organ. After a pause, the orchestra commenced Adagietto. Immediately the noise from above took on another guise. There was a gasp – not from the audience. There was another gasp – this time from Basil Smith as it dawned on him that he was the unseeing witness to the establishment of a new form of Anglo-Italian entente.

Charlie Burns against Kevin Newton did not have the look of a fair contest. The bowler was well revved up by this stage and gave the impression of being about to carry all before him. 'Don't let it hit your pad,' Alan Birch had reminded him between overs. As far as Kevin was concerned, that was the least of his worries. He had expected the bowler to have been nobbled by now, but there was no sign of that. Lacking even the pretensions to batting of David Pelham, Kevin Newton reached a similar decision to that of his team-mate. He wanted this nightmare over and done with. By the end of the over at least three others shared his view.

They embraced. They had not seen each other for five years. Christopher Wormhurst was the younger brother of one of Stewart Thorogood's best friends at university. The five years were skipped in a few sentences and they came quickly to the 'What are you doing here?' bit. In Stewart's case it looked obvious, but was not. In Christopher's case it was not obvious or, even after Stewart had been told, probable. Christopher, a policeman? No, a detective? Stewart's mind boggled as he remembered the drunken eighteen year-old's rampage after a party and the near-riot in the police station which had followed. How the world moved on! Stewart's trip down memory lane came to an abrupt halt as Christopher explained the fatuous task on which he was supposed to be engaged. He laughed apologetically. Stewart Thorogood did not.

Not every member of the audience at the concert in the school hall was hard of hearing. The lapses of the school orchestra during the quieter passages of Bizet's 'L'Arlésienne' allowed increasing notice to be taken of the hidden, alternative performance. Fortunately not everyone was as quick as Basil Smith to establish its nature. The speculation led to a buzz in the audience which served only to undermine still further the struggling musical endeavour. Basil Smith decided he had heard enough of both performances. Between Adagietto and Carillon he made his exit, earning a glare from the world-weary conductor, whether of irritation or envy he did not know.

It would go down in the annals of the Outcasts' Cricket Club that Kevin Newton scored twenty-four runs in a single over against the fastest bowler he had ever faced. It was stirring and occasionally comic stuff. The first ball Charlie Burns bowled was meant to be intimidatory. It was very short and very quick. His fellow-Outcasts had been unaware up to then that Kevin Newton knew what the hook shot was, let alone having the wherewithal to play it. In execution it lacked grace, the footwork was plainly faulty, the arms appeared stiff and his head was in the wrong position; the ball nevertheless disappeared over the pavilion. Charlie Burns's answer was an attempted yorker. His length was not quite right. Kevin Newton, to the disbelief of his team-mates, planted a foot down the wicket and with an outrageous swing of the bat, sent the ball skidding past the bowler straight for four. This displeased Charlie Burns and he went for the short one again. With an ugly smear Kevin Newton sent it head high past a diminutive Under-15 fielder at square leg who, wisely from his own point-of-view and obligingly from the batsman's, took evasive action. The verbal appreciation of his escapalogy which he received from the bowler and Terry Lilgate was somewhat less than understanding.

Although Terry Lilgate urged him in words not borrowed from the coaching manual to 'knock his effing helmet off', Charlie Burns demurred. His two short balls had each been hit for six, his full toss for four. He thought he would strive again for the yorker. This time he produced a beauty. Kevin Newton jumped to one side leaving his bat like a prop at arm's length. The bat must have just covered leg stump for the ball went off the edge like a rifle shot, past the extended left hand of Gus Flabert (the right hand being otherwise engaged) and beat fine leg to the rope. The bowler did not go short of advice from his coach, who was an unrepentant adherent of the blitzkrieg form of cricket. His own theory was a slower ball. It was well disguised and it did not deserve what it got. Kevin Newton backed away, this time towards leg, whilst waving at the ball as though his bat was a soup ladle. He managed to spoon the ball over the slips. Third man moved the wrong way and the ball was over the boundary before it was fielded. Charlie Burns's patience finally snapped and he found himself at one with his coach. He produced a short, fast, rising ball. Kevin Newton took his body to the safety of the off-side whilst whirling his bat, much as a discus-thrower might wind himself up. The ball went off the bottom of the bat in a direction midway between fine leg and square leg. Both fielders moved towards it. The batsmen watched in fascination. The young square-leg fielder, still smarting from the tongue-lashing he had received earlier in the over, kept his eyes firmly on the ball without so much as a glance at his approaching colleague. Before the ball cannoned into them, they had – painfully – cannoned into each other. In deference to their prostrate forms, the batsmen eschewed a run.

During this spectacular over Stewart Thorogood noticed and took encouragement from the obvious, enthusiastic partisanship showed by Christopher Wormhurst. He decided to come (partly) clean. Sketching the background to the match in a few pithy sentences, Stewart Thorogood explained the Outcasts' game-plan. To his relief he found that the detective constable's sense of humour was on the same wavelength as his own. Christopher Wormhurst approved the resting-place chosen for David Simms and agreed with Stewart Thorogood as to its poetic justice. Nor could he see any wrongdoing in the 'assistance' furnished to Philip Bond. Stewart remained silent on the disablement of Jack Dolland.

The temporary disablement of two other fielders provided the opportunity for a top-level discussion between Charlie Burns and the bursar, who had reappeared in a manifestly agitated state. When the bursar had said to Charlie Burns, in the last words which George Jolliface had heard, that he required to see him again 'later', he meant 'now'. The reason for this change of timetable had been occasioned by another difficult phone call the bursar had received from his bookmaker. To put no finer point on it, the bursar's creditworthiness had been unilaterally reviewed. The debt was required to be redeemed within a very much shorter period – or else. These two short words had electrified the bursar. The only possible source of salvation, as he saw it, was the fast bowler on whom the Rockcliffe cricket team was currently relying. He found Charlie Burns at a moment of low ebb. The reminder of a bounty of £1500 might possibly have sufficed to entice him away from a scene of humiliation (as the bowler was inclined to see it). The reckless doubling of the offer by the bursar left Charlie Burns in no doubt. Pausing only to take a long draught from the canister at the boundary edge which he had hitherto disdained, Charlie Burns slipped away unnoticed.

In a not too distant place, after a second spell, another of Rockcliffe's fast bowlers metaphorically took his sweater and drifted happily into unconsciousness.

After what Ray Burrill, in his role as captain, regarded as a worrying delay, the match resumed with the injured players repaired. William Briggs commenced his second over without Tom Barnes realising that he was a fielder light. Four balls later he began a count. By this time Alan Birch had accumulated eight runs with surprising ease. Furiously Tom Barnes summoned his last remaining reserve. It was not until the end of the over that the identity of the missing person became apparent. By this time he had another wicket, even though the Outcasts had got two hundred on the board.

With a full hand of fielders in support, William Briggs managed to restrict Alan Birch to a single. As amazed as anyone by Kevin Newton's performance in the previous over, Alan Birch overlooked his partner's career average. It is said that a player's average tells the truth. Kevin Newton took a relieved swish at a nice, gentle, slow delivery. The ball took a leading edge and went high. William Briggs took the catch.

By this time Herbert Banston was in deep despair. Boys missing, daughter missing, police on the premises (the wrong part of the premises in the case of Detective Sergeant George Jolliface), the school facing possible closure: the headmaster settled for a stratospherically high-risk strategy. Slightly disorientated, Basil Smith was walking past the entrance to the administrative offices when a man appeared clutching a plastic bag. It was thrust in Basil's direction with the promise, 'If you give us a good report, you can expect the same again.' So saying, Herbert Banston shot back into the building.

Basil Smith examined the bag with some circumspection. It was pink and bore the legend of a sex-aids establishment in Frinton. 'Every need catered for' was the promise it made. Basil Smith gingerly peered inside as though some sex aid might jump out to embarrass him. Not so. What was inside lay still and inanimate. With incredulity Basil Smith saw a large quantity of banknotes in bundles. He did the first thing which any upright accountant would do in these circumstances. He found a quiet place and counted it. For an unknown reason he had been presented with £15,000. It seemed a large fee for playing a cricket match.

Inside his office, Herbert Banston wondered whether £15,000 now and the promise of £15,000 to come would do the trick. He had remembered various newspaper articles suggesting that corruption was rife in the Asian sub-continent. Being a man of shocking prejudice, the headmaster had persuaded himself that a local government officer of Asian ancestry could very likely be bought. Nevertheless it was a high price to pay. The nest-egg he had raided had been built up not without difficulty. He thought back over the tricks, ploys and devices he had had to employ. Without new and more lucrative schemes in the future, he would have to put off a few years longer the moment when he could dump the appalling Mrs Banston and depart for a South Sea island with, if not Fawn Felucca, someone who could excite the same animal instincts in him.

Tom Barnes could not understand how or why he had lost his leading bowler. His disappointment was outmatched only by Terry Lilgate's anger. Despite having conceded sixty-three runs off five overs, the captain realised there was no alternative to his having to rejoin the attack. This was what captaincy was about: coping with crisis. In fairness to Tom Barnes, he was a much better cricketer than his record in this match so far showed. By coming on at the school hall end he hoped his luck might change. It gave him one advantage: the umpiring of Terry Lilgate.

While the field was being set, Alan Birch did a runs per over calculation. As a result of delays and the general dilatoriness of the fielding side, they were left with ten overs. That meant a scoring rate of just above six an over. They had been scoring so far at more than twice this asking rate. A possible element of complacency entered into Alan Birch's batting. He played two respectable balls defensively, got a short one and square cut it for two, casually on-drove a full toss for three and then watched whilst Rashid Ali, the incoming batsman, prodded profitlessly at the last two balls of the over.

Alan Birch was convinced that he had the measure of William Briggs. Not even a dropped catch by an evidently distressed wicket-keeper gave him pause. A batsman can get into trouble if he changes gear. It was this which contributed to Alan Birch's undoing. The other contributor was Billy the Kid, a cleverer bowler than his coach, preoccupied with his strike force of pacemen, had so far recognised. By the last ball of the over he had conceded no more than two singles. Alan Birch needed a boundary to keep his side up with the rate. The bowler read his mind and offered him a beauty which curled invitingly and, wonder of wonders, spun wickedly. Alan Birch was into the stroke before he sensed his error. The ball took the edge, not the middle, of the bat and provided the fourteen year-old at square point, first, with a bout of nerves as the ball dropped towards him and, secondly, a catch.

The bursar stared defeat (and, in his imagination, dismemberment) in the face. Something had happened to Charlie Burns. The boy was ponderously tapping the keyboard between intervals of blankly gazing at the monitor and shaking his head. Charlie Burns was desperately trying to clear his head. It was swimming. He could not concentrate. He felt drowsy. After not quite three overs this was ridiculous. The bursar decided that it was ridiculous if not downright dangerous for him to wait any longer. Whilst Charlie Burns continued to fiddle listlessly with the computer, the bursar began to shred files. There was a thud as Charlie Burns slumped forward. Easing him to one side, the bursar did a 'delete all' exercise. Then, returning to his own office, he packed a case. The bursar had decided to do a runner.

The combined batting prowess of Greg Roberts and the Redman twins had never been known to strike terror into the hearts of the bowlers ranged against them. They were particularly unused to coping with the demands of a run-chase, still less the lethal finger of Terry Lilgate. Greg Roberts was left in no doubt by Rashid Ali that he was cast in the subsidiary role in the partnership they were about to form. Without wishing to undermine the morale of his team-mate, Rashid Ali did not conceal his preference for Greg having as little of the strike as possible. An over later he had much the same conversation with Nigel Redman, and three balls after that with Tom Redman. The slide continued in the following over after a brief partnership in which leg-byes and byes had predominated, Gus Flabert's incapacity becoming more and more noticeable, except, it seemed, to his coach.

Terry Lilgate had struck three times. Greg Roberts and Tom Redman had failed to keep their feet out of the way. No other factors were taken into consideration by the umpire. Out they had to go. Terry Lilgate gained his third wicket from square leg. When Nigel Redman hit the ball straight back to William Briggs in his best imitation of solid defence, the bowler (naturally) appealed. Syd

Breakwell had just about satisfied himself that it was a bump ball when he saw his opposite number gesticulating noisily in his direction. He strolled across in Terry Lilgate's direction to be told very firmly that the ball had not been hit into the ground and had carried to the bowler. Syd Breakwell should have given the batsman the benefit of his still doubting mind, but found that he was pre-empted by Terry Lilgate's raised, accusing finger. Believing from where he stood that it was a joint decision, Nigel Redman had sportingly departed. With batsmen nine, ten and eleven clinically removed, all eyes turned towards to the pavilion.

County Councillor Percy Harport meanwhile was on the phone. He had little else with which to occupy himself. His house had been picked clean. Every item of furniture had been removed. Pictures and plates from the walls had gone. The floors were bare. Even the mat which surrounded the lavatory pedestal was missing. Only the BT phone had been left, presumably because it had been thought to be the one object of no value in the house. Or perhaps it had been a charitable gesture by the thieves. In this situation the county councillor had had many calls to make before he could bring to mind the concerns of Herbert Banston. When he finally rang the headmaster he thought that his message would be one of relief. That was not how it was received.

The bursar emerged furtively from his office. His priority was speed rather than discretion, for otherwise his only bag might not have been one bearing the legend in stencilled letters: 'Bursar, Rockcliffe School'. He thought he was making good progress through the school grounds when he encountered an Indian-looking man hugging a cerise-coloured bag. When the man spoke to him, the bursar's first thought was to run, but then he recollected that his would-be assailants did not include an Asian. He stopped. The man thrust the plastic bag towards him saying, 'I think you should have this.' The bursar shrank back, having third thoughts. The fiends. This was a bomb. They had sent someone to deliver it who probably was a fanatic. The bag fell to the ground and a packet of £50 notes spilled out. The bursar had fourth thoughts. He knew money when he saw it. Assassins, he quickly told himself, did not wrap bombs in banknotes. He followed the bag to the ground, peered into its interior and saw that its contents were good. Had he wanted to ask questions (and the moment quickly passed), he was denied, because an embarrassed Basil Smith had shot away, fully believing he had done the right thing. So far as the bursar was concerned, it could not have been better.

This might have been the first occasion on which he had been entrusted with the responsibility, but Ray Burrill clearly understood what the duty of captaincy was. He knew that he faced the biggest test – outside the saloon bar – of his short career with the Outcasts. This was it. The last stand. Cowdrey at Lord's 1963. The injured man had to come to the wicket. It was this imagery which bolstered him in his decision. The comparison was, of course, ludicrous, because he had broken nothing and this was not a Test match. Yet Ray Burrill felt that he was under some sort of test. So memories of his heroes sustained him in the brave steps he took towards the middle. Thirty-five runs were needed to win the match, one ball and five overs to survive. It was the one ball which was dominating Ray Burrill's thoughts.

The search of the school which Herbert Banston now instituted was more thorough and more extensive than those organised to locate missing pupils. This search was altogether more serious. The Indian gentleman had to be found. Surely, the headmaster reasoned, it could not be an impossible task. The probability of there being scores of Indians roaming the grounds had to be extremely low. He was not conducting an Asian Open Day. The person in question ought to stick out from the crowd. And so, he thought grimly, should the lurid pink bag, containing not sex aids, but something far more precious which he could ill afford to lose, especially knowing what he now knew. The director of social services, Aneurin Singh, was on holiday with his family in Cuba.

Tom Barnes, not to mention Terry Lilgate, was convinced that the match was won. The sight of Ray Burrill trudging to the crease did not alter the expectation. 'Bounce him,' said Terry Lilgate, remembering the injured shoulder, but forgetting the extraordinary fallibility of the wicket-keeper. It was a creditable bouncer from a bowler of Tom Barnes's pace, but avoidable by someone as anxious as Ray Burrill to keep all parts of his body away from contact with the ball. Had Gus Flabert not had one hand down the front of his trousers when the ball reached him, extras might have been avoided. They were not. The total advanced by two.

If William Briggs thought that he was beginning to exert a degree of control because he had taken three wickets in nine balls at a cost of two runs, he was about to be re-educated. Like many Indians, Rashid Ali was a naturally good player of spin. In William Briggs's case, actual spin was only rarely achieved. Having played two balls warily, Rashid Ali stepped up to a full delivery and drove it classically past mid-off for four. Two balls later he disdainfully dismissed a short ball over the head of mid-wicket for another. Nor did the closer field setting for the final ball prevent him easing the ball to the side of the square-leg umpire for the single he needed to protect Ray Burrill from Tom Barnes. Terry Lilgate just managed to refrain from thrusting out a foot to stop it.

In his experience, phone calls from Mrs Smith were not always the harbinger of welcome news. With a ritual reference to the amount he may have had to drink and an expression of hope that the 'silly match' was over, Jane Smith commanded Basil's immediate return home because they had been invited to an impromptu party at her sister's. In Basil's eyes, the only redeeming feature attributable to his wife's sister was his wife's sister's husband, who could usually be relied on to have a barrel of real ale on the go in his garage. Whereas Basil might in other circumstances have had a frosty and negative exchange with Jane over such a request, he thought this was a good moment to get credit in the bank by acquiescing. Three factors influenced him. The money episode had left him uneasy. He speculated about some unhappy follow-up. He also worried that with the focus on the batting of Rashid Ali his own continued presence might draw attention to the stunt they had pulled. It was on the latter point that he consulted Stewart Thorogood. Pausing only to introduce Detective Constable Wormhurst to Simon and Sophie Crossley in the scorebox and explain their intention, Stewart and Basil drove off. And, as Basil muttered to Stewart when they were in the car, 'There'd be no bloody beer after the match anyway.' The clincher.

Rashid Ali now had to face the sinister combination of Tom Barnes and Terry Lilgate. The coach might have recovered from the worst effect of his earlier binge, but this was purely relative. Rashid Ali had no difficulty picking up the instruction issued to the bowler: 'Bounce him.' Tom Barnes did not achieve the same effect as in his previous over. The ball was short, it rose and then it rose even further as Rashid Ali pivoted and helped it behind square for six. Tom Barnes began to detach himself from Terry Lilgate's advice. He conceded only two more runs in the over which brought the Outcasts to the 250 mark. More importantly, he ensured that Ray Burrill would be on strike to William Briggs.

The audience in the school hall had thankfully reached the interval and its accompanying refreshments. With one exception they were steeling themselves for the first movement of Mozart's Bassoon Concerto and the finale of Tschaikovsky's Symphony No2 when the headmaster arrived. He was in search of Fawn Felucca, but not quite in the same way as Dean Faulds had been for the last half hour. He found his director of music flushed and as lovely as ever. For a moment he faltered, almost forgetting the reason for his presence. Recovering, he interrogated her as to the whereabouts of the Indian visitor he had asked her to take under her wing. Fawn Felucca could no longer see Basil Smith, but she brightened, telling the headmaster that Signor Faulds would know because they had both been at the cricket. Signor Faulds, she suddenly realised, was another she could no longer see (he was lost amongst his admirers), but the word 'cricket' was sufficient to get Herbert Banston on the move.

Ray Burrill's shoulder was still extremely sore. He tentatively swung his bat and tried to avoid a wince. Next he rehearsed an ostentatious forward defensive stroke. That was less bad. He prepared to face William Briggs, who for a moment flirted with the thought of trying a bouncer. He sensibly opted for line and length – at least that was his aim. The third ball drifted down the leg side and Ray Burrill deflected it, almost neatly. It still earned him two despite an 'Are you sure?' from his partner. And that was all. The remaining balls of William Briggs's over required vigilance and that was the most that Ray Burrill could give.

The return of Gary Pocke to the scorebox, which he would have been wiser never to have left, was dramatic. The door was flung open and the erstwhile school scorer arrived carrying a battered suitcase. 'Bastards,' he yelled. Simon and Sophie Crossley did not feel that this greeting was aimed at them. Nor did it seem to fit the players on the field beyond. 'Bastards,' he barked again, gaining added emphasis by slamming the case on to the floor of the box. He did this with such force – or perhaps it was just old (it had once belonged to Terry Lilgate's grandmother) – that it burst open to reveal an interesting variety of (obviously unsold) merchandise and a scattering of £10 and £20 notes. It was of particular interest to Christopher Wormhurst, who materialised from behind the door. 'Oh, shit,' said Gary Pocke. 'No, drugs, I guess,' replied the detective constable, reaching for his notebook.

Tom Barnes was in determined mood. He hated losing. In any case, Rockcliffe did not lose. Ignoring another 'Bounce him' directive from Terry Lilgate, he steadied himself to bowl a tight over. As he ran in, he was not helped by the sight of the wicket-keeper jigging up and down in a most unprofessional manner. Instead of middle and off, the ball went far wide of off stump, but Terry Lilgate remained motionless and silent. Tom Barnes managed to get the next two balls on target and of a good enough length to deny the batsman runs. A sudden movement from Gus Flabert as he was in his delivery stride caused Tom Barnes to skew the fourth ball to leg and Rashid Ali caressed it past square leg for a boundary. The following ball was intended to be a yorker, but it was too full. Rashid Ali was quickly in position and the shot beat the fielder's despairing dive. The Outcasts had closed to within six runs of their target. They were to get no nearer in the remainder of that over. Tom Barnes produced the ball of his life. How it missed the edge, how it missed off stump and how it was retrieved cleanly by Gus Flabert were equal mysteries.

The headmaster arrived at the boundary's edge for the climax of the match. He had only to look towards the middle to see his quarry. Wearing a cap, not a helmet, Rashid Ali was recognisably Indian. However, it was an Indian clearly bereft of the pink bag which (thoughts of Fawn Felucca aside) was the immediate object of

Herbert Banston's desire. Keeping his eyes glued on the batsman, the headmaster resisted the temptation to invade the pitch. Instead he engaged a junior member of staff in conversation about the movements of the Indian batsman. In particular, he wanted to know whether he had been seen with a pink plastic bag. The junior member of staff, himself an habitué of the Frinton establishment with which he associated pink plastic bags, suppressed a smile and went on to say that the only movements made by the Indian batsman in the last half hour or so had been between the wickets. He directed the headmaster's attention to the number of runs Rashid Ali had on the board. The first doubts began to assail Herbert Banston. He could not understand why, but the fear grew that this might not after all be his man – or his money.

As the match ended, the usual scenes were replaced by others of a very unusual nature. The customary courtesies were virtually non-existent, although the two captains almost shook hands. The young substitute fielders heard the supper bell and took off with a speed and enthusiasm which might have been tempered had they known what was awaiting them. Gus Flabert did not stand on ceremony: he sprinted towards the pavilion for relief from the torment in his groin. (He had spent most of the innings worrying that he was facing the onset of a communicable disease, whereas in fact he had been merely the victim of a schoolboy-type prank administered, as it so happened, not by a schoolboy.) From the direction of the scoreboard, Christopher Wormhurst headed for Terry Lilgate (who was sprinting nowhere) with a view to pursuing inquiries. Gary Pocke, who had squealed, was temporarily handcuffed to the heavy roller. The headmaster made for Rashid Ali. Another figure running in the opposite direction was David Simms, desperate to explain himself to his captain. All the earlier searches had ignored Alan Birch's food hamper. He who had consumed its contents had become its contents until he had finally slept off his gluttony.

By contrast, the Outcasts were in good order. They crowded around their captain. Ray Burrill, the man who had denied them a drink all day, was restored to favour. He had played the first three balls of the final over with the caution they had deserved. He had the luck of being patently dropped by the wretched Gus Flabert whose woes had continued. With three balls remaining he had failed either to score or to give the strike to the more prolific Rashid Ali. He had then rethought his approach. Re-appraisal was similarly being undertaken by the bowler with the assistance of his captain fresh from an exchange with the coach standing at square leg. The dubious tactic, which William Briggs had rejected in his previous over, was now being urged on him. As a desperate try he acquiesced, not knowing that Ray Burrill had decided on heroics. The ball was never more than medium-pace, but it rose obligingly. Ray Burrill threw everything into it in a flat-batted swipe. The wrenching pain in his shoulder caused him to release the bat. It flew at speed towards square leg. The ball had preceded it at greater speed and higher trajectory. The match was won in a double blow. The ball cleared the boundary, but the bat failed to clear the umpire. Terry Lilgate had leapt aside to avoid the ball, but he had not expected the bat to be following it. He collapsed and was promptly sick. The Outcasts agreed that it was a fitting end.

ROCKCLIFFE SCHOOL

Barnes		b. Colson	0
Hamerskill	st. Newton	b. Burrill	0
Bond		b. Colson	0
Briggs	c. Newton	b. Burrill	81
Flabert	not out		48
Tibbins	c. Furness	b. Colson	67
Orman		b. Redman T	1
Simms		b. Redman N	15
Burns	lbw	b. Roberts	19
Dolland		b. Colson	4
Gulfstrode	did not bat		
Extras			30
TOTAL	(for 9 wickets)		**265**

Bowling	o	m	r	w
Colson	5.2	0	50	4
Redman N	12	3	49	1
Burrill	4	2	12	2
Pelham	20	8	56	0
Roberts	3	0	33	1
Redman T	11	3	41	1

OUTCASTS

Birch	c. sub	b. Briggs	91
Pelham	lbw	b. Dolland	22
Faulds	lbw	b. Dolland	12
Colson		b. Dolland	4
Burrill	not out		24
Furness	lbw	b. Burns	0
Newton		b. Briggs	24
Rashid Ali	not out		38
Roberts	lbw	b. Barnes	0
Redman N	c. &	b. Barnes	0
Redman T	lbw	b. Barnes	0
Extras			50
TOTAL	(for 9 wickets)		**266**

Bowling	o	m	r	w
Dolland	4.2	1	48	3
Barnes	10	0	97	2
Burns	2.4	1	26	1
Briggs	6.4	1	46	3

Outcasts won by 1 wicket

CLOSE OF PLAY

T he Outcasts had no reason to dally. The last buffet-less Clacton Express of the day was their aim. They were reliant on the school mini-bus and they could not expect it to make a detour of local watering holes for their benefit. The best bet seemed to be to get back to London by the quickest available transport. There was, after all, a bar at Liverpool Street station which served real ales.

The headmaster singled out Rashid Ali for congratulation and was forced to admit to himself on close encounter that this was not the man to whom he had given his nest-egg. As an afterthought he asked Rashid Ali whether he had seen anyone about the place who looked at all like him. Rashid Ali assumed that the headmaster might be on to their little cricketing deception and so answered in his most solemn tones and with a kernel of genetic truth that he had seen no-one of Indian extraction that day.

Herbert Banston was nonplussed. He was equally puzzled to see the younger of the two policemen who had been in his office taking what looked like an unfriendly interest in Terry Lilgate. DC Wormhurst had radioed for back-up and Terry Lilgate was in the process of being manhandled towards one of two police cars which had raced to the scene. The headmaster thought that the police were meant to be recovering his pupils, not depleting his staff. He also wanted to divert their energies into the hunt for his money, but he was unsure quite how to explain the situation without opening himself to unwelcome questioning.

EVENTUALLY CRICKET

The dilemma was resolved by the policeman himself. Having despatched Terry Lilgate, he turned to see Herbert Banston gazing in his direction. Pointing towards David Simms, he cheerily informed the headmaster that two out of his missing trio were now back in the fold. He was confident that the third would be back 'within the hour'. Christopher Wormhurst thought that these glad tidings might have been received more gladly, but he had to pass on the less good news. He had 'detained' a pupil on suspicion of dealing in what he euphemistically described as contraband and he would need to remove him from the school premises. Terry Lilgate, he said, would be helping with inquiries. The headmaster seemed as impassive in the face of this information as he had on receipt of the 'good news'. Finally he spoke.

Since he had first met the two policemen (Herbert Banston shuddered at the recollection of the second) in his office, there had been two developments. His younger daughter had gone AWOL and so had £15,000. Not wishing to tax the detective constable with conflicting investigations, the headmaster dealt only with the matter which was nearest and dearest to him: the money. A sum of money, a few thousands, had disappeared. It had been 'taken' from him ... by an Indian person ... who could have been a visiting cricketer ... but apparently was not. He offered a description of the man which was vague, and of the bag which, colour apart, was equally vague. He stressed the delicacy of the situation. The investigation must be discreet, but urgent. Christopher Wormhurst moved off with suitable assurances.

After the recital of his life, Dean Faulds separated himself from Fawn Felucca. As the concert ended, their interests began to diverge. Fawn Felucca's thoughts turned immediately to the collection and those of Dean Faulds to cricket. Looking at his watch, he realised he must rejoin his team-mates. The match must be over and there was a train to catch. A glass of wine was offered, but he brushed it aside. Japanese Riesling was not among his favourites (Fawn Felucca had taken advantage of a job lot put her way by Terry Lilgate. At 65p a bottle it had been too good to miss.) Dean Faulds edged out of the hall through a knot of well-wishers whose memories of Sandy Macpherson and Reginald Dixon had been rekindled. He side-stepped the collection box and was clear of the hall before the rumpus occurred. The person who had first encountered no reaction from Florence Trumpington, when offered a glass of Japanese Riesling, had assumed it was a matter of taste (which it might so easily have been). It was only when someone, who had rather too quickly consumed two glasses of this non-vintage flower of the East, tripped over the outstretched feet of the late Mrs Trumpington that news of her passing swept through the hall. No-one regretted the news more than Fawn Felucca, because attention was drastically wrested from the collection on which she had placed reliance.

At first Philip Bond could not understand the flashing light which penetrated the room. In a second or two he thought he detected a blue tinge. It did not take much longer to make the connection. A chill went through his body which had nothing to do with the state of his dress. He had dozed – a not altogether unreasonable aftermath to his afternoon pursuits. His second realisation was that he was alone. Had he been dreaming? No, he rapidly recollected, he did not think he had. But then. Oh God, the match! In a trice he was into his whites and down the stairs, expecting to find a vengeful Terry Lilgate. Wrong. It was a police car, but, the driver apart, its only occupant was the lady who had led him to the house. Sophie Crossley's apology was immaculately done. The car had broken down. There was no telephone. She was so sorry. Where was his girlfriend? The question was entirely disingenuous. On its way to the house the car had sped past Serena Banston trying vainly to hitchhike her way back to the school. Coming upon her in the return direction, having deposited Sophie, Philip Bond asked the driver to stop. PC Wayne Norton directed her towards a rear seat. He doubted his ability to concentrate on the road ahead with that skirt riding up on the front seat beside him.

Having made arrangements for the transfer of Gary Pocke to the police station, suitably accompanied, DC Christopher Wormhurst had a pang of conscience. He had been separated from George Jolliface for too long and, although it might have been more by luck than judgment, the detective sergeant had been right. The missing boys had all been found more or less on the premises. Christopher Wormhurst had also recovered a missing girl and made two arrests on unconnected matters. He felt a need to report. But after twenty minutes of wandering around it began to look as though a policeman had been added to the day's list of missing persons. Eventually, the detective constable wandered back to the point in the school where he had started. The car in which he and George Jolliface had arrived was still there. By chance the first person he met on entering the administrative block was the bursar, not the headmaster. The bursar, being by now all too well aware of what had happened, was quick to direct Christopher Wormhurst to the sanatorium. What he found there led to further inquiries in which his senior colleague played a most unfortunate part. Ever the gentleman, Christopher Wormhurst returned to the bursar's office to thank him for his assistance. It was as he turned to leave that the detective constable's eye caught a glimpse of shocking pink in a waste bin.

The Outcasts had their second experience of the day of Rockcliffe Parkway. The station did not improve with acquaintance. The cafeteria beneath the platforms was closed 'due to working-time directive', which Ray Burrill thought was a novel touch. The plasma screen train indicator informed them to their surprise that the next train for Waterloo, Ashford and Paris was running approximately three hundred and seven minutes late. It then dissolved into a green and yellow maze pattern which was as helpful to the Outcasts' needs as what had preceded it. A poster on the wall had a curvaceous lady in a swimsuit inviting the onlooker to share a Sunday experience with her in Clacton, but the next-door poster dashed expectations with its announcement that the line would be closed on Sundays until further notice 'for extraordinary engineering works'. Absorption of any additional advice and information was curtailed by the sound of an approaching train. The Outcasts hastened up the ramp to the stark and deserted platforms. Ray Burrill just had time to notice that the sausage lay undisturbed on the opposite platform. The garish colours left them in no doubt that this was the Clacton Buffet Express they sought.

Clambering aboard the rear coach, the team unexpectedly encountered a refreshment trolley anchored to a compartment door. Denuded of most forms of refreshment apart from a few cans of mango vitamin juice, it was also deserted. They found Harry

Northwood asleep in the first-class compartment (even temporary staff had privileges). Either Expresso Trains Ltd had not allowed themselves to be burdened by the working-time directive or their temporary steward had slept through a turn-round at Liverpool Street. Ray Burrill decided that he would benefit more from their de-brief than continued slumber. 'Bruised but not broken' was his immediate answer to the question which formed in Harry Northwood's eyes.

As the tale of their (narrow) victory and how it had been plotted began to unfold, Harry Northwood's twitch diminished and the stammer disappeared. The progressive neutralising of the Rockcliffe fast bowlers brought a smile to his face, but he was disappointed that one in particular had not suffered a more ignominious fate. He was very approving of the trick played on Cooperbatch T Gulfstrode. The combined city and corporate knowledge of Stewart Thorogood and Dean Faulds had served to set up the plot. Everyone roared when Dean Faulds repeated his American PA role. The tales went on; the exploits were recounted. Kevin Newton talked them through his heroic innings. His audience did not know whether to be more or less impressed when he confessed that since he had shorn his locks, his helmet had sat lower on his head and he had not been able to see a thing. Dean Faulds was asked about his organ-playing and was relieved that Basil Smith was not present to elaborate.

In such merriment, none of it alcohol-induced, the journey quickly passed. Liverpool Street and its bar hove into view to end one of the driest days in the Outcasts' history. Taking Harry Northwood for eighteen, Ray Burrill invited him to join them for a victory celebration. As Harry had worked the trick himself on many occasions (since his fifteenth birthday), he had no qualms in accepting. First, he said, he had to check in his trolley and dispose of the rubbish. This triggered a thought in Dean Faulds's mind. He had retrieved a white plastic bag which Stewart Thorogood, in his haste to leave with Basil Smith, had left in the dressing room. Dean Faulds fished it out of his cricket bag and tossed it into the black waste sack attached to Harry's trolley with a casual 'Do you mind?' Harry did not.

The Outcasts were moving rapidly into their third round when Harry Northwood caught up with them. And he soon caught up with their consumption. He had not lacked practice since his fifteenth birthday. The gathering became ever more cheerful and ever more lively. It was agreed that Ray Burrill had led them to victory on the field, but Stewart Thorogood was toasted in his absence for having been the master strategist and manipulator. The cheers ran round the group. Other people in the bar looked on with amusement, tolerance and not a little curiosity as this dozen or so people surrounded a larger wicker hamper. The cause of the celebration eluded them. It would have taken a long time to explain. Syd Breakwell excused himself before the singing began.

On Sunday morning Harry Northwood drifted into consciousness with the finest hangover of his young career. He lay in bed piecing together his memories of the previous day. Images floated in and out of his mind. There was a white plastic bag. It had contained an empty bottle of vodka, an empty packet of itching powder from the Chipping Rockcliffe Magic Shop and an almost full jar of vaseline. When he was fully awake, he realised he must have been dreaming.

On Monday morning Rashid Ali remembered little of Saturday night, but had a store of recollections of Saturday daytime. When Neil Danby called at his office, he was told with as much regret as Rashid Ali could muster that he must find another solicitor as he in all conscience could no longer act for him. Rash had learnt too much.

On Tuesday morning the Police, Inland Revenue and Customs and Excise descended on Rockcliffe School in a combined operation to begin investigations which would ultimately lead to its closure. As well as Ray Burrill, Christopher Wormhurst had got the result of his life.

OUTCASTS C.C.

versus

WILLINGFOLD C.C.

THE TWO TEAMS
(in batting order)

WILLINGFOLD C.C.
Edward Townsend
Brian Leyton-Brown
Ben Harding (c)
Jim Abbs
Walter Ryesmith
Geoffrey Jarr
Trevor Edgefield
Bill Forbes (w/k)
John Tod
Henry Pickard
Elvis Coombes

OUTCASTS C.C.
Jon Palmer
Stewart Thorogood
Dean Faulds
Alan Birch
Winston Jenkins
Phil Cole (c)
Harry Northwood
Charlie Colson
Kevin Newton (w/k)
Tom Redman
Colin Banks

PRELIMINARIES

He was not really Uncle George, but that was how he had been known to Phil Cole and his family for years. Wildly generous, endlessly kind, always wealthy, George Chubbington had led with charm and no little luck an immensely successful business life. He had befriended Phil's father (who had been part of the luck) and benefits had regularly flowed to the young Phil in the form of pocket money and gifts. Whenever Phil had looked for sponsors for school or university money-raising schemes, Uncle George had always topped the list. So when the request came, how could Phil refuse?

It was to be a charity cricket match. It would take place in the village where Uncle George lived. As Phil Cole learned more he realised the occasion would not be charitable in the strict sense of the word, more a money-raiser. Willingfold-in-the Myre lay in an unnoticed, but beautiful part of West Essex. The village had a wonderful cricket ground in a perfect setting, but there were two drawbacks: no pavilion and no team. Uncle George was a fanatical cricket enthusiast and could not believe that the village's fortunes had sunk so low. He had readily joined an action group to remedy this state of affairs. In trying to rebuild a team the action group had quickly discovered that the absence of a clubhouse and proper changing facilities and sightscreens and nets and a scoreboard and kit was a handicap to recruitment.

For all his determination to get things right, Uncle George was no Paul Getty. He was ready to put his hand in his pocket to finance a few of the accoutrements which would make cricket possible and even half-enjoyable. He also had contacts. Uncle George always had contacts. He got attention paid to the ground and, importantly, to the pitch. Some benches appeared. Two portakabins arrived, to be followed by a couple of portaloos. Gradually some of last year's players were persuaded to reconsider. A search for new players stretched even over the county boundary. New Willingfold came into existence.

It was important to plan ahead. Uncle George's success in life had depended on long-term planning. He also had an eye to the big project. If Willingfold-in-the-Myre Cricket Club was to have a pavilion, some big-scale money-raising had to be done. That would require people in the village and surrounding area being enthused and thereby seduced into a collective effort. In Uncle George's experience, grand design excited the imagination and boosted the ultimate yield. So there had to be more than one element in the strategy. Uncle George had thoughts about this.

Even on the most optimistic assumptions, it was soon apparent that the necessary amount of money could not be raised solely by reliance on the local populace. Preliminary design work and estimates from a friendly architect (Uncle George's friend) had confirmed this conclusion beyond any doubt. Uncle George realised that they would have to make an application to the National Lottery. It was then a matter of putting in place the ingredients essential to make the application wholesome and appetising to those who would be considering it. On the basis of what he had heard, Uncle George had little faith in those who would be considering it. They seemed amazingly inventive in the production of batch after batch of questions of such complexity and obscurantism in comparison to which an application for a social security benefit looked a piece of cake. First things first, reckoned Uncle George. Let Willingfold show what it could raise on its own before the attempt on the Lottery summit was launched from base camp.

The first Saturday in June, Phil Cole was told. Did he know anyone else who might be free to play? As it happened, Phil knew a whole team which might be free to play and he floated the idea in front of Uncle George. Fine, came the answer with the added promise that they would have the time of their lives. Both men then qualified their commitments. Phil explained that he would have to check the availability of other Outcasts. Uncle George thought he knew what he meant by a good time, but remembered that to ensure it he would need the co-operation of others. There was one thing Phil had to know before talking to his friends. 'What's the ale down there?' 'Ah,' said Uncle George, now realising one of the ways in which he would be able to make the invitation irresistible, 'no problem there. Suggistons. Amongst others,' he added significantly.

As soon as Uncle George mentioned the date, Phil Cole had sensed the opportunity. If the custom and practice of the last five years had been observed, the Outcasts would have been playing Deansbury End. However, the custom and practice of the last five years were very definitely not being observed. Last year's game had ended in acrimony. It was a series of little things punctuating the game which had culminated in rupture of a relationship which had been more cordial than jolly. The Deansbury End cricketers took their matches seriously. They were a sober crowd. On arrival on the first Saturday in June last year, the Outcasts were not.

The fateful outing had been preceded by a call from Charlie Colson to David Pelham, who was match manager and captain for the Deansbury End fixture. Charlie had heard from 'a reliable pal', who knew his ale, that there was a pub in a village near Harlow which had just produced a quantity of home brew described as 'out of this world'. What Charlie's friend had not passed on was the local belief that after four pints you were out of your brains. David Pelham had needed no more than thirty seconds to decide that the schedule would have to be adjusted to take account of this new information. He and Charlie Colson were the two big hitters in the Outcasts' beer consumption stakes. They also regarded themselves as sophisticates in ale selection although their judgment was not always accurate.

How they and other team members would have fared with the Rose and Crown's home brew was, perhaps mercifully, never put to the test. Their coach (Executive Sporting Coachways were still in business at the time) found the Rose and Thicket, the Elizabethan Rose, the White Rose and, when the search for the rose had finally been abandoned, the Boy Bugler. But the Rose and Crown with its precious brew proved totally elusive. Charlie Colson's reliable friend had been somewhat less than reliable in his directions. The Outcasts' perambulation round the Essex and Hertfordshire countryside was not totally in vain. Their misinformed route had allowed them to re-acquaint themselves with Crugmunton's

Champion Ales, McShinty's Magnificent Bitter, Cowshall's Correct Bitter and Rugner's Best Beer. To measure up to his responsibilities as captain, David Pelham confined himself to three pints. One or two members of the party did not show the same restraint. Collectively the team was late in reaching Deansbury End. One of its members was unable to leave the coach and another would have been better advised not to have tried. The home team captain, clearly displeased by the delay, nevertheless undertook to shake hands with each of the Outcasts as they emerged. His reward at the end was to be knocked to the ground as Kevin Newton stumbled against him having missed most of the steps of the coach in descending.

The afternoon had not improved. The Outcasts' bowling had been lethargic and erratic and the fielding inept. Deansbury End amassed almost three hundred runs for the loss (surrender would have been a better word) of only four wickets. In the course of the innings, the home team captain, attracted by a strange sound from the visitors' coach, went on board and took great exception to what he saw. The tea interval had been marred by a remark about the filling in the sandwiches being misinterpreted by the person who had prepared them.

The Outcasts' innings had started well enough. Stewart Thorogood and Jon Palmer, not wholly clear of head but batting by instinct, had put on sixty off eight overs when an unfortunate incident took place. In taking a sharp single, Jon Palmer collided with the Deansbury End skipper who was bowling. By now in a thoroughly sour frame of mind, the skipper forsook dignity and sportsmanship and accused Jon Palmer in a couple of words of not being entirely sober. As an Outcast it was a moot point whether Jon Palmer should have chosen to deny the charge. However, he did with emphasis, banging the base of his bat not on the pitch as he had intended, but on the unprotected toe of his interlocutor. By this time the ball had been retrieved and the bails removed at the bowler's end. Play was interrupted for fully five minutes after which the match continued without Jon Palmer (run out) and the home team captain (carried off).

In eight more overs, the remainder of the innings had disintegrated. Only seven further batsmen presented themselves. One of the missing pair was easily accounted for as he had never left the coach. Controversy surrounded the whereabouts of the eleventh man. A light-hearted remark by Greg Roberts that the missing batsman could be adding to his score elsewhere was seized upon by the burly Deansbury End wicket-keeper whose shapely nineteen-year-old daughter had been reported in the company of a fair-haired man, 'who could have been dressed in cricket clothes'. The situation had quickly spun out of all proportion. The burly wicket-keeper had stormed off the pitch in search of his daughter. If for no other reason, this brought the match effectively to its end. Some other members of the home team were inclined by now to believe of the Outcasts that there was no smoke without fire. There was little by way of comradeship left in the encounter. Some other members of the Outcasts, knowing the absentee to be Colin Banks, their serial Romeo, feared the worst (or best depending on point-of-view).

When, after an awkward few minutes, Colin Banks had strolled into view with no more than a drink on a stick by way of company, there was no need for him to apologise to his team-mates for not being available to bat when required. None of them had remotely imagined that he and the not-out batsman, Tim Jackson, between them would have scored in excess of two hundred runs off twenty-four overs or indeed twenty-four runs off two hundred overs. The burly wicket-keeper and suspicious father was another matter. He was held back from landing any actual blows, but there was an angry confrontation. Colin Banks was wide-eyed in his assertion of innocence. As the questioning continued, he even threatened that he would be consulting his solicitor. The tension was slow to dissipate, but his friends eventually edged him away. His flat-mate, Greg Roberts, could not help noticing as they did so, a grass stain on Colin's trousers which he was sure had not been there when they came off the field at the tea interval.

The last stump of the season had barely been pulled from the ground when a letter arrived from Deansbury End Cricket Club informing the Outcasts' fixtures secretary that no fixture could be offered in the following season. Phil Cole knew that nothing had been found to replace it. An inquiry had come from Scrange-by-Sea, a small village on the Essex coast, but it was not followed up on discovery that it was a team of over-sixties which risked being as disapproving of the Outcasts' style and approach as the men of

Deansbury End. Word came that one of Her Majesty's Prisons in East Anglia was trying to interest its inmates in cricket, but such a venue was not thought to yield much prospect of Crugmunton's Champion Ales, Cowshall's Correct Bitter or Rugner's Best Beer. 'Mind you,' Winston Jenkins had said, 'these days you never know.' Phil Cole himself had added, 'And if we arrive blotto, we could get banged up ourselves.'

After a round of telephone calls, Phil Cole had half a dozen firm commitments for Uncle George's match. The rest were a collection of don't-knows, refusals and not-at-homes. He reported back. Uncle George seemed pleased. He was now able to tell Phil a little more about what was in store. It would be country-house accommodation by courtesy of local families. An all-day beer tent would offer six real ales. They would start with a champagne breakfast ('to get us in the mood'). After the match there would be an ox roast in the evening. 'It's going to be one big party,' continued Uncle George's sales pitch, 'and all in a good cause.' By the time he had finished, Phil Cole for one was sold.

Armed with this filled-out agenda, Phil went back to those of the Outcasts who had indicated their probable willingness to play. Probability became certainty. He then got through to three others to whom he had not previously succeeded in speaking. They seemed keen to sign up as well. Over the weekend word had obviously spread. One or two, who had previously pleaded other engagements, suddenly found themselves unencumbered. By Sunday evening the only two Outcasts absolutely and completely unable to spend a weekend in the country were Rashid Ali (visiting a sick relative in East Africa) and Basil Smith (wife's insistence that they could not put off the annual visit to her parents). Together with Syd Breakwell, their umpire, and scorer Simon Crossley (provided he could bring Sophie) the party had swollen to twenty. A nineteenth Outcast had been enrolled in the person of Harry Northwood, who had recently celebrated his eighteenth birthday. He had turned out to be not a half-bad batsman. He could also drink and, importantly, had a taste for the right kind of ales.

Uncle George was unfazed. There was no problem. All would be welcome to join in the fun. But wouldn't they be imposing unnecessarily on the hosts who were offering beds, Phil Cole felt constrained to ask? Seemingly not. But, Phil had continued, the match could hardly be seventeen-a-side. This was not the nineteenth century. There had been a silence for a moment at the other end of the line. Phil began to imagine that Uncle George was seriously thinking about a match like that. In the end Uncle George had said that they might need a few substitute fielders if the beer flowed well and, anyway, it would be a great weekend away. So it was settled. Or almost. Uncle George asked how they would be travelling. With Executive Sporting Coachways out of the reckoning it was Phil's turn to pause. It did not sound an occasion for cars. Sensing the uncertainty, Uncle George mentioned that he had a contact. Leave it to him. Phil did.

The more the Outcasts spoke about the forthcoming trip to Willingfold-in-the-Myre, the more it took on the character of a day or two in paradise. Information came in a steady stream from Uncle George. The names of the real ales which he had ordered: 'Suggies,' said Dean Faulds with a dreamy look in his eyes when Suggistons was first mentioned, 'My God!' The places where they were to stay: The Manor. The Hall. The Towers. The Vineyards. As David Pelham remarked: 'It looks like a case of having to take a razor and a change of underwear.' There was to be other entertainment about which Uncle George was less specific.

With the exception of Sophie Crossley, the wives and partners took an early decision not to augment the party travelling to Willingfold. Watching their menfolk get legless was a pleasure to which they tended to confine themselves no more than once a year. This supposedly charitable outing, despite some superficial attraction, had all the appearance of a thoroughly drunken revel. It also happened that Margaret Birch had recently accompanied her husband to the annual dinner of the regional pharmaceutical committee of which he was a member. The occasion had been mind-numbingly boring and in no way relieved by the meal they had eaten. Alan Birch had been out-voted in his preference for something up-market. The rest of his colleagues wanted to keep the ticket price no higher than £10. Everyone suffered accordingly. It might have seemed the more astonishing therefore that the obligatory raffle contained a vast number of extremely attractive and valuable prizes. The drugs companies, Alan confided to his wife, worked in mysterious ways, the wonders for their customers to perform. Margaret won a voucher for a weekend for four in Amsterdam – and that had been the twentieth prize in the array. Jane Smith was otherwise engaged, but Adrienne Palmer, Liz Allason (Charlie Colson's steady girlfriend) and Amanda Sutton (Stewart Thorogood's live-in partner) were all ready to throw in their lot.

Sophie Crossley, however, would stay with her husband. Their secret, concealed as successfully as their wedding had been and incredibly for longer, was out: Sophie was pregnant and nearer, much nearer, to delivery than conception. So they would go to the anticipated comforts of Willingfold in place of any adventure in Holland. This time the Crossley tandem could not be risked. Simon and Sophie were therefore more grateful than any of the Outcasts to discover that Uncle George's contact had yielded the promise of a top of the range, luxury, air-conditioned coach with full video facilities. It seemed in advance that it would be nothing like any previous coach in which the Outcasts had travelled to a match. And that would indeed be the case.

The Outcasts had been told all they needed to know in connection with their visit. Uncle George had not burdened them with a description of all the things he had in mind to make the first Saturday in June a day to remember for Willingfold-in-the-Myre Cricket Club. He had rapidly appreciated that a cricket match alone could not be expected to raise the kind of money the club would require to demonstrate to the Lottery people that it was a worthwhile cause. He had racked his brains for other events and activities which might attract punters to the village.

Besides cricket, rugby, golf, tennis and snooker (strictly late at night) Uncle George did not watch much television. In the process of channel-hopping to find one of these diversions, he remembered coming across some extraordinary contest in which people in funny costumes competed against each other in outlandish games. He thought it had been called 'It's a Knockdown'. The vicar later put him right. However, what Uncle George had been sure about was that the event had been watched by a large crowd. Could they, he asked several of the locals, stage such a spectacular in Willingfold? Several of the locals expressed doubts. It was not until the sub-postmistress mentioned that her brother-in-law, who lived in Greater Manchester, had once organised an 'It's a Knockout' and might still have access to the games and equipment that the idea began to take hold.

As the cricket match would be occupying the most obvious piece of open ground on which such an event could be staged, the next question to be faced was location. Uncle George had the answer to that. Adjacent to the cricket ground and separated from it by a hedge and two gates was land owned by a local farmer, Ken Pegley. It was through one of these gates, carelessly left open some months previously (investigation had never revealed by whom), that Farmer Pegley's cattle had wandered. They had made towards the then existing cricket pavilion. Opinions varied as to whether they had been attracted by the voice of Sir Cliff Richard which had emanated from an upstairs window or become agitated by it. What was undeniable was that their stampede had caused the building to collapse. There was general relief in the village that none of the animals had been harmed.

Uncle George had been a generous contributor to the fund which was started to honour the memory and assist the widow of the club scorer, Fred Wheeler, whose body, distressingly damaged by scavengers, had been recovered a week later from the wreckage. Mrs Wheeler had been away from the village visiting their daughter and son-in-law. It was not until her return that it was learnt that her husband's habit was to spend occasional evenings working in the pavilion office on the illumination and embellishment of his scorebooks whilst listening to cassettes of his favourite singer. In the recriminations which followed, blame was apportioned between Ken Pegley and Sir Cliff Richard, but more heavily towards the former as the singer had a lot of other fans in the village. As Uncle George saw it, the former would be ready to have his sense of obligation stirred.

Ken Pegley's field was extensive. There was a large area of level ground before it gave way to a gentle, but distinct slope down towards the Myre. The flat area seemed to be of ideal size for the jolly games once so beloved by television audiences. Having won the farmer's approval, Uncle George's ambitions grew. He envisaged side-shows and then one of his fellow members on the impromptu organising committee had suggested a band. A dog show, beautiful baby contest and bungee-jumping were among other bright ideas (not all implemented). Of course, there had to be a refreshment tent which, after reflection, became two. One would serve teas and the other alcohol. Uncle George firmly ruled that these should be separate from anything happening on the other side of the hedge. He wisely foresaw that lager fans might not mix easily with real ale enthusiasts.

Uncle George and his colleagues had absolutely no idea how many people would turn up for the day of fun and games. The commitment of neighbouring villages was secured by the expedient of persuading them to enter a team for 'It's a Knockout'. With Willingfold itself, this amounted to five and Uncle George had got a shrewd idea from which source the sixth and final team would be drawn. Seating was obviously required. A local contractor offered to rig up a sort of grandstand to hold a couple of hundred people. Otherwise it was planned to have an assortment of seats, benches and deckchairs around the perimeter. Lavatory facilities had to be provided. One of the committee members remembered that the son of his wife's cousin had helped to set up a new business, Portaloodeloo Ltd. On inquiry it was learnt that this company boasted unlimited capacity and flexibility; more importantly, on the strength of the family connection, twelve of their de-luxe models would be supplied free of charge. Everything seemed to be satisfactorily taking shape.

Publicity for the great day was entrusted to an enthusiastic young man who had recently bought a cottage in the village. He worked in the creative media. His name was Darcey De'Arth and he claimed to be a good networker, whatever that might have meant in this context. So familiar did he seem with promotional techniques that his committee colleagues, who were wholly unfamiliar with this aspect of life, conceded total delegation. This lack of supervision proved to be an error. Darcey De'Arth was a genuine professional. He had made no false claims. With gusto he set about putting Willingfold-in-the Myre on the map. He would have done better to have studied the map before executing his plans.

Uncle George's pride at having so easily gained the co-operation of Ken Pegley was somewhat dented when it was pointed out to him that a great deal of pre-event time would be needed for the preparation of the arena. A field which had been home to seventy head of cattle for several weeks was not in ideal condition for the planned activities, especially those which involved tumbling on to the ground. There were some volunteers for the clean-up squad; others, not least Uncle George, were pressed men.

Once the grand design had been outlined, there was no reluctance on the part of others to set up stalls and add variety to the occasion. Looking down the list of potential entrants, Uncle George raised his eyebrows. He would not have expected to have found a snake-charmer in rural Essex. He was less surprised to see Tommy Burnhough's name. Had he confined his carpentry skills to the building trade in which he had worked for many years, Tommy Burnhough would have stayed within the limits of his capability. However, he had persuaded himself to go into design. He had used his spare time – the irregularity of work in the building trade had meant rather a lot of it – fashioning pieces at once simple and crude. The most radical of art critics would have been pressed to have anything glowing to say about Tommy's pieces unless, of course, they had first been viewed in the Royal Academy. Even at the level of country craft they were ugly – and mostly heavy. Not the sort of thing to be bought on a day out without a suitably-sized van. Uncle George shook his head in wonderment.

There were two pubs in Willingfold. The unfortunately named Dirty River (the words had a certain historical resonance in the village) served only keg bitter and a host of fashionable lagers. At the other end of the village lay the Oak and Yoke which specialised in real ale. Neither establishment conformed to the descriptions implicit in their names. The Dirty River had a thatched roof, white-washed walls with lattice windows and a profusion of roses and hollyhocks bedecking its exterior. By contrast the Oak and Yoke had all the charm of a 1960s primary school. However, both establishments had cheerful, outgoing landlords with a strong community spirit. They readily fell in with Uncle George's proposition that each should take sole charge of one of the two licensed refreshment outlets.

Having drawn the big picture and settled the more important features of it, Uncle George felt he could leave the details to be filled in by other members of the organising committee. In so deciding he completely failed to gauge the promotional zeal of Darcey De'Arth.

And so it was that on the first Friday in June the Outcasts gathered at the appointed place at the appointed hour to board the coach which was to convey them to Willingfold. It was a sleek and luxurious cruiser. There were tables between the well-upholstered seats. Two large-screen television sets were mounted at the front. The back section was shared between a WC and a bar. The windows were smoked glass permitting no-one outside to see much of what was happening inside. That Uncle George obviously did have connections was Phil Cole's first impression as he surveyed these unexpected surroundings.

The driver explained that the vehicle was the one being used by the members of this year's touring team. As they were currently in Dublin for a three-day fixture against Ireland, it was fortuitously available and the boss was doing a favour for an old friend. (It figured, thought Phil Cole.) There could be no faulting the standard of comfort on board, but the contents of the bar were a disappointment. Can after can of Fxxxxxx and 4xxxx greeted them. Had it been down to him, Phil Cole would have taken out the refrigerator and used the space more imaginatively for a barrel of proper beer. The journey had not been long under way when David Pelham found a collection of videos in a locker. They were all unmarked. One was fed into the machine and the Outcasts found themselves looking at what appeared to be a batting masterclass. The appearance was deceptive for it was soon realised that only current England batsmen were featured. It took another minute or two to recognise that they had stumbled on a coaching video for the touring team's bowlers. After a while another cassette was selected. This turned out to be kids' cartoons. A third was tried. The opening sequence seemed to suggest that this might be a coaching video for women's cricket – a somewhat puzzling item in the collection. It was only when the lady cricketers on camera began to divest themselves of their kit that the puzzle was solved. The Outcasts felt that, through their access to the coach, they had gained great insights into the defining character of the international visitors and settled down cheerily for the rest of the journey. Syd Breakwell and Sophie Crossley engrossed themselves in conversation as far from the arresting video as possible.

It was agreed by the whole team that they had never seen anything more erotic on a cricket field. In eager anticipation they delved again into the video locker only to be met with disappointment. Neither Bobby Simpson on the World's Greatest

Skippers nor 'Warne Out – the first 100 dismissals' had the same appeal. In the latter case, the Outcasts were able to overcome their curiosity as to whether the contest referred to the chubby Australian's bowling or batting, preferring instead a re-run of the women's 'coaching' video to cover any points they might have missed. Buoyed by this entertainment, the team was in good fettle when the coach turned into the car-park of the Oak and Yoke, the rendezvous appointed by Uncle George.

To the Outcasts' regret even 'a swift half' was ruled out, because the various hosts were waiting to serve them dinner. A briefing would be held back at the pub at 10 pm, but they might like to know that the champagne breakfast would be served in the marquee at the ground at 10 am. After a spontaneous chorus of groans, this was swiftly adjusted to 11 am. The visitors were assigned to their billets which, with one exception, were in easy walking distance.

HOSPITALITY ARRANGEMENTS

The Cottage (G Stubbington Esq)
Phil Cole, Tim Jackson, Syd Breakwell, Simon and Sophie Crossley

The Hall (L Phypps Esq)
David Pelham, Charlie Colson, Kevin Newton, Harry Northwood

The Towers (Mr & Mrs Haverscombe)
Tom Redman, Nigel Redman, Ray Burrill

The Vineyards (Mr & Mrs Dolbee)
Alan Birch, Stewart Thorogood, Winston Jenkins, Dean Faulds

The Manor (Col & Mrs Crickhill)
Colin Banks, Greg Roberts, John Furness, Jon Palmer

Alan Birch, Stewart Thorogood, Winston Jenkins and Dean Faulds reboarded the coach for the short trip to the Vineyards. Others followed Uncle George's instructions and made for the Manor, the Hall and the Towers. Uncle George took under his own wing Phil

Cole, Tim Jackson, Syd Breakwell and the Crossleys. They headed for Willingfold Cottage, which, despite its name, was comfortably larger than most properties in the village. The pub car-park emptied almost as rapidly as it had filled with departing promises of 'See you in the bar later.' Not everyone would fulfil this undertaking.

Willingfold Cottage was a magnificent property. Originating in the seventeenth century, the cottage had been extended by caring hands through succeeding years without ever losing a look of antiquity. It would be hard to say whether this had more to do with planning restrictions or the wealth of its owners. Uncle George had never married. He and his home were looked after by Mr and Mrs Sparrow. When Uncle George was entertaining, their efforts were often supplemented by their daughter, who had gone into catering. She had married and was now called Mrs Eagle. The spread which welcomed Phil Cole and his companions was in keeping with the style of the property. It was a cold buffet of rich variety enhanced in the eyes of Uncle George's guests by the presence of a firkin of Suggies.

After wiping a last, lingering speck of a strongly-scented Brie from his upper lip, Uncle George asked Phil Cole whether he had picked his team for the match. Resisting an impish temptation to say that he had not yet had a chance to inspect the wicket, Phil Cole wrote some names on a piece of paper and handed it to his host. As Uncle George knew nothing about any of the players, their names meant nothing to him. However, it was quickly apparent that there was another purpose behind the inquiry. 'Six spare players,' mused Uncle George aloud. 'Well, five allowing for a twelfth man,' replied Phil. 'I thought I'd let them take turns as necessary.' 'Good thinking,' said Uncle George, 'but they could help me out as well.' He then revealed what he had in mind. Phil Cole was taken aback. He did not feel in the slightest bit confident that he could inflict this indignity on his friends. As he thought frantically what to say without offending Uncle George, he was further taken aback by hearing Tim Jackson, ever the party animal, say, 'Could be a good laugh.' Tim was promptly put in charge of the caper to Uncle George's delight (and relief).

At this point Phil declared that it was time for the necessary pre-match conference in the Oak and Yoke. His readiness and enthusiasm were shared by Tim Jackson. Syd Breakwell demurred.

For obvious reasons of lassitude, Sophie Crossley felt she was unable to make this fixture. Her husband loyally volunteered to stay by her side. 'Splendid,' said Uncle George, 'that gives me an opportunity to show you the state-of-the art cinema I've built in my cellar. I think you'll be impressed.' He then reeled off a series of technical expressions to bolster his claim. It was when he added that the system was shown off at its best with The Sound of Music that Syd Breakwell decided after all that a brisk walk to the pub and maybe a half would be a good tonic before bed.

At the Towers, the billet of the Redman brothers and Ray Burrill, a very different scenario had unfolded. Mr and Mrs Haverscombe were an utterly delightful elderly couple, but the three Outcasts found that their welcome was tinged with embarrassment. Halfway through the day, it transpired, their 'help' had received a message to say that her mother, who lived in Swindon, had been taken ill. Understandably, she had downed tools and fled. Beds were left unmade, dinner unprepared. Chivalry being deeply embedded in their code, the Haverscombes had not for a moment thought of reneging on their commitment. They had done their best to complete preparations for the visitors, but their best had sadly fallen short of what they would have wished. Charles Haverscombe had to think of his heart and Alicia Haverscombe was increasingly handicapped by arthritis. By the time they had made up two beds, they had exhausted their stock of sheets and themselves. Their remaining sheets were in a damp pile in the utility room where they had been left for ironing. Both needed a rest before they readied themselves to tackle the vegetables. Alicia Haverscombe felt equal to the task of placing a leg of lamb in the oven only to discover that before her abrupt departure, the 'help' had failed to buy it and equally failed to acquaint them with this omission. A glance in the fridge indicated by its absence that a side of smoked salmon had not been transferred from the freezer. The Haverscombes realised with despair that there was no chance of it thawing before dinner-time. To revive their sagging spirits they had turned to the gin bottle. Huge tumblers of gin and tonic were pressed upon the arriving Outcasts as a litany of apologies began.

What Mr and Mrs Haverscombe had not anticipated was their good fortune in the particular guests who had been assigned to them. Tom and Nigel Redman had spent most of their adult life ministering to a mother who (in her own mind) hovered precariously between life and death. They had been forced into a high degree of self-reliance. Preparation of meals was for them a stock-in-trade. Indeed, had it been required, they could have spring-cleaned for the Haverscombes. By contrast, Ray Burrill led a very basic bachelor life. He was in no way put out by sight of a mattress covered only by a blanket. Many of his nights – not all of them deliberately – had been spent on floors. What he saw now, had the Haverscombes but known it, was the equivalent of flying first-class.

Accepting a second enormous gin and tonic, Tom Redman told Mr and Mrs Haverscombe that they need have no worries. If he and his brother could be given a free hand, a meal would be brought forth. Ray Burrill was left to make conversation and further gin and tonics. Another litre bottle of gin appeared (Mr Haverscombe had never relinquished to their 'help' any share in the responsibility for keeping the Towers well stocked with drink). In his retirement years, Mr Haverscombe had taken a computer course. Equipped with a powerful 750 MHz machine he delighted in e-mail and the Internet. There was not one of its uses which he had declined to exploit. It was in testing the possibilities of Internet shopping that Mr Haverscombe had come across www.booze-up/kwik.eu. An early trial demonstrated eminently satisfactory results: just-in-time delivery at rock bottom prices. The only downside had been the cooling of a hitherto long-standing relationship with the proprietor of Willingfold's nearest off-licence.

Before serious inroads had been made into the latest litre of gin, the Redman brothers produced a dinner which ran to three courses. The first was a variant of an Italian bean soup. Nigel Redman had started with a single can and had somehow extended its contents. This was followed by an omelette surprise which in its variety of contents certainly surprised the Haverscombes. Tom Redman had found bits of this in the fridge and bits of that in the pantry. Served with oven chips and frozen peas, it was suitably filling fare. It could not fail to be enhanced by a Corton-Charlemagne, Grand Cru which Mr Haverscombe brought up from his cellar. By the time fruit salad had been placed in front of them, none of the diners was disposed to notice, let alone comment on, the almost singular species of which it was composed. The Outcasts completed their good deed by washing up before setting out for the Oak and Yoke and allowing their hosts the early night which by this time they craved.

In marked contrast to the easy-going atmosphere of the Towers, the Manor was a home where formality reigned. A maid opened the door to Colin Banks, Greg Roberts, John Furness and Jon Palmer. Before showing them to their rooms, she introduced them to Colonel and Mrs Crickhill. They were standing in a large reception room off the hall. Greg Roberts assumed by their appearance that they were on their way out to a function. The Colonel was wearing a well-cut dinner jacket and his wife an elegant full-length red dress above which lay a cascade of pearls. The Outcasts accepted a sherry (the only drink on offer) and embarked on what turned out to be a stilted and uneasy conversation. Colonel Crickhill seemed shy and reserved, hard to imagine as someone who had once commanded a fighting unit. His wife struggled to find anything that she might have in common with these young men who looked far removed from her own offspring, who were both high-flying army officers. This uneasy period of standing around holding a minute glass of an alien amber fluid was brought to an end by Colonel Crickhill when he suggested that his guests might like half an hour in which to change for dinner. It was only then that the true significance of their hosts' attire dawned on them.

The maid directed them to their quarters whilst explaining some of the temporary problems which were being experienced at the Manor. 'Work' was being done on the second floor and so some of the spare bedrooms were not available. Off a long galleried landing, the Outcasts were shown two rooms which they were to occupy. The maid apologised for the one containing a double bed and, suppressing a giggle, hoped they would be able to manage. At the furthest end of the landing there was a bathroom containing a huge bath, but no shower. Again an apology. The other bathroom at the top of the stairs was out of action. The local plumber was on his yacht in Florida and not expected back for three weeks.

They met in the twin-bedded room claimed by John Furness and Jon Palmer on the basis that Greg Roberts and Colin Banks, being regular flat-mates, would have no difficulty mucking in together.

Noting that it was a very large double bed, Greg and Colin acquiesced without rejoinder. There was something more immediate to worry about. Uncle George had given no hint that they would be expected to dress for dinner. Perhaps he had not known the old-fashioned style of the Crickhills. Yet alone a dinner jacket, their guests did not have a jacket of any sort between them. They had no ties and the nearest thing to a collar was in the form of a sky-blue polo shirt (with an expensive designer label) owned by Greg Roberts. Colin Banks had a rather loudly-striped collarless shirt. For the rest they were equipped with an assortment of T-shirts, sweatshirts, jeans, khakis and tracksuits. There had never been an Outcasts' uniform and so they could not even sport two identical kits between them unless ....

If the four Outcasts had been discomforted by the expectation that they were meant to dress for dinner, it would be hard to gauge the thoughts which passed through the minds of Colonel and Mrs Crickhill when their guests descended in cricket whites. (Wisely the four had not committed the social solecism of wearing a cap.) The same code which had led the Crickhills to suppose that you should dine in formal wear prevented them making any comment about the Outcasts' appearance. A bell rang and Mrs Crickhill led the way in silence to the dining-room. Dark panels and candlelight provided an atmosphere in which whites looked even more bizarrely out-of-place. Grace was said. Servants appeared. Napkins were placed on laps. Food and drink began the rounds. It was plain, but well-cooked fare. The wines were very drinkable. No difficulty for the Outcasts there.

Sparking a round of cheery dinner-table conversation proved much more difficult. It was a chance reference to a character in a TV soap by Greg Roberts which set things off at one end of the table. Suddenly Mrs Crickhill was electrified. Did Mr Roberts watch EastEnders? How interesting! The merest twitch of assent from Greg Roberts prompted an outpouring from his hostess, who, it turned out, had watched every episode since the programme's inception. Greg, who had not seen nearly as many, but plenty more than he would have wanted to admit to his fellow team members, found himself well able to interject with relevant comments. Shortly after this two-way exchange got going, John Furness answered a question from Colonel Crickhill about whether he had any other leisure pursuits apart from cricket. Ignoring a dirty laugh on the part of Jon Palmer and giving him a sharp kick under the table, John mentioned his role as a drummer in an occasional jazz band. Unbelievably the Colonel, whose enthusiasm for cricket was decidedly low-key, was a jazz freak. Another animated conversation ensued leaving Jon Palmer and Colin Banks across the table from each other to talk about the forthcoming Test series and the composition of the England team about which they both knew as little as they did about jazz and EastEnders. The Outcasts, having wondered how soon they could decently tear themselves away from the Crickhills' table, almost missed last orders. However, they should have known that in the Oak and Yoke this was a somewhat abstract festival. Too late to change out of their whites, they were greeted with great hilarity and predictable wisecracks. They were the last to arrive for the team talk.

Just ahead of them had come the party staying at Willingfold Hall. The butler had greeted David Pelham, Charlie Colson, Kevin Newton and Harry Northwood with the news that Mr Phypps 'most regrettably' had been called away on urgent international business and that he, Mr Grouse, had been instructed to make them 'most royally' welcome. He, Mr Grouse, was sure that they would find everything to their complete satisfaction. He, Mr Grouse, would spare no effort to ensure their stay was enjoyable. There had been much more along these lines whilst baggage was carried upstairs, quality accommodation (all singles) allocated and the time of dinner announced.

The welcome had been effusive for a combination of reasons. Grouse, the butler, was having to make good for the absence of his employer. This would have been necessary in any case. However, as the butler suspected that the international business which had taken Mr Phypps away was by no means urgent, but rather French and shapely, he felt an extra obligation to take good care of the house guests. The presence of such guests also gave Grouse a degree of relief from otherwise dancing attention on his employer's elderly and irascible father whose physical disability kept him bound to his room. His two-way radio connection with the kitchen meant that he could never be entirely forgotten. In the absence of Mr Phypps Junior, Grouse was left with a free hand as to the manner and style of the hospitality to be dispensed. Grouse was a high-quality entertainer when operating at his employer's expense. The fatted calf had been well and truly slaughtered for the visitors' benefit. Mrs Enzyme, the cook, had not spared herself in the preparation of the meal whilst Grouse had spent an enjoyable hour selecting wines and port from Mr Phypps's collection. This industrious tasting was the fourth reason for the butler's effusiveness. He was several steps ahead of the Outcasts on the path to intoxication. And Grouse had plans to make it a long path.

Paté de foie gras, herb-crusted halibut, casserole of pheasant, crême brulée and a crumbly blue stilton were appreciatively consumed by the Outcasts with the help of a series of fine wines and vintage port. Grouse deliberately fomented an argument over the '52 to persuade his guests to compare it with the '64 which he had already decanted. When a somewhat heady procession took off for the pub, there was plenty left over for Grouse and Mrs Enzyme to enjoy a mountainous late night feast. Grouse had given David Pelham a key and a warning. If something went bump in the night, it was likely to be Mr Phypps Snr, whose quarters were above them. They were not to worry about the old man's presence in the house and any disturbance which it might cause. It was an unfortunate omission on Grouse's part not to have given a matching assurance to the elder Phypps.

Bill and Lydia Porter had been in charge of the Oak and Yoke for around five years. Now in their mid-forties, both had turned to country inn-keeping as a relief from the stresses of sanitary engineering and nursing in Birmingham. The Oak and Yoke had provided them with a lower income, but greater peace of mind. An hour after the Outcasts' party (incomplete as it was) had assembled in their public bar, Bill Porter observed to his wife that, had business been at this level since their arrival in Willingfold, they could probably have afforded by now to have fulfilled their ambition to buy a hotel on the Costa del Sol. There was no doubt that the Outcasts were in good thirst. The presence of both McShinty's and Suggiston's provoked the need for continual comparison in a vain effort to establish consensus as to which was the greater brew.

In spite of this utterly futile, but thoroughly pleasing exercise, Phil Cole managed to convey the news to those present who would and who would not be playing the next day. With four of his intended team unexpectedly missing from the pub, this might have been seen as a high-risk exercise. Mystifying to Phil though it was that his friends should fail to succumb to the lure of the ale, he doubted they would miss a champagne breakfast which was now fixed for the more gentlemanly hour of eleven o'clock. It was probably because of the utterly futile, but thoroughly pleasing bout of fine ale consumption that Tim Jackson was able to sell to his non-playing comrades the unlikely proposal that they would make up an excellent squad for 'It's a Knockout'. The mind-numbing reality of this commitment would not sink in until the next morning. For the moment there was a boozy bonhomie. Having, as he thought, sorted out his team and, with Tim Jackson's help, kept everyone happy, Phil Cole settled down to enjoy himself. The only other relevant thought which passed through his mind was the absence of anyone who looked like or claimed to be a member of the opposing team. He concluded that they must be keg drinkers and therefore ensconced in the village's other pub. It had been remiss of him not to have obtained some insights from Uncle George about whom they would be facing.

Despite the boisterous atmosphere, Phil Cole's mind flicked through the Outcasts' season to date. It had hardly been vintage. Since the visit to Rockcliffe School, they had played four matches, winning one, losing two and abandoning the other for reasons which had nothing directly to do with the weather. Consistent form had been shown by virtually no-one, principally because few members had consistently turned out to play. The win over Purldene had owed everything to a century from Jon Palmer and a six-wicket haul based on a rare burst of real pace by Colin Banks. Unfortunately, neither had been able to turn out (sober) in subsequent matches. A dogged fifty by Harry Northwood and a sustained bout of big hitting by Winston Jenkins were the only worthwhile memories of the two defeats. The bowling had been entirely forgettable. Of the last match in May prior to the descent on Willingfold, a veil was best drawn. Phil Cole shuddered at the memory and quickly sought forgetfulness in another pint.

All good things must come to an end. When Bill Porter sensed that the rate of consumption of his visiting patrons was beginning to slacken, he decided to call a halt. There was a long day ahead tomorrow (almost today) and the publican shrewdly calculated that the Outcasts' capacity would be suitably augmented by their exertions and the high temperatures which were forecast. There was no doubt in his mind from comments passed that it would be his beer tent and not that of his village rival which would receive their support.

It was as well that their places of lodging were only minutes away on foot, although in some cases the foot was not one hundred percent sure. First to peel away were Phil Cole, Tim Jackson and Syd Breakwell. Despite having moved on to his favourite Scotch early in the session, Syd's instincts as a former policeman ensured that they reached the Cottage without mishap. His early training on pedestrian-crossing control still stood him in good stead. Once indoors, they could hear rather than see that the last mountain was currently and climactically being climbed. Uncle George hopefully inquired whether they would like a nightcap and 'Mary Poppins'. (Uncle George had an unconsummated love affair with Julie Andrews.) The sight of Simon and Sophie Crossley emerging sleepily from the door to the cellar cinema sufficed to convince the returning party that their destination should be up rather than down. They were not first to bed, but nor were they the last.

At the Towers, the Redman twins and Ray Burrill would have settled gladly for Mary Poppins or even The Wizard of Oz if it would have spared them the crisis which greeted their return. Surprised to see the house ablaze with lights at such a late hour, they found a weeping Mrs Haverscombe being comforted by her husband. Both were in their dressing-gowns and clearly distressed. A clue to the cause was not hard to find even by strangers to the house whose senses were enfeebled by drink. A puddle of water lay in the middle of the hall. Further investigation showed it to be not the only one. The cold water tank in the loft had burst its bottom. The Haverscombes, whose room was directly underneath, had been drenched in their bed. That they were suffering from shock was obvious as well.

The shock of what they saw worked for the Outcasts in an opposite sense, galvanising them into a state of responsibility. Water was turned off, but not before some strong tea was made. Damage assessment was undertaken. Part of the house was a mess; part had escaped. The Haverscombes were persuaded to take the guest room which the Redmans would otherwise have had. Sleeping on the settee was not an option as the lounge lay on the side of the house under the master bedroom. The water from the loft had continued its descent albeit with reduced force. The lounge carpet resembled the pitch surrounds at Old Trafford after a sharp shower. Another puddle had been found in the kitchen, but its source was traced not to the defective water tank, but to the Haverscombes' dog, a Yorkshire terrier. He had suffered a nervous reaction to this unaccustomed tumult. Upstairs the mattress with its single blanket had metamorphosed from a first-class single berth to an economy class threesome. After carrying out some rudimentary mopping-up operations, it was still a thankful place of sanctuary for Tom Redman, his brother and Ray Burrill.

Their experience was light relief by comparison with what befell those returning to Willingfold Hall. Their approach was neither quiet nor discreet. In no way would it have conformed to the model recommended in the Burglars' Manual of Best Practice (8th Revised Edition, 1997). And, of course, in no way did David Pelham, Charlie Colson, Kevin Newton and Henry Northwood regard themselves as thieves in the night. Unfortunately, this perception was not shared by Mr Phypps the Elder. In flat contradiction of the statistics produced by the County's police force, old Mr Phypps had allowed himself to become obsessed by the belief that cases of burglary were on the increase. Furthermore, no places were more vulnerable than large country houses when thought to be deserted. Mr Phypps's suspicious mind had been inflamed by a diet of crime novels and television dramas which filled his lonely days. He was also increasingly dotty.

Such was the rowdy cheerfulness of the approaching foursome that they were undeterred by the first shot. It could surely have been no more than a car backfiring. The thought came rapidly to Charlie Colson that they had seen no cars, but not quite as rapidly as the second shot which splintered the trunk of a young silver birch growing by the side of the drive. No mistake this time. The Outcasts leapt for cover which was fortuitously provided by some rhododendron bushes on the other side of the drive. Any lingering doubt that they had stumbled into a war zone was removed by a

voice (more a frenzied shriek) which informed them, 'You won't get away from me, you bastards. You're not going to get inside this house.' And then for emphasis, 'Bastards!' This was followed by another salvo.

Just as shock of a different kind had had a sobering effect on Tom and Nigel Redman and Ray Burrill, so too did this unprovoked attack work wonders on their team-mates. Even so, they found it difficult to assess their situation with total clarity. The disturbance had produced no reaction from elsewhere. Peering through the bushes with extreme care, David Pelham could see no light whatsoever in the house apart from the glow which surrounded the silhouette of the madman with the gun. Grouse had not even remembered to illuminate the porch light before passing out on the kitchen floor. Both David Pelham and Charlie Colson possessed mobile phones, but had left them behind as neither instrument had registered a signal since entering the village. If, they figured, Grouse had not been alerted by the commotion, he might have fallen into a drink-induced sleep (for which there had been some evidence before their departure). Kevin Newton came up with the thoughtful suggestion that both Grouse and Mrs Enzyme might be dead, shot by an old man who had gone berserk. Another sudden shot from the upstairs window gave a whiff of credence to this outlandish theory. The three of them were beginning to contemplate retreat into the outer blackness of Willingfold (there were no street lamps in the village) as the least worst option, when they were interrupted by a low, but penetrative whistle.

The school attended (and soon after examinations to be abandoned) by Harry Northwood had, somewhat unfashionably in this day and age, boasted an army cadet force. Participation was voluntary, but a remarkably high proportion of the eligible year groups had enrolled. This owed something to the fact that the alternative activity in Wednesday afternoon's timetable was a gardening class which was not voluntary. In practice, this took the form of working in the gardens of the school and its senior staff, and helped to limit the cost of professional assistance. Not in any way militarist or militant by nature, Harry Northwood had found himself responding well to cadet force training. He had been identified as officer material and had risen to the most senior rank in the corps. Under battle conditions in the grounds of Willingfold Hall, his capacity for initiative and drive, despite his consumption of an excess of alcohol, had a beneficial outcome.

As his disappearance had been unnoticed, so his reappearance at the crawl, army-style, was a shock. 'I've found us a refuge,' Harry whispered, and David Pelham hoped that English language was not one of his forthcoming A-levels. Keeping out of the line of fire as another random shot rang out followed by a condemnatory 'Bastards!', the Outcasts crept round to the other side of the house. With better night vision than the other three, Harry Northwood led the way to an immaculate summerhouse on the fringe of the lawn furthest from the Hall. Its door was open. (The grizzled ex-sergeant who helped in the training of Harry and his fellow pupils had taught a few tricks beyond the scope of the official manual.)

The quality of furnishing of this outhouse was the equal of anything to be found in the Hall itself. There were two extremely plush settees, a reclining chair, a marble-topped table, a music system and a bar. All this could be seen with the help of two low-wattage lamps. The independent electricity supply which illuminated them also powered a fridge, the contents of which Harry Northwood had already identified. For the benefit of his companions, he brandished a bottle of genuine Russian vodka and a tin of Beluga caviar. This was the place where the owner of Willingfold Hall, when blessed with female company, was wont to conduct his al-fresco entertaining. The Outcasts had to decide whether, on this side of the house, they were safe from the old man's fire and could break in and find refuge in their bedrooms or whether they should stay put.

The walk back to the Manor had been without incident. The guests had been given a key, Mrs Crickhill having reluctantly concluded that the Outcasts would not be deterred from the pub by a showing of the first-ever episode of EastEnders and that she would not be awake when they returned. Bed for both her and her husband had been sufficiently welcome that their slumber had been instant and profound – fortunately proof against the blundering upstairs journey of their visitors. Colin Banks, in particular, had drunk more than was wise for someone due to play cricket – even fun cricket – within a few hours.

Not all the guests in the Manor fell asleep as readily as their hosts. In the room occupied by John Furness and Jon Palmer there was a television set. Channel-hopping whilst extricating himself from his clothes, John Furness came across a scene which he thought was sufficiently sexually explicit to command his further attention. Half-an-hour later he was a disappointed man. Jon Palmer's drift into sleep was delayed by the excited and later frustrated commentary of his room-mate. Next door, rhythmic snoring told a different story.

Two hours into the night, the house was still. The television channel had gone off-air with John Furness sprawled in a state of semi-undress, lulled to sleep finally by a test card. It was then that Colin Banks awoke. He needed the bathroom. Sleeping naked as was his custom, there was no item of clothing he could conveniently find without disturbing Greg Roberts. As he was only likely to bump into John Furness and Jon Palmer, he took the risk of entering the corridor and fumbling his way towards the bathroom at the end. Having used the light in the privacy of the bathroom, he was more disorientated on the way back to his room. Thankfully he slipped back into bed and into sleep, noticing that his companion had been undisturbed.

What had detained the party at the Vineyards beyond even the flexible opening times of the Oak and Yorke had been a meal of the utmost elegance. Alan Birch, the Outcasts' travelling gourmet, was joined in his enthusiasm by Stewart Thorogood, Winston Jenkins and Dean Faulds, not all of whose incomes allowed regular dining of this style. The hosts, Mr and Mrs Graham Dolbee, were out to impress. Food and drink was their thing, or, more particularly, it was the thing of Mrs Graham Dolbee, whose alter ego was the celebrity TV chef, Bunty Buscombe. Having beavered away in relative obscurity whilst acquiring her skills, Bunty had finally taken the nation by storm in a programme called Spicy, a title which referred as much to her language as to the meals she prepared. This had led to her own series, The Empty Plate, in which she had widened the range of both her cooking and her vocabulary. Books and videos had followed to the point where Mrs Dolbee's income had started to rival that of her stockbroker husband. Not even Alan Birch, who took an interest in such matters, had made the connection between Mrs Dolbee and Bunty Buscombe. The omission was put right with a vengeance as course followed course, each with its accompaniment of excellent wine. Every plate was duly emptied as indeed is the objective of any proud chef. None of the wines from the vineyards from which the house derived its name was among those served at the Dolbees' table. They were unblushingly dismissed by Graham Dolbee as mainly for the wine-box trade. Any lingering thoughts of going out to the pub were removed by the presentation of an impeccable dessert wine followed by a fine old Armagnac. Digestion was complete.

The Dolbees' guests slept soundly and recuperatively, proving once more the beneficial effects of a perfect combination of good food and good wine. Not only was sleep induced, but dreams too. Winston Jenkins found himself in a match wherein thirty-six runs were required to win off the last over. Naturally, he did the necessary. Alan Birch was at once Bradman, Constantine and Compton in scoring a hundred for England against a World Eleven. In Stewart Thorogood's case he was a combination of Larwood, Tyson and Trueman at top speed on a spiteful pitch, but despite his taking wicket after wicket, the innings never came to an end. Dean Faulds's dream was composed of altogether different images, too indelicate to recount.

Willingfold-in-the-Myre awoke to a day which would be long remembered by its populace. The first person to approach consciousness was Greg Roberts, who turned over and discovered that he was alone in bed. As this was not an uncommon situation for Greg, he rolled back again and thought no more of it or for a while of anything else. The first person out and about (milk was delivered only on alternate days in Willingfold) was Darcey De'Arth. He was a man with a mission and the mission was to put Willingfold on the map. Calling in every favour he could muster, he had arranged for himself a series of interviews on local radio and regional television. The commitments held. Darcey De'Arth was fortunate that in the preceding twenty-four hours there had been no priority news such as the discovery of a singing donkey or announcement of a wedding to be performed underwater, either of which would have been guaranteed to lose him his slot. Willingfold would have collectively blushed if residents had been awake to hear these broadcasts. Darcey De'Arth had been confined to the earliest parts of the various programmes, as it happened, to allow a newly-discovered toddler pop group more time to get to the studios. Even so, he had made good use of his time. Willingfold-in-the-Myre, to people who did not know it – and they could be numbered in millions – came over as a rural paradise. Its 'village festival' would be a 'knock-out' event, the biggest fun day of the third millennium. With lots to do for the whole family it was an outing not to be missed. Darcey remembered to mention all-day licensing. He also threw in the word 'charity' at random intervals.

There were two things which Darcey De'Arth failed to say. The word 'cricket' did not pass his lips. Nor did he expand on the subject of transport. In fairness, it would hardly have been worth mentioning buses. The public transport omnibus to Willingfold was as the stagecoach to the emerging settlements of the American Wild West. Whilst it had never been attacked by Indians, it seemed vulnerable to mechanical breakdown, flat tyres and driver absenteeism. It was at best a weekly service and Saturday was not its day. Nor was there rail transport. Willingfold had been spared the indignity of having its track torn up by Dr Beeching in the last century, because not even in the heyday of the railway in the previous century had anyone thought that the village was worth even so much as a halt.

What Darcey De'Arth could usefully have said was that Willingfold's connections with the national road network were tenuous. The principal road into the village was from the east. It stemmed from a junction with the main road which was easily missed even in perfect conditions, as the lone white finger signpost was increasingly obscured by a prolific, luxuriant bush. The local highways authority, lacking in funds, had been unable to afford a man and equipment to tackle the bush. Forced to adopt a policy of masterly inactivity, it relied on the goodwill of a local farmer to perform a public service. Goodwill was absent. The farmer kept pigs.

The road to the west was not much more than a lane which ought properly to have been advertised as suitable only for light vehicles. However, there was a need for it to be traversed from time to time by agricultural machinery and so advice to the wider motoring public had been withheld. It is just possible that, had Darcey De'Arth known at the time of his broadcasts what he was to find out only on his return journey, it might have occurred to him to offer some practical tips to motorists. Along the lane between Willingfold and the main road to the west lay the beautiful but decaying Muckersby Bridge, sadly overlooked by Constable in his and its prime. It was actually situated across the county boundary from Willingfold and was therefore the responsibility of a different cash-strapped highways authority. Having ignored for years the pleas of farmers and the residents of Willingfold to strengthen the bridge for everyday utilitarian purposes, the highways authority had finally succumbed to pressures from the Rural Heritage and Culture Council to restore the bridge for environmental reasons as part of the county's millennium programme. The work was due to start at the beginning of July. As a preparatory gesture, one-way operation over the bridge, controlled by temporary traffic lights, was instituted at eight o'clock on the morning of the first Saturday in June. However, even as he waited three minutes for the lights to change, Darcey De'Arth's mind did not allow itself to be diverted by this little practical difficulty from the noble aspects of his 'village festival'.

The first that anyone in the police or motoring organisations knew of what was planned in Willingfold came from hearing Darcey De'Arth's voice on radio. Those who knew the village laughed at the obvious exaggeration. Those who did not know the village dismissed it from their minds.

Darcey De'Arth came back to a village which was slowly coming to life. Grouse, the butler at the Hall, was among those returning to wakefulness. With an evil smile and an aching head, he thought back to the previous evening whilst preparing the coffee he needed for himself and which he imagined would suffice for those bound for a champagne breakfast at the cricket ground. Before his thoughts turned to the old man on the second floor, he went in search of Mrs Enzyme. The cook had finally escaped his attentions by locking herself in the broom cupboard under the main staircase to which she alone had the key. Although it was a large broom cupboard, as broom cupboards go, she had spent an uncomfortable but not sleepless night. The only compensation, she told herself, was that a night in the kitchen with Mr Grouse would have been no more comfortable and probably a lot more disturbed.

At the point when Grouse was ready to ascend the stairs with a tray for his employer's father, a sudden movement in the garden caught his eye. To his amazement, a man wearing only underpants was urinating at the edge of the lawn. He had had the grace to keep his back to the house and was startled when Grouse raced up behind him. 'Sorry, mate,' said Harry Northwood, 'but I didn't want to disturb anyone in the house.' Harry's consideration was not reciprocated by Grouse when he had advanced on the summer-house. Three crumpled bodies were sprawled on cushions adorned by a similar number of vodka bottles. In studied contrast, four scoured tins of caviar were neatly stacked on the top of the fridge. A number of cigarette butts were ground into the tiled floor. The place stank, though whether more pungently than the kitchen in which Grouse had woken was a moot point which would be forever untested. If Grouse had any feeling of guilt over his own abuse, he was quickly able to transfer it elsewhere by this unexpected turn of events. Beyond acknowledging their return to consciousness, he used no words to convey displeasure. He relied on looks and exclamations and sighs to hint that he, Grouse, might have been placed in an awkward position vis-à-vis his employer. However, the invisible parcel of guilt had not yet finished its journey. When David Pelham had recovered his poise and Harry Northwood his trousers, Grouse was acquainted with the events which had led them to the summerhouse. The word 'shot' had much the same effect on the butler as old man Phypps's second blast had had on the silver birch. Grouse wilted. Then he turned and fled back to the house.

Ignoring the tray which he had so meticulously prepared a few minutes earlier, brushing aside Mrs Enzyme repatriated from her broom cupboard, Grouse took the stairs as fast as his now throbbing head would allow. The door of Mr Phypps Senior was locked. Neither banging nor shouting produced any response from within. Cold fear began to grip the butler. Realising he had not picked up his master-key from the kitchen, Grouse cursed and ran down the stairs passing the emboldened Outcasts coming up. Three more minutes elapsed before the door was finally opened. Grouse took two steps forward and one very suddenly back as he found himself looking down the barrel of a gun.

At the Towers the day had begun badly. There was no water except where it was least wanted. By isolating some circuits, a partial amount of electric power seemed to be safely available. Nigel Redman made some toast for the Haverscombes. The immediate priority was to find a plumber, but finding one who was up to the job on a Saturday in the vicinity of Willingfold seemed a tall order. And then Ray Burrill remembered the Porters. At the same time, the Haverscombes remembered that they were meant to be attending speech day and prize-giving at their grandson's school in Leicestershire. This joyous event, at which young Alexander was due to receive the history prize, had been driven entirely from their minds by the horrors of the night. For the second time in her short acquaintance with the Outcasts, Alicia Haverscombe wept.

Prizes at school, after all, were not two a penny. Neither of the Haverscombes could remember winning one. Their son had completed his education without winning a prize and, for that matter, with only thin results at A-level. So this was in the nature of a red-letter day for the family. Alexander was clearly to be hailed as an intellectual prodigy. The truth was more complicated. Alexander's year group had been given a project entitled 'Hitler and the Course of World War Two', to which the award would be related. Alexander had chosen to argue that it was the failure of Hitler to understand cricket which had proved the fatal flaw in his ability to direct the management of the war. It was an approach on which no previous historian had stumbled. Alexander's dissertation contained some interesting analogies and seductive scraps of evidence, but was not of sufficient weight to win the actual prize. To encourage the boy, who in truth was in the lower band of intelligence quotient, an award for originality had been introduced.

But a prize is a prize, and its presentation a moment to be savoured. Were the doting grandparents to be denied the pleasure?

Had Virginia Crickhill been a different kind of girl, she might have screamed. Her remaining entirely cool and calm owed everything (almost everything) to her professional training. Not only had she become an extremely competent officer in the armed forces, but she had been seconded for special duties. She had regularly worked under cover and was expert in dealing with tense situations. Her parents knew nothing of the details of her work, but her father was experienced enough to have a shrewd general idea. They could never be sure when they would see her. They had to accept that she would come and go. Often, as she had explained, she could not predict her timetable and therefore her leave opportunities. Colonel and Mrs Crickhill were used to finding that there was one extra for breakfast. On this occasion she had turned up after midnight and, not unusually, found the house in darkness. Taught never to emit a sound she had crept to her room where the sheets were ever-aired.

In a pre-dawn adjustment of her sleeping posture, Virginia Crickhill stretched out her left arm and had not expected it to connect with more than an expanse of the ever-aired sheets and pillow. Instinctively she knew that what her arm had encountered was more than bed linen. Her reaction was not to flinch. The arm, extended in innocence, became a powerful weapon of defence. Having gripped its object, which most certainly did flinch, its owner reached for the cord of the light above the bed. Colin Banks stared wide-eyed at his Amazonian captor whilst he tried hard to breathe. Virginia Crickhill also stared. Even in the middle of the night after a bout of drinking, Colin Banks presented an agreeable sight to a woman. She was quickly persuaded that this was an unlikely terrorist assailant and jaw-jaw seemed to hold more possibilities than war-war.

At Willingfold Hall, shock overtook shock. The merest pause was long enough to establish that there was no threat from the gun. The man against whose chest it rested was not conscious. In a belated show of concern for the person of whom he had charge, Grouse made a grotesque attempt to administer the kiss of life. But it was too late for that. Not for nothing had David Pelham once been a volunteer for St John Ambulance (it had actually guaranteed him access to all home matches at Stamford Bridge) and what he had been taught then now allowed him to make a professional diagnosis. Dragging Grouse away, he said, 'Get off. Can't you see? He's a bloody stiff.' There was no real doubt about it. Mortimer Dalrymple Phypps would never watch another cricket match. Once this fact had sunk in, Grouse became extremely lachrymose. It did not take the attending Outcasts long to realise that these were not tears of grief, but more of fear that his job could be imperilled. For a while he was good for nothing and the Outcasts felt obliged to take charge, pumping essential information from him while he gulped hot, sweet tea, which he would have preferred laced with whisky, but was too chastened to ask.

Another charged with assembling essential information was Ray Burrill at Willingfold Towers. The Haverscombes had been despatched to Leicestershire with extravagant and emphatic assurances that everything would be taken care of in their absence, including Boycs the dog. Their protests as dutiful hosts that their guests' visit to Willingfold might be ruined were finally overcome. To salve their conscience in the face of Ray Burrill's assurances that he could both supervise the visit of tradesmen (as yet to be contacted and even in one case to be identified), the keys of Mrs Haverscombes' car – an elderly Mini – were entrusted to him to aid his mobility. After their departure, it was agreed that the Redmans would do some shopping – on account at the village stores – and then proceed to the champagne breakfast. Ray Burrill was prepared to sacrifice this feast for the sake of helping the Haverscombes, but hoped (not too fervently) that he would be free in time to play his part in 'It's a Knockout'. His day was to prove more complicated than he could possibly have anticipated.

At first it was relatively straightforward. Lydia Porter said that whilst she was no longer an active plumber, she would come along and assess the situation with a view to offering advice. The electrician, Walter Ryesmith, was at home cleaning his pads in preparation for the match. He declared himself willing to help the Haverscombes by coming out to check the electrical system and make it safe. Ray Burrill was also able to contact a decorator. There were two listed in the telephone directory with Willingfold addresses. By now into his stride, Ray Burrill did not bother with a second opinion and chose the first name by alphabetical order. He then made himself another cup of coffee (bottled water had been not the least of the acquired groceries), tickled the tummy of the lively Boycs and settled down to await arrivals.

Needs at Willingfold Hall were less easily met from local resources. The late Mr Phypps's general practitioner was based in the nearby hamlet of Nether Willingfold. It transpired that he was out on his rounds, but would be paged. His surgery receptionist somewhat acidly remarked that she could not say when he might be able to get to the Hall, because Dr Olgate's priorities were the living and not the dead (a claim which would not go unchallenged in the area he served). Police Constable Tod's telephone was on divert to divisional headquarters where the voice seemed uninterested in the report of an unexpected and unexplained death. An exasperated Charlie Colson, who was making these calls on the prompting of Mrs Enzyme, was finally provoked into penetrating the apparent boredom at the other end of the line by adding that it looked to be the work of a Chinese Triad. 'Blimey,' was the electrified response this earned from divisional headquarters, 'I'll report it to Inspector Chang.' Charlie Colson was left wondering whether it was now his turn to be wound up. What he could not be expected to know was that Syd Chang was the only Sino-British officer in the Essex Constabulary. The Inspector was better equipped than most to assign credibility to the suggestion that a gang of Chinese desperados was roaming the Essex countryside with felonious intent. Police Constable Tod could not cut himself off from headquarters and he was instructed to drop whatever he was doing – he was ironing his whites – and get himself to the Hall. Willingfold had no undertaker, but Messrs Doom and Son from the nearest market town promised a hearse by noon.

Not having had to view the body and now safe from any undue attention from Grouse, Mrs Enzyme had got quickly into her stride. Well aware of the forthcoming champagne breakfast and its likely contents, she counselled a good foundation of cereal and hot buttered toast. This she would prepare after running baths to allow the Outcasts to soak away the effects both emotional and physical of their nocturnal experience. Later she knew that she had to do teas at the match. Before then she had to coax some life and sense back into Grouse. The words 'What about young Mr Phypps?' did it.

Making speed through Cambridgeshire in their Jaguar and shaking off their cares in the process, Charles and Alicia Haverscombe were congratulating themselves on their extraordinary luck in having on the premises, in their hour of need, such helpful and competent young men. Alicia Haverscombe had been particularly taken with the young one who was training to be a vet (Ray Burrill). 'What a nice young man,' she murmured at five mile intervals. 'It's a comfort to know that Boycs is in safe hands.' She sighed. 'And offering to take charge like that. I do hope he'll know to get the right people. I left out a list for him on the kitchen table. As long as he doesn't let that dreadful man Coombes and his uncouth son into our house.' Five miles went by. 'What a nice young man,' she said again, and then let the worries of Willingfold slip from her mind. What had also slipped from her mind earlier was to draw Ray Burrill's attention to the list on the kitchen table. As the backdoor had slammed behind the Redmans on their shopping expedition, so the piece of paper had fluttered to the floor where it had been retrieved by Boycs and taken playfully to his bed to be torn into tiny pieces.

Uncle George had set off from Willingfold Cottage well ahead of his house guests, leaving them in the good care of Mrs Sparrow, who shared the belief of Mrs Enzyme in the wisdom of a solid foundation to any champagne breakfast which her employer was organising and her daughter preparing. Uncle George was anxious to check all was in order, not just with the champagne breakfast and preparations for the match, but also with the rest of his organising committee whose main responsibilities lay the other side of the hedge. The marquee which had been hired for the benefit of the cricketers and the cricket club committee was not from the poorest end of the range. It was a striped affair, as was Uncle George's blazer. The marquee company limited itself to blue and white, whereas five colours could be detected in the covering of Uncle George's ample figure. Pink predominated in the lining of the marquee whereas Uncle George's blazer was complemented by cream shirt and trousers. The casual onlooker might have supposed that this appearance denoted the captain of the side. The casual onlooker would have been wrong. Uncle George no longer played cricket. He was purely the stage manager, and he was bent on a good production.

Fulfilling his captaincy role, Phil Cole, with a bacon sandwich and mug of coffee as ballast, was the first of the Outcasts to reach the marquee. The whole scene was undeniably picturesque. The sun was already bearing down and bathing the ground in a warm glow. When Phil Cole caught up with him, he found that Uncle George with a champagne glass clamped to his hand was himself exuding a warm glow. Greeting Phil he said, 'You must get your chaps to have a few glasses of this. Best cure for a hangover I know. This is the vintage stuff. It's not from your average supermarket, you know.' Uncle George continued to proclaim the restorative qualities of good champagne as other Outcasts gradually came into view. Phil Cole was anxious to detach him from this exercise in corporate geniality. He needed him for a few moments to talk cricket.

Meanwhile the majority of the hospitality homes of Willingfold had settled back into a sort of normality as the Outcasts exited in the direction of the cricket ground. Colonel and Mrs Crickhill were surprised (as ever) to see their daughter come downstairs for breakfast, curious that she appeared to be exhibiting warm friendship for one of their guests and amazed when she threw into the conversation that she might go along to watch the cricket. Such behaviour was wildly at odds with the withering comments she had been wont to make whenever in the past she had come upon her brother engrossed in a Test match on television. Mrs Crickhill's reaction ('Well, perhaps I'll bring a picnic which we can have together') did not seem to engender much enthusiasm in her daughter.

Nor was Grouse much enthused by the task which Mrs Enzyme insistently pressed upon him. Their employer had to be told. Grouse knew that this was easier said than done. He was disinclined to share with Mrs Enzyme the likely nature of Mr Phypps's European business. When his boss did not want to be disturbed, he covered his tracks well. From hotel bills he had extracted from Mr Phypps's jacket pocket or found in a waste bin, Grouse knew of one or two favourite haunts and the favourite pseudonyms chosen to go with them. By ringing these places, Grouse risked revealing to Mr Phypps how much he knew. Nagged by Mrs Enzyme he made discreet inquiries, but they were fruitless. That left the mobile phone, but Mr Phypps always said that 'on no account' was that to be rung. As Mr Phypps's relationship with his father had never seemed to Grouse to be the most cordial, let alone loving, there was doubt as to whether news of his demise would rank as sufficiently exceptional to overcome the bar. Grouse hesitated.

Ray Burrill had been left on his own at the Towers with only Boycs as a companion whilst he awaited the arrival of the erstwhile plumber, Lydia Porter, who had answered his SOS call. The others, he thought, would be quaffing champagne. To sustain him, he had only his virtue and a copy of an old Wisden which was the sole representative of cricket on the bookshelves of the household. He absorbed himself in the account of how the last four English wickets at Headingley had produced 248 runs. He rubbed his eyes and read it again to be sure. It scarcely seemed possible.

In the matter of champagne, however, both Ray Burrill and Uncle George had miscalculated. With one or two notorious exceptions, the Outcasts were not champion champagne swiggers. Nor were they in the business of getting light-headed on champagne in mid-morning when they had the whole day to get legless (if necessary) on the six fine real ales they had been promised. If not exactly clear-headed, the players readying themselves for the afternoon's match were still closely related to sobriety. Having, in the end, done little more than dabble in the champagne breakfast, most of the Outcasts (not counting those seeking Dutch courage for 'It's a Knockout') had let their attention wander to the construction of sets for 'It's a Knockout' and the erection of a bouncy castle.

Having wandered, attention became riveted on the last-named. Inflation had not had to proceed far before it became evident that it was no castle. What appeared was the huge top half of the anatomy of a well-endowed woman – very much in the pink. Her outstretched arms formed the sides of the structure and the operative part was an extended lap. The (very) well-endowed woman had a face which bore a lascivious smile. This was the only bouncy castle the suppliers had – and the children could not be denied. However, it was thought more discreet to turn the structure round so that only a smooth pink back fronted the arena. Thus the woman had a good view of the cricket from a very deep mid-wicket position. For a batsman at the (missing) pavilion end, it was to prove an uncomfortable presence.

Cricket was brought back firmly on to the agenda when a young man poked his head round the corner of the marquee and inquired, 'Mr Chubbington?' Phil Cole, who had been in the process of bearing down on Uncle George, got the impression that Uncle George was not overwhelmingly pleased to see the newcomer. Sneaking a glance at his watch, his welcome could have been more effusive. His 'Dear boy' lacked his usual enthusiasm. 'A touch early, aren't we? We aren't due to start till twelve thirty.' With admirable cool, the young man replied with a look which conveyed the message that it appeared a start had already been made. However, he continued with words of pure cricket intent, 'Thought we might have a bit of a pre-match knock-up.' Pause. 'Of course a glass of bubbly might dissuade us.' His attention caught by use of the words 'we' and 'us', Uncle George peered out of the marquee to see a group of men gathered in front of the portakabin marked 'Home'. As though adjusting his thoughts, he outwardly recovered his poise. 'Naturally, dear boy. Come and have a glass before you change.'

Introductions were then made. Phil Cole gradually began to get the picture. For what he regarded as an important exhibition match to reinforce the Willingfold cricket club's claim for Lottery recognition, Uncle George had decided that the team itself needed reinforcement. Having single-handedly reconstituted the club committee, Uncle George had been in a position to be persuasive. Without prejudice, as he had said many times, to the captaincy of Trevor Edgefield, he thought it would be helpful to take advantage of the temporary availability of Ben Harding. This was the new arrival who had made short work of the glass of champagne of which he had taken delivery from Uncle George. Ben's family lived locally and Ben was just back from a postgraduate tour of the Antipodes. He had played for his university and was potentially a rather better-than-average club cricketer. Perfect, Uncle George had thought.

As champagne and conversation flowed (in that order), Phil Cole began to piece together an appreciation of what had been planned. The importance which Uncle George had invested in the match had led him to ditch several of the players who had last played for Willingfold. The remaining band had been supplemented not only by the fortuitous reappearance in the village of Ben Harding but by the recruitment of the best available cricketers from neighbouring clubs without a fixture that day. It might have been a scratch team, but Uncle George reckoned it was better than anything Willingfold could have fielded on its own. Over a further glass it was agreed that the game would be forty-five overs per side (the new fashion) with a nine-over restriction on each bowler. Tea would be taken as a half-hour break between innings.

Either side of getting changed in the portakabin bearing the legend 'Visitors' (under which someone uncharitably had written 'Cast-outs'), the Outcasts continued to be fascinated by what was happening beyond the hedge. Ben Harding and the other new recruits continued to be fascinated with the drink and other entrails of what had not otherwise been the most whole-hearted champagne breakfast of all time. As the deadline approached, the Outcasts appeared to have a fuller complement than the home team, although Nigel Redman had warned Phil Cole that they could be a man light for the 'It's a Knockout' team. Walter Ryesmith was the penultimate arrival. The electrics at the Towers had survived the deluge largely intact. As a precaution, two light circuits were taken out until drying-out had fully taken place. With that, Walter Ryesmith had swapped his equipment bag for his cricket bag and headed for the ground. PC Tod had taken a little longer over his assignment at the Hall. The constable was not used to dealing with sudden deaths and their inevitable concomitants, bodies. This was normally a job for doctors and ambulance men. It was obvious to the constable that old man Phypps had neither shot himself nor been shot despite the presence of the gun. Beyond that he was not prepared to speculate. If some clever-dick detective wanted to check the room for prints, let him, thought PC Tod. He was relieved when the doctor arrived and satisfied when he pronounced 'probable heart attack'. 'Natural causes' was his own description to Divisional HQ, and then he rushed back home to rid himself of his uniform and clamber into his freshly ironed whites.

Apart from those caused by unaccustomed drinking of champagne, there were a couple of hiccups to be overcome before play could begin. Fred Wheeler's mantle as club scorer had fallen on

Ron Mills. On that sunny June morning it had not been the only thing to fall on Ron Mills. His greenhouse had unaccountably collapsed on top of him whilst he had been tending his tomatoes. His wife, Doris, was now tending to him and had sent word that Ron would be counting nothing today beyond the stars in front of his eyes. A grumbling twelfth man, Tom Haresmith, was pressed into service.

By contrast, the last-minute incapacity of Willingfold's umpire, Norman Abbs, was seen more as gain than loss. Norman Abbs had served the club for many years as player, groundsman and, latterly, as umpire in what had been by common consent a descending order of merit. No-one doubted that he knew the game, but, as he had grown older so he had become more fussy and dogmatic in the way he supervised it. He had not been helped over the last three years by the development of a cataract in his right eye, a condition which was a secret shared between himself and the National Health Service, which had not yet been able to offer him treatment. As his vision had become clouded, his judgment had not. Certainty had replaced doubt, occasionally to the total incredulity of the players involved. Despite this, no-one had been willing to take on the duties of umpire and so Norman continued to rule.

Pure chance had led to the interruption of Norman Abbs's reign. In the post that morning he had received an unexpected envelope containing notification that he had won £25,000 on the Premium Bonds. This was the more fortunate in that he held only five bonds and even these he had inherited from his wife. It had been a cheerful start to the day as he contemplated the Caribbean cruise for which he had always hankered and about which the late Mrs Abbs had always been so dismissive. Based entirely on hearsay, Norman Abbs believed that there were rich, lonely women to be found on cruise ships. Turning his mind from exotic rum cocktails sipped against the background of a multi-coloured sunset, he even had the more practical thought that without prejudice to a Caribbean escape, he could now afford to pay for a cataract operation. He was therefore spritely in both mind and step when he reported for duty at the cricket ground. There he joined a champagne breakfast which, so far as Uncle George was concerned, had outlived its usefulness. With good cause to celebrate, Norman Abbs spurned the breakfast and concentrated on the champagne.

Inside three quarters of an hour, he was no longer spritely in either mind or step. Found slumped amongst a pile of empties, he was prised from his white coat with some difficulty whilst muttering something unintelligible about rum punch. The gap was no sooner created than it was filled by Colonel Crickhill, who happened to be conversing with Uncle George when the news broke. 'Haven't done it for a while, but I'm sure it'll come back to me,' were the Colonel's reassuring words as he prepared to pair up with Syd Breakwell, but it was more a case of noblesse oblige. Uncle George was left to ponder the impact on his plans of this unexpected development. He soon had another reason to frown.

Uncle George had been generous, indeed lavish, with his hospitality in respect of the visiting Outcasts. In respect of what was involved in the cricket match itself generosity had not come into it. Such information as Phil Cole had acquired had had to be dragged out of his host. Having chatted a little with his opposite number, Ben Harding, Phil had begun to feel that there was a hidden agenda. This was true. It was an agenda with one item on it: victory. Uncle George wanted Willingfold to win. Privately he had determined that this was an essential outcome in pursuit of what he regarded as his strategic aims: to lift the cricket morale of the village and to impress the National Lottery people that Willingfold had what it takes. Not least their share of the necessary monies.

Before Phil Cole went out to toss, he was beckoned by Uncle George in a conspiratorial manner. 'A word about the pitch, dear boy. It tends to get a bit tricky later when it's worn.' And then, if this was not already a clear enough hint, 'I'd bat if you get the chance.' The first whiff of fumes from the start-up of a burger stall in the adjoining field was not the only thing to hit Phil Cole's nostrils as he strolled to the middle with Ben Harding. He sensed an unmistakable smell of rat.

A similar sensation had overtaken Ray Burrill at Willingfold Towers except that in his case it was not a metaphorical rat. Whilst he awaited the arrival of Lydia Porter to assess the plumbing repairs, Ray had become conscious of a strange odour. At first he suspected Boycs, but Boycs was an extremely well-trained dog in that respect. Then he wondered about drains. He moved about from room to room. The smell waxed and waned, but he was unable to identify its source. By the time Lydia Porter arrived, its existence was undeniable. Her nose puckered as soon as she crossed the threshold. Ray Burrill almost had to insist that it was the water tank and not the drains which were the reason for her being summoned. As they went upstairs towards the loft entrance, the fumes got worse. They had to force themselves up the loft steps to find not only a defective water tank, but a defective rat as well. Called out a couple of weeks ago, the council's rodent control executive had laid poison which had by now claimed its first victim. The dying rat had curled up by a hot water pipe against which its lifeless body had started to cook. Some time had to elapse and some remedial measures had to be taken before the plumbing inspection could be resumed.

Phil Cole won the toss. There then followed an elaborate charade. Phil paced up and down subjecting the pitch to a close inspection. He pressed his foot on it in one or two places. Getting down on his haunches, he caressed the surface with the palm of his hand. Having seen something similar in a televised match, he took his flat key from his pocket and pressed it into the pitch. Seeing Colin Banks at the boundary edge he called across to him, 'Got a minute?' Colin detached himself from his female companion with a reluctance which suggested that he did not have even a second to spare. He ran out to the middle with a 'What the hell is all this about?' expression on his face. Phil Cole whispered something to him and Colin nodded. Another whisper followed by a nod. And again. 'Right, then,' Phil called out in the direction of Ben Harding, 'we'll have a bowl.'

Uncle George stared at Phil in dismay. This was not what he had wanted. He had envisaged the local side chasing victory in a grandstand finish with the crowd cheering every shot. Now he was less sure. He could not fathom what Phil Cole might have seen in the pitch that he had missed. Colin Banks meanwhile stared at his captain wondering why on earth he had been summoned out to the middle to be asked about his plans for the evening's drinking. He was answered with a wink. Phil Cole was unsure whether there was any advantage in fielding first, but at least he felt he had implanted a degree of doubt in the other side as well. As he crossed the boundary line, the umpires passed him in the other direction. They were in animated conversation.

FIRST INNINGS

Colonel Crickhill felt obliged to repeat his disclaimer for the benefit of his fellow umpire. Syd Breakwell was reassurance itself, suggesting that the Colonel should take his cue from him. This was not advice which would have brought comfort to cricket headquarters. Syd Breakwell's knowledge of the game was conceded to be good; it was just that he often had a funny way of applying it. Having cleared the Colonel's mind of a faint colonial memory that an over contained eight balls, Syd Breakwell persuaded himself that he would be able to 'carry' his partner.

The Outcasts' side which Phil Cole led on to the field was in better shape than might have been expected after their nocturnal experiences. They had breakfasted more wisely than Uncle George had hoped. Perhaps their generally good spirit provided yet further evidence of the uplifting effect of cricket on people who step forward on to a pleasant ground in warm weather for a contest between bat and ball, especially when buoyed by the prospect of a gigantic booze-up at the end of it. Last on to the field was Colin Banks, who seemed reluctant to be parted from his recently acquired lady friend. Last on the field, but it turned out to be first into action as Phil Cole assigned him to what from memory was called the pavilion end. Striding out to do battle came Edward Townsend and Brian Leyton-Brown, both imported players for the day. If appearance was any guide, they looked useful cricketers. It would not have helped Phil Cole to know that Edward Townsend, in the season to date, had already scored two centuries for his club. Brian Leyton-Brown had done nothing so dashing, but by steady accumulation had acquired an average of just over forty. Within three overs both were – to use a familiar cricket term – back in the portakabin.

Those who knew Colin Banks were aware that he had days when he was on song and others when he was completely out of sorts. In a magnificent first over he succeeded in terrifying batsman, wicket-keeper and Uncle George. Phil Cole's first thought had been to set the standard field which he knew Colin favoured. This was a compromise between attack and defence. His second thought was to remind himself of the kidology on which he had embarked. After a word with the bowler he posted a third slip. From the moment he began his run, Phil sensed that Colin was out to impress. There was nothing particularly fast about his first ball. What was noteworthy was that it was in the right place just outside off stump. It had not always been possible to rely on such accuracy when Colin Banks began a spell. The second ball was quicker and Edward Townsend, without two glasses of champagne inside him, should have been able to turn it to fine leg, but he had been unable to adjust his eye to the conditions. He was not destined to have long to make the adjustment. Colin Banks's third ball was distinctly fast. It narrowly failed to take the edge of Edward Townsend's bat or the outstretched fingers of Kevin Newton behind the stumps. Third man was the third man to miss it and four byes resulted. Colin returned to the attack with menace on his face and a gleam in his eye. His fourth delivery was fast and short and unexpected. Edward Townsend jerked back with his bat raised in protection of his face. The ball rose from the shoulder of the bat and third slip had all the time in the world to make the catch.

Ben Harding came in at first wicket down hardly noticed by the Outcasts who had gone into a huddle (*à la mode*) further to inject doubt into the minds of their opponents and Uncle George. 'Come along, gentlemen,' huffed Syd Breakwell and the side resumed its fielding pattern. It immediately had to alter the pattern on discovery that the new batsman was left-handed. The alteration required in the bowler's line was not achieved so readily and four more byes were conceded. Ben Harding was the first to admit after the game that he was lucky not to have succumbed to the last ball of the over. It was an almost perfect yorker. There was a frenzied flurry of bat and pad causing the batsman to overbalance and land in an undignified, possibly champagne-induced heap. His wicket remained intact. There was a concerted and sustained appeal. However, it was all too early in the piece and too confusing for Syd Breakwell. He felt he had to give the batsman the benefit of the doubt. It also crossed his mind that two dismissals in the first over might send a disastrous signal to his fellow umpire.

Stewart Thorogood did not pretend to the same pace as Colin Banks and certainly not to the pace he had displayed in the opening over. Nevertheless, under prompting from Phil Cole, he felt he had to attempt the same degree of accuracy and aggression. The result was a respectable over which cost no more than a single. Brian Leyton-Brown looked to be judging the pace of the wicket and seemed in no discomfort. This was soon to change once Colin Banks had got his hands on the ball. The first delivery of his second over fizzed past off stump. Apart from being quick it was otherwise harmless. The ball which followed was a yard quicker and short of a length. It was completely misjudged by the batsman who took it painfully in the midriff. A minute or so passed before he could resume. The next ball was deliberately dug in short and, lacking full composure, Brian Leyton-Brown confined himself to getting out of harm's way. He only just succeeded. Had a replay been available he would have been shaken by what he saw. Colin Banks was not the last to claim that the ball which dismissed Brian Leyton-Brown was the finest he had ever produced. Of fullish length and very quick, it (unexpectedly) broke back, cut the batsman in half, missed the wicket-keeper by a wide margin and raced to the boundary. Unfortunately for the batting side it had disturbed the leg bail in its progress and they were 9–2.

Uncle George was aghast. This was turning into a nightmare scenario. He was by now thoroughly unsure what he had let himself (and the village) in for when buying so readily into Phil Cole's suggestion that he could supply a whole team for this match. From everything which Phil had said to him, Uncle George had been convinced he was being presented with light-hearted cricketers who were mainly in it for the booze. On the evidence of two and a half overs, it was beginning to look like a grudge match. It could end up being a fiasco. The Lottery project would be doomed. Uncle George retreated into the marquee and ordered another bottle of champagne to be opened. His anxiety was premature.

For Ray Burrill at the Towers, anxiety was mounting with good cause. Lydia Porter had departed. He was on his own with Boycs and the lingering smell of the deceased rat. The ex-plumber's verdict had been stark and uncomplicated. There was no alternative to a new tank. The only consolation with which she left Ray Burrill was that she knew someone who might be able to help. She would do her best, but meanwhile she had a pub to run. Boycs had twice brought Ray his lead with a begging expression on his face, but he remained unsatisfied. Ray was obliged to hang around for the decorator he had called. Moodily he flicked through the Overseas Cricket section of Charles Haverscombe's worn copy of Wisden noting in passing another triumph by New South Wales in the Sheffield Shield despite their opponents variously having available the services of Wes Hall, Rohan Kanhai and Gary Sobers.

At this low point in their innings, the Willingfold team had at its service only Jim Abbs, the youngest of six sons of the indisposed umpire. Jim was a nervous young man in his mid-twenties with only a limited amount of cricket behind him. He fell into the category of being a natural ball player, but football and hockey had had the major part of his attention. Coaxed by his father and latterly by Uncle George, he had turned out a few times for the village. He was stocky by build and a good striker of the ball. He was not normally nervous, but to someone a little under-prepared, the sight of Colin Banks tearing in and pitching short did not gladden the heart. Had he been in a position to do so, Ben Harding might have changed the batting order, but he was not and there was no-one in control in the dressing-room. The displaced captain, Trevor Edgefield, had taken a back seat and was content (maliciously so) to let things take their course.

If Jim Abbs had been nervous as he walked out to take his guard with two balls of the over to go, his condition had deteriorated by the over's completion. He swore that he never saw the first ball. Kevin Newton also swore. He too had missed the ball, but it had not missed him. Before his gloves had time to intervene he had been hit in the chest. His recovery necessitated a further delay. It was a moot point whether he or the batsman was the more enthusiastic about facing the next delivery from the rampant Colin Banks. Again it was very fast, but dug in too short. Jim Abbs flashed, but missed. Kevin

Newton was not yet in any condition to undertake anything vigorous and his movement in the vague direction of the ball was token. By now third man had begun to recognise the key role which he appeared to have been assigned. He managed to get himself in position and retrieved the ball before it could reach the boundary. If he surprised himself, he also surprised the batsmen for they failed to run.

Stewart Thorogood produced a pacy over of good length which tested Ben Harding's defences without ever threatening execution. He had an encouraging word with his partner between overs, but Jim Abbs did not feel particularly encouraged as he watched Colin Banks accelerate towards him. Halfway through the over he felt a little better. All his bodily parts were intact and he was unbruised. He had left alone or evaded or been lucky (there was scope for different assessments), but the shaking had stopped. The fourth ball, perhaps a shade slower, he actually met with his bat in fairly good imitation of a forward defensive stroke. The fifth undoubtedly veered towards leg and Jim Abbs helped it on its way. He was off the mark and his relief showed. The field crossed over for the left-hander. This did not help the bowler's direction. Correcting for the previous delivery, he was nearer Ben Harding's leg stump than his off. His length failed him too and the batsman punched him satisfyingly to the deep mid-wicket boundary.

Jim Abbs found Stewart Thorogood more to his taste even though the bowler allowed him no liberties. Jim began to feel that he was in charge as, short of scoring, he did much as he wanted during the over. Colin Banks looked noticeably less menacing as he ran in at the beginning of his fourth over. The first delivery was quite quick, but it was too wide of off-stump for Syd Breakwell's comfort. Willingfold was treated to the sight of the dramatic Breakwell signalling of a wide complete with pirouette. Another fast delivery was legitimate, but short. Ben Harding cut, handsomely, and was unlucky to be limited to two. But luck was not denied him for long. Speed and direction now began to ebb away from Colin Banks. The remaining balls of the over were medium-fast and hittable. Three of them were hit very hard indeed, earning three boundaries. Colin's bubble had burst. It had been magnificent while it lasted, but his extra-curricular activities had finally caught up with him.

Curiosity and temptation finally caught up with Grouse at the Hall. He punched into the telephone the numbers he was under instructions not to use. After a few seconds his master's mobile phone began to ring and ring and ring. Grouse was about to end the call when there was a click, the sound of breathing and then a response. 'Hello.' It was a woman's voice. Grouse grimaced although it could hardly have been out of distaste. He began his inquiry. 'Is Mr. Phypps there, please?' The answer was negative. 'Do you know where he is?' This too got a negative answer. He tried again, but still got no further forward. Grouse was puzzled. The woman's voice did not fit in with what he had imagined his employer's assignment to be. If anything, it sounded familiar. The same thought must have occurred to the person at the other end, for suddenly she said, 'Is that you, Mr. Grouse?' Mr Phypps's mobile phone had been answered where he had left it – on its charger in his bedroom where it had eventually been traced by Mrs Enzyme, who had been cleaning on the landing. The mystery of Mr Phypps's whereabouts remained unsolved.

It seemed quite easy, but at the end of Stewart Thorogood's fourth over Jim Abbs realised that he had not succeeded in adding to his side's total. Phil Cole conferred briefly with Colin Banks, although without the slightest doubt in his mind that he had to rest him. He spoke some kind words and hoped that Colin could give him another fierce burst later in the innings. He then summoned Winston Jenkins. Winston's steady (at best) medium pace could hardly be rated frightening, but being big and black he might instil some initial wariness in batsmen who did not know him. The ploy, reckoned Phil, was worth trying. And at first it worked. The deception was aided by Winston, at Phil's suggestion, taking a longer run-up than usual. To the credit of Winston Jenkins, he bowled with respectable accuracy until the last ball of the over. This was pulled for six by Ben Harding with fluent ease, a stroke which Uncle George thought to be worth another glass of champagne.

Apart from Uncle George's personal accolade, Ben Harding's fine shot had also earned a generous round of applause. This brought the attention of the players to the fact that their efforts were being observed by a growing number of people. As 'It's a Knockout' was not due to start until 2.30 pm, those visitors who had (wisely) set out early for Willingfold, were killing time by watching the alternative attraction. The public bar in Farmer Pegley's field had opened at one o'clock. With the sun above and a beer below it was an agreeable diversion even for those unfamiliar with the finest points of the game.

Stewart Thorogood felt at ease with himself. With no ill-effects from the wonderfully balanced menu on which he had feasted the previous evening, and boosted by no more than a single glass of champagne, he was moving well and his action was smooth. He had found a bit of late swing which seemed to be keeping the right-hander quiet. Perhaps he could get one to move the other way. Fired by Ben Harding's aggression at the end of the previous over, Jim Abbs was keen to get on with it. They had started to steer the innings out of danger. The next thing was to assert control. However, despite Jim Abbs's determination, control remained with Stewart Thorogood. The batsman hit the balls with which he connected harder, but fruitlessly. The bowler waited until the last ball of the over to try his inswinger. It was a beauty. It totally surprised the batsman. It also took the umpire unawares. Colonel Crickhill was the picture of uncertainty. Seeing this and where the ball had gone, Ben Harding shouted for a run. It was an ancient ruse, but it sufficed. The colonel's doubts vanished. 'Not out,' he roared as if this had been his intention all along – and for good grace he did not even signal a leg-bye. Stewart Thorogood swallowed hard.

The crowd was swollen at this point by the arrival of Ray Burrill, who had at last been able to make his escape for a while from the Towers. Lydia Porter had rung with good news. She had located a suitable water tank and a man able both to deliver and fit it. Saturday service would carry a premium, but doubtless, she supposed, the Havercombes' insurance would cover it. Ray Burrill was equally ready to suppose, only too glad to get some action. The man and the tank should be on site within an hour, Ray was told. He had turned from the telephone to the side-door where a commotion (a combination of vehicular and canine noise) heralded the arrival of the decorator. He said that he would need to take a good look around to make an assessment. 'It might take an hour,' he said, adding, 'is that a kettle?' Ray Burrill thought that he had been presented with an opportunity to get up to the cricket ground and also to check on requirements regarding 'It's a Knockout'. First, he had had to get the decorator to move his van so that he could extract the Haverscombe Mini.

Jim Abbs thought he would take a careful look at Winston Jenkins before taking any liberties. After three deliveries which had neither swerved nor deviated, Jim Abbs cast off caution. Perhaps he signalled his intention a little too obviously by asking for a fresh guard. At any rate Winston Jenkins read his mind. Winston knew from all too much painful experience that when batsmen realised he was not in the mould of great West Indian fast bowlers, he was likely to be hit far and wide. One of his defences had been to experiment with a slower ball. It did not always work. Sometimes it travelled further and wider. On this occasion it was well executed. Jim Abbs was comprehensively fooled. His intended drive turned into an ugly thrash. The ball contacted only the edge of the bat and ballooned over the slips. Luckily for the batsman it fell in no-man's land between the slips and third man. He took a single and time to reflect. Ben Harding clipped the next ball for two and might have had two more but for a fine diving stop by Harry Northwood who was lurking between point and gully feeling thirsty.

Yes, Stewart Thorogood had said on being asked by his captain, he was more than happy to continue at what for want of a better description was known as the farm end. By the end of the over he was less happy. He started with a full toss which Jim Abbs gratefully smacked straight past him for three. In correcting his length Stewart produced a good ball for Ben Harding which the batsman was content to block. Its successor was not so good. It erred on the leg side, was again full in length and begged to be hit. It was, skimming to the deep mid-wicket boundary. Trying again to correct, Stewart's next ball fell short and was cut square for another four. The applause for the village side's fifty was quite generous. Stewart told himself to concentrate and the chastisement had the effect of limiting the rest of the over to a single.

At this stage Phil Cole, not with any great expectation, thought he should persevere with Winston Jenkins. Within minutes there was another fifty to celebrate. Winston began his third over with two dreadfully short balls. Intended to intimidate, they rose off the pitch only to a height which was comfortable for cutting and pulling. Ten runs accrued and the fifty partnership was posted. At this juncture Winston abandoned his longer run, reverted to his usual eight paces and kept further damage down to a couple of singles.

Unlike the unfortunate Fred Wheeler, the club's scoreboard had survived the collapse of the pavilion. It comprised a rudimentary metal frame on which tin plates were hung. For want of anything better to do in the absence of her female friends in the Outcasts' entourage, and a desire to be close to her husband, Sophie Crossley had assumed control. She had acquired two young assistants in the shape of the brothers Skynn, Robert aged 12 and David aged 10, whose pleasure seemed to be heightened by banging the plates together as they were changed. Simon Crossley concentrated on keeping his meticulous record, much more detailed than was being attempted by his dragooned opposite number, Tom Haresmith. Simon was attired in a pair of bright yellow slacks and a cotton top of black and yellow horizontal stripes. He failed to appreciate why, as the boys came near him, they kept saying 'Buzz.'

The scoreboard could convey only a limited amount of information, but enough to keep spectators aware of the recent landmarks. They also knew that Ben Harding, even if they did not know his name, was himself on the brink of a very entertaining half-century. However, some spectators were by now looking at empty glasses and anticipating rather more comic entertainment in the arena reserved for 'It's a Knockout'. Their children were also tugging at sleeves and wanting to be off to the stalls and sideshows. That other attractions were now available beyond the hedge was emphasised by the striking up of the band.

The search for a band had been beset with difficulties. Bands with local connections were already booked on such a popular day as the first Saturday in June. The amount budgeted for payment of the band was a major restriction on choice. In the end the best the committee had come up with was an ensemble calling itself the Variety Players of Much Heydon, which someone recalled as having given satisfaction at a Women's Institute tea party last year. Not many bars of music had been (literally) executed before members of the committee were wondering what the source of that satisfaction had been. In the passage of twelve months a transformation had overtaken the Variety Players of Much Heydon. Those with any real musical talent had moved on to pastures new, leaving behind the gallant triers amongst whom could be counted the conductor. The band did not have to play long before it became apparent that it had only a restricted repertoire – so limited in fact that the use of the word 'Variety' in its title might have given rise to question in the context of the Trades Descriptions Act.

Not everyone deserted the cricket. Against the flow, one of the helpers rushed up to Uncle George to say that more manpower was needed at the main entrance to the arena. The paying public (£3 for adults, 50p for children) was arriving in unexpected strength. The entry stream would have to be split. Change was also becoming a problem. Uncle George was inclined to be dismissive. He was sure that it was a temporary hitch, and in any case responsibility for this part of the operation was supposed to be delegated. He finally agreed 'to come along in a minute' and, pleased to know there was going to be a good turn-out, he resumed his concentration on Ben Harding's approaching fifty.

Ray Burrill was also concentrating on the cricket when he found himself being swept off his feet by a big blonde girl who seemed to be wearing far too much make-up. It took him a moment or two to recognise Tim Jackson. His friend's usual suave and debonair appearance was very effectively lost under a blonde, plaited wig, an excessive applicatiion of rouge and a milkmaid's costume. Tim was anxious to check Ray's precise availability, for otherwise they risked being a man short in their 'It's a Knockout' team. Tim's appearance almost drove Ray Burrill to declaring his total non-availability, but he was assured that he was not wanted for the milkmaids' game. As he went through the programme, Tim Jackson seemed to be taking the event as seriously as he might the afternoon's racing at Sandown, but not so seriously that he could not be persuaded to take a pint in the cricket marquee whose bar was now open.

From a distance, Phil Cole failed to recognise Tim Jackson in his new guise, but his eyes followed Ray Burrill and his new-found friend with envy as they retreated into the marquee. It was becoming warm work out in the middle and a quick pint of suitable ale would have been a pleasant diversion. However, he could not allow himself to be diverted from a decision which needed to be made. Stewart Thorogood had bowled his first five overs so economically that Phil had won the bowler's approval for the suggestion that he might bowl his full allocation in a single spell. After Stewart's sixth over, Phil had begun to harbour doubts about this strategy. He approached the question of a seventh over gingerly, inquiring whether in view of the rising temperature, Stewart might after all prefer a break. But, no, Stewart had adjusted himself physically and mentally to the idea of bowling his nine overs straight off the top. What he did not bother to mention to his captain was that he calculated that this would give him a window of opportunity to down a pint or two without detriment to his batting at a later point in the day.

So Stewart Thorogood took the ball. Phil Cole was soon wishing otherwise. With Jim Abbs on strike, Stewart thought he would try his new-found inswinger again. It proved to be newly lost. What might at best have been a swinging yorker taking out leg stump was a straight full toss which Jim Abbs recognised well enough to stroke through the covers for four. His first boundary made him feel good. With his appetite whetted, he despatched a respectable second ball through mid-off for another boundary. The third ball fell short and, in full flow, Jim Abbs successfully unleashed a square cut. By now Stewart Thorogood was less at ease with himself. As he tramped back to his mark, he muttered repetitively to himself 'Outswinger.' The indoctrination had its effect. He produced a good outswinger which, in the context of the over, the batsman did not expect. Attempting another flowery drive, Jim Abbs edged between the first and second slip which Phil Cole had been on the point of removing. After a fumble by third man, the batsmen ran two.

At this juncture both captains intervened, the one to quieten down his partner and the other to fire up his bowler. Neither succeeded, but one was lucky. Grumpily Stewart Thorogood started in again. Fluency was nowhere evident. The outcome was a short ball on leg stump. Jim Abbs could not believe his luck. He was in a mood for it to go miles. And it did – but upwards. Instead of a clean pull which would surely have earned four, Jim Abbs in search of the bigger prize got underneath it and an ugly swipe succeeded only in an edge which sent the ball soaring. Even then he might not have been dismissed. Whilst the ball was climbing towards the heavens, earthly creatures below were in confusion as to where it might drop. Kevin Newton, the wicket-keeper, advanced to within a few feet of the bowler's follow-through. They looked upwards and then at each other. Kevin Newton could see on Stewart Thorogood's face an expression which recalled the catches he had dropped off Stewart's bowling – there had been several, especially before Kevin had forsaken his long fair hair – and indecision might have reigned a while longer if Phil Cole had not commandingly called 'Keeper.' Kevin Newton redeemed himself in Stewart's eyes. Jim Abbs departed.

According to the list he had left in the changing-room, Ben Harding had expected the incoming batsman to be Trevor Edgefield. It was not to be. Marching towards him was Walter Ryesmith, who Uncle George had described with insight of dubious profundity as a better number six than a number five. If sudden success had gone to Jim Abbs's head, his change of fortune had steadied Stewart Thorogood. Resisting the temptation to have a go at the new batsman with his cherished inswinger (Ben Harding had got back to the non-striker's end by the time the ball had been pouched), Stewart concentrated on his outswinger and had the satisfaction of seeing Walter Ryesmith guide it obligingly into the hands of Alan Birch at second slip. Uncle George's assessment of relative merits could not be further tested as there continued to be no sign of the batsman allocated to the number five spot. Walter Ryesmith's replacement was Geoffrey Jarr, a small, balding man who looked older than his years. It was believed amongst his friends that signs of premature ageing were explained by the hours he put in as a cost accountant. In reality it had more to do with a hyperactive social life.

Coombes the decorator eased his position in the one wholly dry chair remaining in the lounge of Willingfold Towers. Having poured himself another cup of tea from a teapot which had already caused a scorch mark on the painted wooden table, he leant back, planting his feet (still in their boots) in a restful posture on the same table. He sighed and looked about him. It was clear that the whole room would have to be redecorated. This had been rather less clear before his arrival. Undoubtedly the paper was damp and sagging in places on the one wall. The fact that it was now peeling and torn on the other three was a direct result of Coombes 'testing' it. Similar professional attention had led to the same conclusion in the master bedroom and the hall. Coombes's estimate was already escalating into thousands when his tea break was interrupted by a shrill burst of barking.

Phil Cole was not wildly enthusiastic about another encounter between Winston Jenkins and Ben Harding. He had alternatives up his sleeve. There was, of course, his own brand of medium pace, but he was experiencing a captain's modesty in taking the ball ahead of others. That at least was how he rationalised it to himself. Realistically, he saw Ben Harding as a class act and did not think that his bowling would be treated any differently from that of Winston Jenkins. Then there was Charlie Colson. Phil was not immediately attracted by the prospect of Charlie's not far from medium pace inswingers. On their day they could be quite useful in keeping one end quiet. So far this season, Rockcliffe notwithstanding, no such day had been found. The Colson specials had taken heavy punishment. Nothing in Charlie's appearance on the field hinted that his form might have changed. Vodka, not being a regular part of the Colson regime, had left its morning-after mark, which Charlie had sought to erase with Uncle George's champagne. The visible evidence of cure was at this stage inconclusive. There was no question of the early return of Colin Banks whose mind seemed elsewhere. That left leg spin, and Phil Cole wanted to leave it a bit longer. Against the likes of Ben Harding, Phil Cole did not see Tom Redman as a strike bowler, but more as a struck one. So it was Winston Jenkins who resumed.

Whether it was the fall of two wickets in successive balls or his own impending half-century was not certain, but caution seemed to infuse Ben Harding. Equally, fearing it might be the last over he would be asked to bowl, Winston Jenkins applied himself with diligence. Ben Harding took a comfortable single off the third ball and Geoffrey Jarr was content to play himself in. With Stewart

Thorogood on a hat-trick, the die was cast. Phil Cole realised that he could not deny him his eighth over and so, rather than holding one over of his permitted ration back, he might as well have his ninth as well. However, the landmark of the over was to belong to the batsman and not the bowler. Stewart did not in any way disgrace himself, but his second ball was flicked away wide of fine leg and Ben Harding collected the three runs which brought him an elegant fifty. Uncle George led the cheers of a diminished crowd. Geoffrey Jarr continued to play himself in.

Uncle George was about to turn into the marquee for the glass of champagne which he was convinced Ben Harding's fifty justified when he experienced a strange phenomenon. One of the nearby portaloos moved. Uncle George rubbed his eyes and looked again in that direction. The little hut appeared to quiver. Was it heat haze? Uncle George was inclined to ask himself. Or was it? ... He snatched a glance at the empty glass in his hand. Looking up, there it was again. The structure definitely shook. If only for his own state of mind, Uncle George had to investigate. It was not until he was a foot or two away from the portaloo that the situation became clear. The cabin appeared to be moving, because someone inside was pounding on its door and shouting to attract attention. The muffled voice had gone unheard amidst the general hubbub. Nor obviously had anyone else sought to use the facility, because when Uncle George turned the handle from the outside, the door opened. An agitated Trevor Edgefield, who had been trying for the last twenty minutes to achieve the feat from the inside, almost fell out into the open air. It was a while before Uncle George could stem his torrent of foul language. After he thought he had calmed down the released prisoner, Uncle George chuckled. It may have been the champagne or a streak of lavatorial humour which had stayed with him since childhood, but it was as ill-timed as it was unintended. Finding a new target for his wrath, Trevor Edgefield used some harsh words to convey what he thought of Uncle George and his cricket match and disappeared into the dressing-room. A few seconds passed and loud laughter was heard therein, proving that Uncle George was not the only person to be tickled by the absurdity of someone being locked in a lavatory.

The adventure of Trevor Edgefield went unnoticed by the players on the field, but it was to have a consequence. Phil Cole gave Winston Jenkins the benefit of the doubt and another over. The bowler got away quite lightly as most of it was bowled to the new batsman, who got himself off the mark off the last ball. The score moved on to 83–4. A visibly tiring Stewart Thorogood made a final effort, but was unable to induce any more errors. Geoffrey Jarr was immaculately cautious and it took a misfield to earn him two runs for a ball he stabbed out on the leg side. Stewart Thorogood finished with figures of 2–33 off his nine overs and began thoughts of refreshment.

Putting off for as long as possible the introduction of a fourth bowler, Phil Cole allowed Winston Jenkins a sixth over. This time luck was not with him, for Winston found himself bowling exclusively to the well-established batsman rather than the nervous beginner. Ben Harding clearly felt that he was not exactly undermining the foundations of his team's innings by applying himself to Winston Jenkins's bowling with a degree of force. A straight, unexceptional ball he turned off his toes past the square-leg umpire for two. The next was straight driven for another two. Winston Jenkins's direction began to wobble. He was cut behind square for another two. A wider ball was thrashed through the covers for four. Winston over-compensated on the other side of the wicket and was tickled for two to fine leg. Only with his last despairing effort did he elude Ben Harding's bat, having found from somewhere a fastish leg-break which surprised everyone including his captain. As Phil Cole said to him, 'If you could promise me six more like that, I'd give you another over. But, as it is, I think I'll risk a change.'

'Bloody traffic,' were the words with which Frank Pirgrove had introduced himself at the Towers. These had quickly been followed by 'Bloody dog.' Boycs barked at strangers. He particularly barked at strangers with ladders, and he could see that Pirgrove the plumber was carrying ladders in his truck. 'Bloody weather,' Pirgrove went on, mopping his brow. 'I could murder some tea.' He had noticed that Coombes had come to the side door with a mug in his hand. The kettle was set to work again whilst Pirgrove and Coombes were not. Strangers when they met, they appeared to be firm friends by the time Ray Burrill returned. It appeared that Pirgrove had been hungry as well as thirsty. The sight of the fresh ham brought back earlier by the Redman brothers had excited Coombes's taste buds. Only a third of a loaf now remained. An empty tin of baked beans and a stained pan showed that the men had not gone without hot food. An opened but unconsumed tin of soup was part of the débris on the kitchen counter. 'Bloody mushroom,' Pirgrove had said, having neglected to read the label, believing that red labels meant tomato soup, for that is what in the Pirgrove household they invariably did.

After a good lunch it was natural to have a rest with a cup of tea and, in the case of Frank Pirgrove, a cigarette. It was in the lounge that Ray Burrill found them. The new water tank remained firmly in the back of the truck. The only thing so far removed from the vehicle was a piece of plastic sheeting which Frank Pirgrove had stretched across the Haverscombe's settee not to protect it from his dirty overalls, but to shield him from its dampness. A cigarette end had slipped from his fingers, missed the china dish he had selected as an ash tray and burnt a hole in the carpet. He was asleep and Coombes was hunched over the crossword in a tabloid newspaper with a puzzled expression on his face. Boycs, who had been left to roam, chose that moment to return from some garden adventure and greeted Ray Burrill with a friendly bark. 'Bloody dog,' said Frank Pirgrove, stirring and then starting as he saw Ray standing over him.

At the cricket ground, the tempo had slowed. The interior handle on the door of the portaloo had been repaired before it could claim any more victims. Willingfold's score was becalmed below the hundred mark. Not even the champagne was flowing. Uncle George's empty glass had been parked at the end of the bar counter close to the source of his special supply, but its owner had finally transferred his attention to what was happening on the other side of the hedge. That was where the noise and the atmosphere now seemed to be concentrated. The number of people left watching the cricket had dwindled to the level one would have expected to encounter at Grace Road in April. The game was something less than riveting.

A double change of bowling (part enforced) had taken place. Overcoming modesty, Phil Cole had opted for himself as Stewart Thorogood's replacement at the farm end. The plan then was to give Tom Redman's leg-spin a try from the pavilion end. If this combination did not work, Phil reckoned that he would have to risk Charlie Colson whilst switching Tom Redman to the opposite end. However, it did seem to work. Geoffrey Jarr looked intent on crease occupation and attempted nothing aggressive. More curiously, Ben Harding was playing an innings of fits and starts, a burst of aggression leading to a period of almost strokeless consolidation. Five overs yielded two runs. Festival hardly seemed the word.

Uncle George saw his relationship with events beyond the hedge as paternal, but distant. Having overseen the broad outline he had left the detail to others, in his assessment, 'more used to that kind of thing'. One look told him that he had overestimated the capacity of most of his committee and severely underestimated the capacity of Darcey De'Arth. Already a large crowd was milling around, except anywhere near the band which was engaged on its third repetition of a selection from 'The Chocolate Soldier'. The beer tent was doing good business. With one or two exceptions, the stalls and side-shows appeared to be operational. A long queue of people awaiting entrance could be seen stretching down the road. Fortunately, there was an abundance of car parking space on fields belonging either to Ken Pegley or the parish. Less fortunately, there was not an abundance of seating surrounding the area in which 'It's a Knockout' would be enacted. They had at least provided a temporary 'grandstand' built with scaffolding. Otherwise there was a variety of makeshift chairs and benches not more than two deep. Very few spaces were left. Buttonholing one of his colleagues on the committee, Uncle George dropped one or two helpful hints designed to ease congestion. He then drifted back to the cricket. It was what Uncle George could not see which might have alarmed him.

Not being a bank holiday, the first Saturday in June would not have been expected to be exceptionally busy on the roads. An early sign that this expectation might not be fulfilled came in a phone call to the Hertfordshire sub-divisional headquarters of the Road Services Association (RSA). Jim Dukes had just unwrapped the foil from the sandwiches made some hours earlier by his wife and from their aroma was trying to guess the filling which had been selected for him for this shift. Cheese, celery and sweetcorn on granary with just a hint of horseradish. Smashing! His Betty made wonderful sandwiches – always something new. She could not cook to save her life, but she made wonderfully inventive sandwiches. The first portion was halfway to his mouth when he was interrupted by the buzz of the instrument on the console in front of him. Jim Dukes was the duty agent. In the RSA, all internal staff were agents, only men on the road were officers. Officer Fred Bear (he was mercilessly teased) called to report 'a bit of bother' on the main road to the east of Willingfold. There was standing traffic in both directions, but no sign of an accident. Jim Dukes checked that neither police nor ambulance had received a 999 call and submitted a verbal report to his regional office. His hand was groping for his sandwich, his mouth salivating for its tangy taste, when the buzzer sounded again.

Willingfold surged past the one hundred mark eventually with a burst of scoring, but without much in the way of recognition. The number of spectators had declined to minority status. Even her young helpers had departed, leaving Sophie Crossley in sole charge of the scoreboard. She was puffing slightly whilst trying to keep up with events on the field. The Redman-Cole combination had slipped from grace. Buoyed by two maiden overs, Tom Redman, instead of relaxing into his stride, had become over-ambitious. In trying to bamboozle Ben Harding with flight he lost first his length followed shortly after by his composure. His third over yielded ten runs and his fourth fourteen. By contrast Phil Cole, whose first three overs had cost one run, took things too easily. Geoffrey Jarr came to the conclusion that there were no mysteries in Phil's bowling and began to play shots. It was when this batsman had the opportunity to face Tom Redman again that Phil Cole realised how rash he had been to grant him a fifth over. After a silky single from his captain, Geoffrey Jarr displayed some smart footwork and twice lifted Tom Redman on to the roof of the marquee/pavilion. Taking a single himself off the last ball of the over, he contentedly leant on his bat and contemplated more goodies to come. The one-fifty mark had now been passed as well. And Sophie Crossley was as aware as anyone of the speed with which the last fifty runs had come.

Realising that he would need to use Charlie Colson as Tom Redman's replacement at the pavilion end, Phil Cole persuaded himself to keep going at the other. The wicket he obtained had very little to do with this tactical appraisal or any significant improvement in the quality of his bowling. Geoffrey Jarr was feeling content. This match was providing him with some useful practice and assisting his return to form. He had been especially pleased with his two sixes and he looked forward to telling his regular team-mates in his home village about his dashing play (which was not what they usually witnessed). After a sweetly-timed push which eluded cover's right hand and earned him two, Geoffrey Jarr would be less eager to describe his dismissal – but in any case the story would go ahead of him. Whilst the bouncy castle was not as instantly recognisable as usual, the rising number of children in the adjacent arena could not be fooled: the 'castle' was in full occupation. As the children bounced, so to some extent did the whole structure. Whether by chance or by co-ordinated effort in one giant leap, the figure of the woman quivered and rather more than her head momentarily appeared over the hedge. It was the very moment when Geoffrey Jarr was attempting to pull a ball which Phil Cole had speared towards leg. It was an unfortunate distraction and it induced a false stroke. Mid-on was able to take the catch and with incredulity the batsman had to go. In his moment of pleasure, Phil Cole could not even dare to hint that he had been playing for that. A still smarting Trevor Edgefield at last got his chance. There were two balls left in the over. He made good use of them.

The road which fed Willingfold from the west was now full to capacity and the tail-back had begun to have a knock-on effect elsewhere on the road network. Agent Jim Dukes's lunch-hour was punctuated with ever greater frequency by calls from his colleagues on patrol about an unusual concentration of traffic in the area. Willingfold had not yet been identified as the magnet. The cheese, celery and sweetcorn sandwiches on granary with just a hint of horseradish lay neglected as Jim Dukes found himself in the middle of a highly unusual traffic incident which seemed to be deteriorating by the minute. Regional office informed him with gravity that it was calling out the reserves. This was the RSA's equivalent of mobilisation, but without any actual declaration of war.

Frustration amongst motorists was mounting. Annoyance was vented in a variety of directions. Those who were not bound for Willingfold could not understand the delay in their journey. They cursed the Minister for Transport and Public Safety, the highways authority, the police and, for want of more particular focus, the Government in general. One man cursed his mother-in-law for inviting the family to visit in the first place. Those whose destination was Willingfold had the same targets for criticism including, in one case, the mother-in-law as passenger who kept saying they should have left earlier. But these people also complained about the destination which was proving so hard to find and so complicated to reach. Queues of standing traffic were now so extensive that street vendors had begun to gather to offer drinks, snacks, newspapers and even, inexplicably, flowers.

Trevor Edgefield looked around him and then settled to receive his first ball from a Phil Cole encouraged as any bowler is by the capture of a wicket. The delivery was modest and received most immodest treatment. Trevor Edgefield vented the anger and humiliation which had been welling up in him into the creation of a savage straight drive out of the path of which the bowler neatly stepped. No-one else chose to intervene and Umpire Crickhill imperiously waved a four. If his first stroke reflected the batsman's anger and humiliation, the second added cunning. It was cleverly placed for his purposes just wide of mid-off. 'Two', shouted Trevor Edgefield and raced to the bowler's end. There he turned, took two convincing strides down the wicket and then yelled successively 'No,' 'OK,' 'Wait,' 'No' and 'Sorry' before retreating to the safety of the crease. He was greeted by the cheerful smile of the bowler and Phil Cole was surprised to see it so broadly reciprocated. Ben Harding had been utterly stranded and Kevin Newton had had sufficient time, even for him, to complete the run out without fumbling.

As Bill Forbes, Willingfold's long-standing wicket-keeper, plodded out to the middle, another person raced on to the field of play in Phil Cole's direction. It appeared to be the knave of hearts, but on closer inspection was found to be Tim Jackson. 'Panic stations,' he announced. Ray Burrill had not re-appeared and they were a man short for the carrot

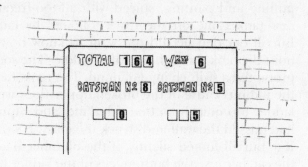

game which was the one after next. Tim wanted to borrow a fielder. In the ordinary way Phil Cole would never for a moment have agreed to this. Perhaps thinking that he had broken the back of Willingfold's batting, maybe believing that the home side would lend him a substitute or possibly just elated by the fall of two wickets in one over, he succumbed – and Harry Northwood was detailed.

When he looked beyond the advancing figure of Bill Forbes there was no sign of the Willingfold captain with whom he might have sought a friendly word about the loan of a substitute fielder. Ben Harding was doing what all good batsmen do when they have been sawn off at the knees; he was having a moment's sulk in the dressing-room. Being a portakabin it was not too well insulated. A youngster, who had chosen to lean against the rear whilst sucking his ice-cream, received a gratuitous extension to his vocabulary. The other Willingfold players, reading the signs, had scattered. Not even Uncle George could be seen. Tom Haresmith at the scorer's table had been a reluctant twelfth man for the home team and he could certainly see no reason why he should oblige the visitors. Phil Cole shrugged and turned his attention to deploying to best advantage the ten men remaining to him.

Ray Burrill had had just sufficient on-the-job training as a vet to have learnt something of the art of patience. Owners with sick animals could goad a saint, and so Ray had a store of resilience with which to counter the appalling state of affairs awaiting him at Willingfold Towers. He had the sense to recognise that it was these men or nothing. He therefore set about coaxing co-operation from them whilst he cleared up the débris of their extended lunch. ('It were only a snack,' Coombes had said defensively.) Amidst much puffing and panting, spiced with all-too-frequent swearwords, the new tank came off the truck followed by ladders and tools. Ray Burrill decided he did not want to know how the two men would hoist the tank through the loft window. The sound of breaking glass prompted a swift change of mind. The tank, he discovered, was only the indirect cause of the broken upper-floor window. In moving the ladder too quickly to one side ('me 'and slipped'), Frank Pirgrove had missed the wall and struck the glass. It would have been better, Ray Burrill fumed silently, if the plumber had asked him to move the car, because the bottom legs of the ladder had also 'slipped' and made nasty indentations on the side panelling of the Mini. Feeling less than complete confidence in the men's assurances that they would 'soon have this lot sorted', Ray Burrill determined to stay on site and sacrifice his team's performance in 'It's a Knockout'. The decision was understandable, but unfortunate. Had he gone, the car would not have been in position to break the fall of the old tank as it exited from the loft.

At nearby Willingfold Hall, Grouse was not a happy man. Deserted by Mrs Enzyme and told to get his own lunch, Grouse was alone, not counting the body of Mortimer Dalrymple Phypps which was still awaiting the attention of Messrs Doom and Son. He, Grouse, had been left in charge. He racked his brain to work out the best way of explaining to his employer on his eventual return what had happened. A father, on his son's departure apparently still blessed with reasonable life expectancy and expressly entrusted to Grouse's care, was now dead in circumstances about which Grouse, notwithstanding the views of the doctor and the police, felt uneasy. Young Mr Phypps would want to know how his father had got hold of the gun. Grouse himself wanted to know how the old man had sneaked it into his room. He had the nagging feeling that delay was aggravating the situation, but, he tried to reassure himself, it was not his fault that the deceased's son was incommunicado. Where the hell was the hearse, he asked himself between mouthfuls of cold meat loaf and pickle? Where the hell was Mr Lawrence Phypps? Both were much nearer than he might have thought.

Charlie Colson realised that he was being used on sufferance. He was honest enough to recognise that he had been in poor form thus far in the season and in poor form after the previous evening's adventure. He knew he had to concentrate hard if he was to muster some accuracy. He received aid from an unexpected quarter. The old stalwarts of the Willingfold team, as Trevor Edgefield and Bill Forbes saw themselves, were in no hurry to throw their wickets away in any kind of mad dash for runs. In particular, the former, revenge having been exacted, had a point or two to make and for a while this was to have priority over making runs. To Charlie Colson's delight and his captain's surprise, he was able to send down three overs for no more than a couple of runs. Phil Cole achieved similar niggardliness at the other end. Extras matched what came from the bat. When Ben Harding emerged from his self-imposed purdah he was not best pleased to find that the fruits of six more overs had been a mere eight runs.

Nor was Phil Cole entirely satisfied. Short of a fielder, short of wickets and short of inspiration, he reckoned that the Outcasts were already facing a stiff target. It would prove even more distant if members of the side refreshed themselves too heartily at the tea interval. These late-order Willingfold batsmen had proved more resilient than he had expected. Having seen the blow with which Trevor Edgefield originally announced himself, Phil Cole realised that the circumspect play of the last few overs was the prelude to a slog in the final few overs. The final few overs were now virtually upon them. It was time to find out whether his fastest bowler, Colin Banks, was up to bowling his share of them.

Carloads of people were still arriving to witness what some hours previously Darcey De'Arth had been carolling as a millennium village festival. The extended journey in the heat of the day had done nothing to improve tempers. Arrival of itself did not dissipate the discontent as by then people could hear the band whose fourth attempt to put across vocal gems from 'Bless the Bride' had not noticeably improved performance. There was a queue for admission, there was a queue for the lavatory, there was a queue for ice-cream and there were so many people lining the 'It's a Knockout' arena that newcomers could scarcely get a glimpse. Heads of families did what heads of families do in such circumstances. Some looked for officials in charge to whom to complain; others made for the beer tent. Most went to the beer tent.

Road conditions to the west of the village made that the worse approach. Officers of the Road Services Association – by now plentifully on the job – were aware of this, but powerless to do much about it without authority from the police. A hastily convened meeting at constabulary headquarters deliberated over the situation, but as none of the participants had ever heard of Willingfold or possessed any knowledge of the terrain, a worthwhile plan of action was a long time in gestation. Meanwhile the badly-timed one-way working arrangement at Muckersby Bridge was wreaking maximum havoc.

It is an ill road-works obstruction that does nobody any good. Lawrence Phypps, in an unaccustomed white van, was stuck behind a hearse. The temporary traffic light was at green, but that made no difference. It had been green before, but they had still not moved. Lawrence Phypps shifted uneasily in his seat and searched his rear-view mirror and his wing mirror. He was sure they were there. There had been an unmarked car behind him for too long for it to be a coincidence. Local knowledge had allowed him to execute a risky manoeuvre into the final turn for Willingfold. They would probably have worked out by now where he was headed. They would be somewhere behind in this line of traffic. They would wait. Suddenly the thought struck him that perhaps they might not. He glanced in the mirrors again and cursed this unexpected hold-up. As his eyes swivelled back, he was confronted by a man in black who caused him almost to freeze in fright. 'Got a light, mate?' Recovering, Lawrence Phypps told himself that this was surely not the way the Customs and Excise began an interrogation, however apposite this might have been to his particular situation.

To his irritation, Phil Cole found Colin Banks less than enthusiastic about re-entering the fray. His mind seemed to be on things other than cricket. He could barely keep his eyes off his female companion and seemingly his lips off the rim of a glass. Phil Cole noticed the faint trace of foam above Colin's mouth. If it had not been for some encouragement from Virginia Crickhill, Colin might have gone on resisting. Finally a compromise was struck. He would bowl the last three overs from the pavilion end. By then, he had assured Phil Cole, he would be up for it. That left the captain with little alternative but to persist with Charlie Colson and the space of an over to choose between Winston Jenkins and Tom Redman at the other end.

Phil Cole's suspicions underlying his projected bowling changes was entirely justified. Whilst he had been conferring at the boundary edge, Trevor Edgefield and Bill Forbes had met in the middle. A change of gear was agreed. 'Leave it to me,' advised Trevor Edgefield. However, as they separated, Bill Forbes was not reconciled to a one-man campaign. He fancied his chances as well against the likes of Charlie Colson. Opportunity came with the second ball which swung in too fully and towards leg. He picked it up well and deposited it one bounce over the mid-wicket boundary for four. He straight-drove the next for two. He felt good. When Charlie Colson tried to spear a faster ball outside off-stump, Bill Forbes leant back and thrashed it high towards extra cover, where to his dismay it was caught by a large blue rabbit.

'That's out,' said Umpire Breakwell to the astonished batsman. His verdict was delivered with a certainty which he should not have felt. Bill Forbes was obliged to suppress his doubts. Halfway back to the changing rooms they were revived when he was accosted by Uncle George waving his arms. Uncle George's first contention was that the rabbit was not a legitimate substitute. This theory was quickly disproved when the grinning face of Harry Northwood had been identified. Next door it transpired there had been a delay in starting the carrot game and the participants in their rabbit costumes were temporarily redundant. Mindful of his other responsibilities, Harry had reverted to the game of cricket. Uncle George's second argument was that a fielder should not be wearing gloves, but Harry had the answer to that. The rabbit costume covered only the outside of his hands. The palms were uncovered. The catch had been clean. Uncle George did not like it, but Syd Breakwell at his officious best did. The game had to proceed without further assistance from Bill Forbes and Uncle George. In the confusion, no-one grasped the real point of law involved.

After this short delay, John Tod was the person who replaced Bill Forbes at the wicket. There was no time for a chat with Trevor Edgefield. The latter was on strike, the batsmen having crossed before the controversial catch, and Syd Breakwell was showing every kind of impatience to get on with the action. The exchange was destined not to take place. Trevor Edgefield struck Charlie Colson's next delivery beautifully through the covers, but was denied a boundary by the fast-moving rabbit who flung himself full-length, white bob-tail heaving, to interrupt the ball a foot from the line. Stewart Thorogood threw the ball back while Harry Northwood recovered. The batsmen collected three. Not being the fittest of men (policing in Willingfold was not the most active of professions), John Tod had been unsteadied by the vigorous running of his partner. He pushed forward at a slanting delivery from Charlie Colson, was struck on the front pad and sent on his way by Syd Breakwell, who failed to consider whether the ball might have gone down the leg side (by the width of a set of stumps).

Elvis Coombes was a known quantity as a batsman. That is why Henry Pickard, who was not, was next man in. Nevertheless, this was promotion. Any one of his regular team-mates in the Hertfordshire village club for which he usually played would be loud in Henry Pickard's praise as an off-spin bowler, but would smile and change the subject if his batting was mentioned. Centuries earlier he would have batted eighteenth. For the moment, the level of his skill was disguised by the nonchalence with which he leant on his bat at the non-striker's end. Trevor Edgefield for one was fooled.

It was decision time for Phil Cole. It was no use bowling a reluctant Colin Banks. He had to settle for his fast bowler's assurance that he would be 'up' for three overs at the end of the innings. Intermittently through the dramas of the preceding over there had flitted memories of the most recent efforts of his two alternative bowlers. Winston Jenkins had gone for twelve and Tom

Redman for fourteen. Before that it was a blur, but he was confident that both had been expensive. Yet neither had bowled at the batsman now at the crease. Trevor Edgefield looked a gritty player. Could he be teased out by spin? And then Phil Cole studied Henry Pickard. He saw a well-built athletic-looking man with the potential to hit slow bowlers many a mile. Like Trevor Edgefield he was fooled. He beckoned Winston Jenkins.

Lawrence Phypps had absorbed the shock with remarkable ease even though it had been an unconventional way of learning of his father's death. The man in black had been joined by another. In the conversation which ensued it was not long before their unity of destination became apparent. Bit by bit the entire situation was revealed. The Doom brothers, whilst relatively new to the business of undertaking (they had previously been in scrap metal), had nevertheless become accustomed to encountering grief in its various forms. They had never before encountered it in the form exhibited by Lawrence Phypps. He beamed and at first the Doom brothers completely misunderstood him when he told them that they were the very men he needed.

The well-established wisteria which many visitors agreed was a feature of Willingfold Towers had taken a severe mauling during the operation to deliver the new water tank to its place in the loft. Ray Burrill had been making tea at the insistence of Frank Pirgrove who reckoned that a good cup of tea was what kept him going. This had not been Ray Burrill's experience, but he had been anxious to maintain the goodwill of the only two workmen available to him. He was acquainted with the damage to the wisteria as he rounded the corner with the mugs of tea. It has to be said that it did not provoke much concern on his part, because this was also the moment of realisation that the crash he had heard a few moments earlier was not of the old water tank hitting the ground. It had been interrupted in its journey earthwards by the Mini which was now distinctly minier than when he had last seen it. There was no need to be an expert in car construction to doubt Coombes's cheery promise that it could soon be 'knocked back in shape'. Before he could argue, they were interrupted by the sound of splintering wood.

Uncle George was not on hand to witness the disintegration of the Willingfold innings. He had retreated to the cottage to make a telephone call. His hope was to get a ruling from Lord's which might yet salvage Bill Forbes's wicket. There was something deeply unsatisfactory about being caught out by someone in a rabbit suit. He was sure that it could not be right. The phone rang a very long time before it was answered. Uncle George was not a man who regarded himself as in any way class-conscious, but it took him only a few seconds to realise that he was not speaking to the keeper of the laws of cricket. In fact he had not spoken at all before a female voice informed him, 'There's no-one 'ere, luv, they've all gone to the races.' Uncle George tried to speak, but he was interrupted. 'It's no good, luv, I'm only the cleaner. I was doing the floor in the Long Room. I only just 'eard the phone. I 'ad to rush all the way. Oh, you'll 'ave to excuse me while I sit down. It's me arthritis. They tell you you don't feel it so much in the warm weather, but I think doctors these days don't know nothing. It takes us old ones to tell 'em.' Uncle George bridled at this ready assumption of his age, but there was no time to speak before he was plunged into what was evidently going to be a prolonged medical litany. It was into its third minute when Uncle George began to appreciate that it might have no natural end. He replaced the receiver and swore to himself that he would table a motion for the MCC's next annual general meeting.

'For God's sake,' Phil Cole had said to Winston Jenkins, 'keep it straight and a bit of pace wouldn't hurt.' But it did. The faster Winston tried to bowl, the faster the ball seemed to come off Trevor Edgefield's bat. That he was managing to keep it straight made no difference. He was simply hit straight, three times to the boundary and also for a couple of twos. His only dot ball was his last when he failed to get out of the way in time and he found himself stopping another fierce drive with his foot. There was a delay before he could resume his place in the field for the next over. The Willingfold score had leapt to 195–8.

After this carnage Phil Cole did not know what to expect from Charlie Colson. Nine runs had come off Charlie's last over although he had taken two wickets. There were seven overs to be bowled and it looked to Phil as though Trevor Edgefield and what remained of the tail would be giving them the charge. Charlie Colson was not really a bowler for the death. Phil remembered with a shudder an earlier match in which, as a result of poor juggling with the attack, there had been no real alternative to Charlie bowling the last over. It had gone for twenty-five. He said nothing as Charlie prepared to bowl to Henry Pickard and limited himself to an encouraging pat on the bowler's shoulder.

'Line and length,' Charlie Colson kept muttering as he prepared to run into bowl. 'Nice and steady does it,' he further advised himself as he moved up towards the wicket. The result was nice and steady – in the form of a full toss which looped invitingly towards the batsman. Henry Pickard gulped. Then he swished. He gulped again as he turned to see his stumps in a mess. 'Well bowled, mate,' Kevin Newton called rather gratuitously as Henry Pickard went on his way. Trevor Edgefield looked on in disbelief. So to some extent did Phil Cole. As he gave Charlie Colson another pat on the shoulder, he wondered about the calibre of Willingfold's number eleven batsman who was deemed not good enough to bat above Henry Pickard.

There was a belief deep down inside Elvis Coombes that he could bat. It was not a belief shared by anyone in the village who had seen him play. Yet the delusion of Elvis Coombes went even further. He was convinced that he had the makings of an all-rounder. This was based on no independent advice or assessment, but on watching himself practise strokes in his wardrobe mirror. He planned to reveal to the village that there was now a new Elvis Coombes. He had watched the ball which had accounted for Henry Pickard and sneered. He would have hit that out of the ground. He walked out swinging his bat in a great arc – he had seen batsmen on television doing that. When he drew alongside Trevor Edgefield he was told, 'Don't do anything stupid.' It was not said with any conviction. As Trevor Edgefield knew too well, Elvis Coombes was very stupid.

Elvis Coombes remembered to ask for a guard. He chose middle stump. Then he remembered to look round the field. Not a blue rabbit in sight – Harry Northwood had joined his other team. Elvis smiled broadly. Charlie Colson trotted in. He had reached the umpire when Elvis Coombes held up his hand and stepped back from the wicket. Pointing, Elvis claimed that there was movement behind the bowler's arm. This was barely credible. There were by now virtually no spectators and members of the Willingfold team, anticipating the inevitable, had already retreated into the marquee where tea was to be served. Trevor Edgefield groaned. He sensed that this was purely a ploy on Elvis's part. The batsman settled again. Charlie made his second approach. Once more Elvis stopped him. 'Got summat in me eye,' he complained, dropping his bat. ('It'll be my fist in a minute,' Trevor Edgefield hissed through clenched teeth.)

Feeling extremely pleased with himself and confident that he had unsettled the bowler, Elvis Coombes now reckoned himself ready to have a go. A trifle miffed, Charlie Colson tried again. His feelings got the better of him. It was not a good ball. He tried for extra pace. It was short and going down the leg side. With almost indecent delight Elvis Coombes launched himself at it. Hit properly it would have gone many a mile. But this was Elvis Coombes, not an all-rounder, nor a batsman. He struck it, but high on the bat. It steepled upwards. Phil Cole had plenty of time to choose between bowler and wicket-keeper to make the catch. He made the traditional selection and Kevin Newton took his second catch of the afternoon. For him it was almost a record. For Elvis Coombes, par for the course. For Charlie Colson, the improbable figures of 4–11. Tea was taken. When they resumed the Outcasts would need 196 to win.

TEA INTERVAL

The mood inside what had now become the tea marquee was not universally cheerful. To be sure, the food was wholesome if simple and straightforward. Mrs Enzyme and her team were good manufacturers of the basic sandwich. Plate upon plate was attacked with gusto by members of the Willingfold side who had had a head start on the visitors. It was the juxtaposition of the tea urn with the barrels of real ale which disturbed Phil Cole. Too much beer too early was unlikely to have a flattering effect on the Outcasts' batting. He was not sure of his persuasive powers in urging restraint. Colin Banks was already well sunk into a pint which Phil knew was not the first of the afternoon. Charlie Colson was embarked on celebration of his four-wicket haul with seemingly no thought about what might further be required of him. Other team members appeared ready to join him. Thankfully Jon Palmer and Alan Birch seemed happy to settle for tea. Phil Cole, who was dying for a beer himself, decided on a 'two pints and a sarnie' strategy whilst trying to convince his friends that there was more to this match than met the eye. The Outcasts, he pressed, should not allow themselves to be rolled over by Willingfold.

Uncle George's legendary cheerfulness had drained away from him. He was cross with the MCC. He was cross with the umpires who had allowed such a poor decision in the case of Bill Forbes. He was cross to find that the Willingfold innings had subsided almost seven overs short of the full forty-five over allocation. His irritation grew as fellow members of the organising committee trooped up with messages about things going wrong with events next door. Uncle George would have settled for something going wrong with the bouncy castle if it removed the ghastly apparition from his sight, but it was still there, as lurid as ever. Somewhat impatiently he agreed to pay another visit to the Pegley field. He noted with pleasure that he had chosen a moment when the band had seemingly taken a breather.

Last to arrive in the marquee were Trevor Edgefield and Elvis Coombes. They were in lively disputation and it was not being conducted in gentlemanly tones. How much lower mutual recrimination might have sunk was not to be known for the sour exchanges were interrupted by the ringing of a mobile phone. Such a sound was not altogether commonplace in Willingfold, because the village was one of the few remaining places where signals from the various networks were problematic. In the view of some people Willingfold was an oasis of tranquillity. The phone belonged to Elvis Coombes and he seemed no better pleased with the conversation on which he was now embarked than with his quarrelling with Trevor Edgefield. Protesting that what he really wanted was his tea, he eventually succumbed to his father's instruction to 'get round the Towers with a couple of industrial driers double-quick'.

The police were at last beginning to exercise an ameliorating influence on the situation outside the village. However, they were a long way short of having it under control. Even then what had been achieved owed nothing to any strategic plan from on high and everything to some thoroughly pragmatic decisions taken on the ground. A motorcycle officer had squeezed his way through to Muckersby Bridge and unilaterally uprooted the traffic control system imposed by the highways authority. The flow of vehicles into the village gathered pace. To the east a diversion was set up which at least took out of the equation vehicles not planning to come to the village. That still left a great many bent on salvaging something from a supposedly great day out in Willingfold as advertised on radio and television. Meanwhile at police headquarters a thoroughly harassed commanding officer pored uncomprehendingly over maps and wondered whether he should call in the Deputy Chief Constable.

Inside Willingfold the great day out was taking on nightmarish characteristics. Crucial to the success of an 'It's a Knockout' contest is the controlling influence of the compère. The only person whom Willingfold had been able to obtain – the only person they had been able to afford – was a minor television personality. On the day it was discovered that his personality in the flesh was rather less than his television persona; for that matter his flesh was rather greater than the camera betrayed. A low-key 'It's a Knockout' in an obscure rural village on a quiet day might have been within his compass. Not all these conditions applied in Willingfold on the first Saturday in June. The participating teams were proving hard to organise and a growing and largely unsighted crowd was becoming restless. The minor television personality had to contend with two further snags. His familiarity with 'It's a Knockout' was limited and his brand of repartee did not travel well outside the studio. A semblance of order was maintained only because of the sheer comic helplessness of the contestants, to which the Outcasts' team contributed not the least share. In the end, spectators contented themselves alternately with jeering at the compère and giving excessively loud cheers to the games players.

Not all the people who had paid money to be present on Farmer Pegley's field were content. As Uncle George could see, the latest arrivals, in particular, were faced with a fast-diminishing range of treats. The ring of people standing round the 'It's a Knockout' arena was virtually impenetrable. All edible items ranging from ice-cream to burgers had gone. The cake stall had been cleared. The tombola was exhausted. Even Tommy Burnhough had managed to sell some of the heftier of his grotesque carvings, but only because by standing on them people had got a better view of the games. A teddy bear stall was reduced to one tiny yellow bear. The charmer's snake had unaccountably died. Most of the competitive side-shows had run out of prizes. Guessing the name of a singularly repulsive-looking doll or the weight of a fruit cake was not a compelling pastime. In any case, so many guesses had been made by now that the exercise was becoming unmanageable. Least of the worries was that the band had gone on strike, demanding more money for playing to such a large audience. It was a threat which Uncle George was happy to face down – however long it took.

The beautiful baby contest had finished a few minutes earlier in acrimony. The wife of the Chairman of the Parish Council had graciously agreed to act as judge. Now, ungraciously, she wished she had not. The competition's organiser had failed to define the upper age limit for entrants. This had given rise to some very disagreeable exchanges before finally an undeniably cherubic ten-month old was excluded. Then there was protest from latecomers held up by the traffic when their offspring were timed out. The mood of the wife of the Chairman of the Parish Council had not improved when she had cradled to her bosom the utterly delightful Caroline Dunk. The baby girl had gurgled, laughed and then puked down the front of the judge's white blouse. The resulting vivid stain suggested that the parents had given young Caroline something totally inappropriate for lunch. There was more unpleasantness when the wife of the Chairman of the Parish Council selected her winner. She had chosen, she said, without hesitation the most beautiful baby girl she had seen in many a year, someone who was bound to turn young men's heads in the future. Too late she discovered her mistake. Little Hilary Chambers was a boy. Immediately the parents of Caroline Dunk had alleged bias and warring groups sprang up. The situation had taken a while to cool. Informed of this sorry fiasco, Uncle George thanked God that they had not proceeded with the dog show.

The fortune teller was still in business, but this was a mixed blessing. Madam Arcadia, who in the non-astrological sphere was Mrs Florence Dinge, had been late in arriving having been unable to predict the traffic jams surrounding Willingfold that afternoon. Those who had booked Madam Arcadia could not have known of the traumatic upheavals which had beset Florence Dinge in recent months. A woman who had previously radiated joie-de-vivre had become glum and care-worn. Her balanced view of life was lost. She now dispensed an undiluted stream of gloom and pessimism. Adults and children were emerging from her booth at best thoughtful and at worst in tears. They were equally bereft of enjoyment for the remainder of the afternoon. The lucky ones were those who were spared the warning of an early death in the family.

This had not been a privilege shared by Lawrence Phypps. He had been dealt the actuality of death, but had reconciled himself to it with equanimity. In appearance with opportunism. In actuality with relief bordering on pleasure. His relationship with his father had never been easy. It was not so much his debauchery, for in that he was merely emulating his father's early years as the latter only too well recognised. It was more his failure to settle into a worthwhile professional career and earn money which had annoyed his father whose own considerable wealth had been acquired by that route. Mortimer Dalrymple Phypps had no intention of excusing his only son from earning money by supporting him with his own. However, a worthwhile professional career had been denied to Lawrence Phypps for two reasons: lack of qualifications and lack of temperament. Strongly possessing the desire to have money, he looked for easier and more informal routes to obtaining it. Residence in his father's house – one concession the senior Phypps had made with an eye, as ever, on his own interest – had given Lawrence a cloak of respectability through which his seamier projects had not penetrated. When in the village, he had mixed well and was seen as a good neighbour. His legendary hospitality was founded (mainly) on his father's money.

Lawrence Phypps suddenly felt liberated. Such filial devotion as he had ever possessed had grown weaker as his father had grown older, increasingly incapacitated and more eccentric. The prospect of dodgy deals as a way of sustaining a tolerable lifestyle began to fade as he began to contemplate the wealth which would surely be his. He had not progressed far in his planning for a finer future when he was dramatically revisited by the present. The hearse had moved over the hump of Muckersby Bridge. Lawrence Phypps was about to restart the engine to do likewise. The van door was pulled unceremoniously open and a voice said 'Out.' This customary courtesy announced the arrival of HM Customs and Excise.

Much as the famous slope at Lord's is not immediately apparent to the untutored eye, so Ray Burrill had failed to notice the gentle incline towards the Haverscombes' garage at the Towers. He would have sworn that the grounds around the house were level. As he viewed the wreckage he now knew better. Geometrically there would not have been much more than a degree or two in it, but at the moment of impact Coombes' van had developed appreciable momentum. In fairness to Coombes, the soundness of the garage's construction may have suffered over the years or may have had some intrinsic defect (it had been built by Coombes himself); in fairness to the Haverscombes, Coombes would have been wise to have applied his handbrake. It was uncertain what had finally propelled the van on its journey, but there was no uncertainty as to the outcome. The garage was largely demolished, the van largely unscathed. The bull-bar had been an embellishment organised by Elvis Coombes.

Sweating and cursing, the younger Coombes arrived at the Towers with the industrial driers ordered by his father. There was no second van or truck within the Coombes business empire and Elvis had had to heave them to the Towers on foot. He was in time to see the family van being reversed back to its original position. His instinctive question – 'How've you managed that, then?' – was not well received. He was peremptorily told to get 'those bloody driers' into the house. The normally well-ordered defecatory behaviour of Boycs, the Yorkshire terrier, had been upset by the tumult of the afternoon. This was of no concern to Elvis Coombes, but there were calamitous consequences as he tramped through to the Haverscombes' lounge. He was then collared by his father for another job up in the loft. Protesting loudly that he was needed to open the bowling for Willingfold, he ascended the ladder into the rodent-scented roof space. Ray Burrill meanwhile was forced to abandon thoughts of cricket and concentrate instead on the availability of carpet shampoo.

The white van was empty. There could be no doubt about it. If you could discount a hold-all containing a pair of well-worn faded blue jeans, a grimy sweatshirt, dirty socks and some extremely personal toiletries, there was nothing, absolutely nothing, in the cargo area of the vehicle. The particular contraband in the mind's eye of the customs officers was simply not to be found. Reluctantly these officials of the crown concluded that the chassis and other remote corners of the van could not conceal more than the odd bottle of spirits or packet of cigarettes. Resignedly but dissatisfied they backed off. There were muttered remarks which might have been interpreted as half-apologetic. As it appeared that traffic was now moving again, if only in one direction, the customs officers returned to their vehicle and for want of a better option, trailed Lawrence Phypps into Willingfold. The hearse had been ignored.

The blow-torch and Elvis Coombes were two elements in the cosmos not designed to be brought in close contact. This universal law was broken by Frank Pirgrove who mistook Elvis Coombes for a competent assistant. The resulting fire was quickly brought under control, but not before the plumber's temporary apprentice in startled retreat had put his boot through the ceiling of the room below. In his struggle to free himself, Elvis disturbed a large area of plaster. This had the effect of putting the fire damage to the roof timbers in almost favourable perspective. 'No more than heavy scorching,' pronounced his father, after telling a bemused Ray Burrill that the smoke from the loft, not to mention the dust from the bedroom, had made him thirsty and that a cup of tea would come in handy.

If Ray Burrill thought he was presiding over a deteriorating situation at the Towers, Phil Cole in the cricket marquee had much the same impression. Up to a point, his strictures had worked. The first seven in the batting order had kept within the two-pint limit, give or take a pint. Charlie Colson, expecting to bat eight, if at all, had moved ahead of them with Kevin Newton, celebrating two catches and niggardly wicket-keeping, in close pursuit. Tom Redman had had only his tea and a pang of conscientiousness over Ray Burrill which had led to his departure for the Towers. Colin Banks had drunk at least two pints before the tea interval started and so he had made a show of sticking to only two pints during the tea interval. The other restraining factor was hanging on his arm.

Had the match restarted then, Phil Cole would have felt reasonably satisfied. It was the jingle of bells which directed his gaze towards the outside. The Morris dancers had assembled on the cricket ground unnoticed by those in the marquee whose minds had been on other pleasures. There was something formidable about their ensemble. Like the Coldstream Guards at Hougoumont in 1815 they gave the impression of not being easily dislodged. Their routine proceeded with a determination about it which defied challenge. In any case there were more of them than there were cricketers. They had also drawn support from the attenuated activities next door. Phil Cole cursed. He interrupted Uncle George, but his host denied foreknowledge of this latest attraction and racked his brain to think of which of his colleagues on the organising committee had been damn fool enough to slip this one past them. Uncle George was in fact doing them an injustice. This particular band of Morris dancers would insinuate themselves like cleavers in a flower bed if ever they got word of a village fete. Words aplenty they had heard from Darcey De'Arth early that morning. Faced with a delay of uncertain length, the Outcasts felt released from obligation and turned back to pay further attention to the six barrels of excellent ale.

The expression on Grouse's face underwent rapid change. There was relief as he saw the hearse approach the front door, dismay as it swept past and disappeared round the corner of the building, puzzlement on sight of the white van, apprehension as he saw who was at the wheel as it too went in the direction taken by the hearse and finally annoyance when, moments later, a dark saloon arrived at high speed, scattering gravel in all directions. Grouse looked disapprovingly at the two men who emerged, noting their shiny suits. He had seen their type on many previous occasions. Double-glazing salesmen – he was sure of it. He was slow to convert from this view even after verbal explanation and waving of badges. Whether Customs and Excise officers or double-glazing salesmen, they were equally unwanted.

Finally putting aside aggressive bluster, Grouse adopted a 'This is a house of death, this is a family in mourning' tactic. The melodramatic wringing of hands and rolling of eyes were in danger of being overdone, but the performance was saved by the entry stage right of the brothers Doom carrying what was undeniably a coffin and inquiring as to the exact whereabouts of the deceased. They were followed by Lawrence Phypps looking suitably grief-stricken. The final coup de théâtre was provided by Grouse, who literally threw himself at the feet of his employer in a display of weeping and wailing which had more to do with Grouse's desire to absolve himself from any possible responsibility for what had happened than to exhibit genuine, heart-felt grief.

Tom Redman returned to a Willingfold Towers very different from that which he had left in the morning. He arrived in time to witness an untoward scene which hinted at deeper trouble. A figure in white emerged from an upper window. Missing his footing on the ladder, Elvis Coombes tried to save himself by grabbing first at a cable fastened to the wall and then the neighbouring drainpipe. The results were spectacular. The cable slowed his fall before the television aerial ensemble to which it was attached came crashing earthwards. By clutching the drainpipe Elvis Coombes avoided a collision with the aerial, but he had not slid far down before it broke away bringing an extensive section of guttering with it. His final drop to the ground was no worse than to leave him winded and the bed of peonies, his resting-place, badly crushed. As Ray Burrill remarked to Tom Redman, the damage would have been less if the whole of Elvis Coombes and not just his boot had descended through the bedroom ceiling. What the boy needed, said his father, was a strong cup of tea. Ray Burrill's prescription would have been different, but he led Tom Redman towards the kitchen to tell him the whole story.

Grouse had his strengths, but also his weaknesses. His bravura performance mixing sorrow with menace was enough to see off the men from Customs and Excise, who in any case had had their previous certainty punctured by the empty van. To Grouse's surprise he received the cheerful thanks of his employer and no recriminations over what had happened in his absence. The Doom brothers went about their business. It did not occur to Grouse to wonder why the hearse had not been parked adjacent to the front door. Nor did he find anything amiss in the length of time which passed between the undertakers returning to the hearse and their driving away with a cheerful wave from the bereaved. Grouse had so typecast Lawrence Phypps as a dissolute living off his father's money that he had failed to understand that there might be other defects in his character. Grouse could see no further than that his job appeared to be safe. He would drink to that – later.

The exhibition of parachute jumping had been timed to follow the ending of 'It's a Knockout'. The games had come to a somewhat heated end. The climactic contest had involved contestants being ducked in large tubs of water whilst rescuing objects contained therein. The exercise was well under way before it was appreciated that someone had decided to enliven proceedings by introducing a quantity of red dye into the tubs. The crowd was more amused by this than by discovering whether completion of the game would have allowed the Wizards of Willingfold to overtake the points total accruing to the Marpledon Marvels. The joker had been well and truly played. The situation was beyond the scope of the minor television personality, who tried to make light of it. His feeble jokes finally enraged two red-faced contestants, who seized him and immersed him in the nearest convenient tub. This further piece of jollity appeased spectators even if the contestants were left rowing with each other in the middle. Before the situation got out of hand the sound of an aeroplane caused heads to turn aloft. The contestants, whether unscathed or dyed, scattered.

At the Towers Ray Burrill put down the teapot and picked up the telephone. It was Mark Haverscombe. His mother had had one of her little turns and so his parents would not be able to travel back to Willingfold until at least the following morning. Mark Haverscombe was full of apologies and Ray Burrill was full of reassurances. Ray offered a silent prayer and thought how much bigger Mrs Haverscombe's turn might be if she could see her house now. But he said nothing to her son apart from giving best wishes and taking a telephone number. Elvis Coombes and Tom Redman had gone back to the cricket ground. Ray was left in the company of the elder Coombes, Frank Pirgrove and John Wisden.

SECOND INNINGS

Ben Harding took the safe option and opened the bowling with John Tod. Ben's card had been marked by Uncle George. However, foreknowledge did not extend to the Outcasts' capabilities with the bat. It had not been difficult to estimate their capabilities with a barrel of beer. The Willingfold captain's inner feeling suggested a formula of steady and straight. Those were the words of wisdom he conveyed to John Tod. From the way the over began, it seemed that the bowler's limbs were having difficulty in processing the message from his brain. The first ball was wide down the leg-side and Colonel Crickhill correctly so called it. The next ball was wide of off stump. The batsman let it go and so did the umpire. John Tod swung his arms furiously to loosen his limbs. There was no immediate effect. His third ball favoured the leg-side by such a margin that it eluded both the wicket-keeper and the fine-leg fielder. Colonel Crickhill was more alert to leg-side wides and duly signalled the boundary. John Tod tried again. Once more Jon Palmer did not have to touch the ball as it passed a foot outside his off stump. The bowler puffed his way back to his mark, beginning to wish that he had not succumbed to a second slice of Mrs Enzyme's coffee cake.

By contrast his captain was beginning to wonder whether they might not all have been better off had they still been in the marquee sampling Mrs Enzyme's coffee cake or other delights. The resumption of the match had been entirely fortuitous. The men who had jumped out of the aircraft over Willingfold on that first

Saturday in June might not have shared the prowess of front-line troops of the Parachute Regiment. In terms of dislodging the enemy they proved equally proficient. Or one of them was. That was all it took – that and a slight failure in technique. A parachutist had drifted away from the formation and found himself descending not towards Farmer Pegley's field, but the cricket ground adjacent to it – an occupied cricket ground. Not for long. Aware of a stirring in the crowd, one of the Morris dancers looked skywards. One glance was sufficient for a panic-stricken warning cry. With not much more than a final jingle and a final jangle the dancers fled. Uncle George and Ben Harding had seized the moment. Willingfold's men had taken to the field with such alacrity that they were ahead of the umpires. It was unclear whether the crowd's applause was for the safe landing of the parachutist or for the military precision with which the pitch had been repossessed.

The applause had given way to mirth as John Tod struggled to master his sense of direction. With his fifth delivery he achieved it. However, the full toss was struck magnificently through the off-side for four. This unnerved John Tod and he produced another wide for Colonel Crickhill to certify. To his credit the bowler bounced back with a pacy delivery which Jon Palmer was not expecting. He jammed his bat down on it just in time and it leaked out backward of point for a scrambled single. Stewart Thorogood, who had drunk one pint more than was strictly advisable, could have done without a scramble before facing the bowling for the first time. He was lucky. John Tod slid off target again and Stewart was able to watch two successive balls pass harmlessly outside his off stump and through to the wicket-keeper. The Outcasts had somehow acquired in the first over five percent of the total they needed.

This dreadful first over confirmed Ben Harding in a decision he had already taken. He would not use Elvis Coombes as the other opening bowler. If John Tod was meant to be the more reliable of the two locals, he hated to think what the large, shambling young man would be like. Uncle George's warning was already imprinted on his mind: stupid, temperamental and erratic, but quick. This could be a forecast for something dire, in view of Uncle George's assurance that John Tod was a plod in every sense, but reliable. He had to lead from the front, Ben Harding told himself. So he began to mark out his run from the farm end.

His captain's analysis of what was best was not immediately shared by Elvis Coombes. He saw himself as someone who blasted out batsmen, and fast bowlers who blasted out batsmen traditionally did so at the start of an innings. That was his simple belief. It had been fortified by hours spent watching tapes of the great fast bowlers of yesteryear. Elvis Coombes particularly enjoyed the bodyline series and regretted that the quality of recording at that time did not allow the full drama of events to be captured in the way which was possible with today's cameras. There was not much of the spirit of festival cricket flowing through the veins of Elvis Coombes. He had begun to strip off his sweater before realising that the captain had other plans. He was about to protest, but Ben Harding pacified him with the reminder that Allan Donald usually bowled first-change in limited-overs matches. The reason for the South African's preference had no relevance whatsoever to what was taking place in Willingfold, but Elvis Coombes allowed flattery to fool him. In strict truth he was relieved not to be bowling straightaway; his escapade at the Towers had left him, he realised, with a sore back.

Ben Harding was a useful cricketer – well above par for this level of the game. Bowling off ten paces, he gave an appearance of athletic ease. His speed was brisk and he used the seam well. Fortunately for the Outcasts, Jon Palmer was a protagonist of roughly equal ability. Less fortunately, the equally able Stewart Thorogood was on this outing just rough. The over restored respectability for Willingfold, but the batsmen survived, the one with elegance and the other with pure luck. Ben Harding found his line and length from the start. Jon Palmer was never in danger, but had to exercise maximum care until he eased one wide of second slip for a brisk single – a little too brisk for Stewart Thorogood's liking. As he took guard to receive the final ball of the Harding over, he had to rub his eyes to clear his vision. He settled, but the ball which came towards him was a blur. He at least judged its line right and was comforted by the sound of bat on ball. An exclamation from the crowd told him that all might not be well. He turned to see the blur resting at the base of the stumps. His lunge had only stunned the ball and it had rolled back on to the stumps. Through watery eyes Stewart Thorogood saw that the bails were still in place. The Outcasts were 12–0.

This score was accurately displayed on the simple scoreboard where Sophie Crossley continued to be in charge. By now her team of helpers had been restored and augmented. Robert and David Skynn had collected a couple of their friends who had been attracted more by the possibilities of mayhem with the metal bashing than by proper regard for the solemnities of cricket. Strict supervision was necessary, but Sophie found this could be maintained from a sedentary position. It was infinitely more comfortable than jumping up and down herself. By teatime she had been thankful to sit quietly with Simon to calm the discomfort she was feeling. Simon had collected two cups of tea and some coffee cake from the marquee, but otherwise they had kept well away from the hubbub it contained. If Sophie had been relieved by the start of the tea interval, her husband had been relieved when the match had eventually restarted. Simon, after meeting Sophie, had – nervously – undergone a fashion make-over. Sophie was working upwards. During the break in play she had returned to the subject of ear-piercing to which Simon had reacted with great alarm. It was not that he was altogether opposed to the idea, but he feared he would find himself the butt of a great deal of Outcast scorn. Yet Sophie could be very persuasive. He gladly buried himself in his scorebook.

It was perhaps as well that Simon Crossley recorded a wealth of detail when he scored, because this kept him busy even when the tempo of play slowed. For it was slow now. There was nothing to vie with the rash of runs which came in the first over. On the one hand, coaxed by his captain and, on the other, anxious not to diminish himself in the eyes of those for whom he had constabulary responsibility (there had already been a call of 'Come on, Plod' from somewhere in the crowd), John Tod pulled himself together and bowled a respectable over to Jon Palmer from which no more than a single came. With huge concentration Stewart Thorogood blocked the last ball. The next over from Ben Harding was a repeat of the pattern. John Tod's third over cost only two and then Stewart Thorogood was exposed to the start of an over by Ben Harding. Like John Tod before him, Stewart Thorogood needed to perform an act of supreme concentration. His did not have to last an entire over. The name of the game was to remove himself as quickly as possible from the firing-line and keep himself away from it until he could get his head straight. To a rather full-looking delivery from Ben Harding, Stewart Thorogood's answer was a dab past point for a single. That at least was the theoretical response. In fact with his bat coming down at the wrong angle, he got an inside edge. The ball passed by the off stump with not much more than an inch to spare in a direction which was as unexpected to the wicket-keeper as it was to the batsman. To Stewart Thorogood's relief, there was still a single in it. He was equally relieved when a leg-bye was taken off the last ball.

A sense of relief was beginning to settle over Ray Burrill as well. This may have owed something to the soothing effect of reading Wisden, but half-an-hour had passed without any fresh calamities. The house's cold-water system – the begetter of all the difficulties – had been put back in working order. Frank Pirgrove ordered a triumphal brew before leaving. Over yet another cup of tea, Coombes had made light of overcoming the other problems. Knowledge of the delayed return of the Haverscombes helped to lull Ray Burrill into false optimism. The dampened rooms were drying out. Coombes was trying to salvage the guttering and downpipe. He had promised that the shed would be rebuilt better than new and that the bedroom ceiling was 'no problem'. The TV aerial replacement would require specialist attention in the following week. And then there was the car. Ray Burrill stirred himself. Perhaps there was something he could do to improve the balance sheet. He put down Wisden having just marvelled that as many as seven players had achieved the double of a thousand runs and a hundred wickets in first-class cricket in the domestic season it recorded. Ray Burrill thought that the lawn could do with a cut. He went in search of the Haverscombes' mower.

Four more relatively unproductive overs had passed. There might not have been many runs, but the opening partnership was unbroken. Phil Cole felt pleased with the situation. However, his pleasure was not shared amongst what by now had become a very substantial crowd. Lured into a village from which early escape looked difficult and having depleted the festival on Farmer Pegley's field, many visitors had resorted to the next-door entertainment. The only other commodity to keep pace with demand had been the beer and that only because of a mistake on the part of the supplier. A new clerk in the sales department had misheard the Dirty Rivers' landlord and sent forty kegs rather than fourteen. It was a fortuitous error. It meant that a large number of people could attain that happiest of combinations, watching cricket with a pint in hand. The throng ringing this village cricket ground would have cheered the hearts of county treasurers across England. Neither Willingfold nor the Outcasts had played in front of such numbers. Disappointed in other directions, this was not an uncritical crowd. It was soon apparent that there was little appreciation of stubborn play.

'Feeling better?' Jon Palmer put his arm round Stewart Thorogood's shoulder in congratulation. John Tod was tiring. He failed to maintain his length and the resulting short ball was crashed to the cover boundary by Stewart Thorogood as though waking from a dream. The boundary was timely not only to revive the scoring rate, but also to neutralise the restiveness in the crowd. A reproving glance from Ben Harding helped John Tod to rediscover his length for the next ball. Frustratingly for him it was carved over the slips for another four. This false shot won a good reaction from spectators whose natural propensity was towards the broader arts of 'It's a Knockout'. They even seemed to enjoy the two enormous but profitless heaves across the line which were part of Stewart Thorogood's repertoire during the remainder of the over.

Ben Harding did not at first pick up any significant change in the situation. Two boundaries in the over he attributed to his having kept John Tod going for one over too many. He deliberated as to who should follow him at the pavilion end. Having himself conceded only three runs off five overs, Ben Harding's only question was whether he should bowl himself out or keep back two or three overs for the end of the innings. He saw no reason to make a double change. Six balls and twenty-one runs later he did.

A police car containing two officers of the traffic division of the local force had eventually crawled into Willingfold. For the first time an on-the-spot appreciation could be conducted. An early decision followed. The officers radioed through to colleagues to stop any further traffic coming into the village from either direction. Amazingly, there were still some people who thought that there might be something to salvage from their outing. They did not take kindly to being told that they must stay on the main roads and keep moving, especially as much by way of motion was hard to achieve.

At this point in the afternoon, visitors to Willingfold could roughly be assigned to three groups: those remaining on Farmer Pegley's field, those on the cricket ground and others who had wandered into the village to see if it had any alternative claims to fame. In the first group various categories could be identified. The appetite of children for bouncing on the vulgar bouncy castle was undiminished and their parents stood around maintaining a watchful eye. There was still a queue at Madam Arcadia's tent where misery continued to be dispensed. There were the drinkers – no misery amongst them. And then there were the inevitable mischief-makers.

Deprived of entertainment by the early end of the 'It's a Knockout' games, a bunch of young men was looking for something in the same vein to keep them amused. One, who was an engineer by trade, found that the portable loos could, without too much difficulty, be detached from their anchorage. Shielded by his friends he managed unobserved to free two of the cabins. He reckoned that it would not take much by way of internal momentum for them to begin their journey down the gentle slope towards the Myre, which was flowing well. Bets were placed on which would enter the stream first.

The winner was the portaloo containing the minor television personality. But it was a close run thing. His cabin had a full eight seconds' advantage before its neighbour began to move. Perhaps it took some moments for the minor television personality to understand what was happening or perhaps his lack of reaction was due to fright, but it was not until the final acceleration began that he was seen to be trying to open the door. The agitation of the person in the other cabin caused it to move much more quickly once it had started, but it was still second into the water. The distance was judged to be a foot. No photo was required. As it happened, one was taken by a commendably vigilant young photographer, who worked for the County Bugle. There were repercussions in the village. The wife of the Chairman of the Parish Council, who had been attempting running repairs to her blouse, did not take kindly to being seen in a state of undress, up to her knees in water and on the front page of the local weekly. She (mistakenly) supposed that this was a revenge attack by parents of babies she had judged less bonny, but was unwise to make her accusation public. The effect on her husband's career in local government was not favourable. What was not so well reported was the fact that neither of the cabins, having been built to the most exacting European Union standard, had disintegrated on impact. This was a point which the manufacturers were later to stress by way of added assurance to future clients.

The roar which greeted the culmination of the superloo race was soon matched by the cricket watchers as Jon Palmer began to address himself more forcibly to the bowling of Ben Harding. It would not have been right to say that Jon Palmer used the long handle. Jon's batting was classier than that. What he did use was his feet. He nimbly danced down the wicket and lofted Ben Harding's first ball back over his head one bounce for four. Ben Harding did not expect a repeat dose, making no change to his length or his field. The second was a huge hit for six. This time the bowler adjusted his field and put a man out deep. It was not enough. Jon Palmer took the risk, but kept the ball on the ground. It was too well-timed and too well-placed to be intercepted. Ben Harding pitched his next delivery short of a length only to see Jon Palmer rock back and punch it backward of point. It took a fine piece of fielding by Edward Townsend to prevent the boundary. He ended up full-length having slid ten feet or more in a spectacular rescue. His discomfiture was well appreciated by the crowd. The bowler's discomfiture continued when Stewart Thorogood top-edged another boundary to bring up the fifty partnership. More cheers. The last ball skidded into Stewart's pads, but Umpire Breakwell did not see it the same way as the bowler ('Going over the top, I fancy').

Having come from an impeccable educational background, Ben Harding prevented himself doing the same thing. Nevertheless, he wished the crowd had not cheered the decision.

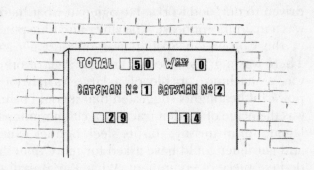

To the visible disappointment of Elvis Coombes, dismissing any lingering ache in his back, the person chosen to succeed John Tod at the pavilion end was Henry Pickard, who bowled thoughtful off-spin. Elvis, whose standard fare was unthinking, wild pace, could not see the point. 'You give me a go,' he advised Ben Harding pointing at Jon Palmer, 'and I'll knock 'is block off.' Ben Harding inwardly groaned. He had to calculate at which point in the innings he could unleash the local thunderbolt with least risk to the outcome. For the moment he was content to enhance what he felt might be a safer option. To his relief and the crowd's displeasure, Henry Pickard delivered a testing over which cost nothing but a leg-bye.

With this restoration of calm, Ben Harding was almost tempted into continuing at the opposite end, but then, on seeing Jon Palmer on strike, he again looked for the safer option. This time it took the form of Brian Leyton-Brown. Anxious to do more with the ball than had been possible with the bat, he immediately found a good line bowling seam up and just short of a length. At the other end Henry Pickard remained tidy. A quiet passage of play followed. Many in the crowd judged this to be the right moment to recharge glasses. There was movement towards the main beer tent. Uncle George had protected the marquee enclosure with notices stating 'members only' – a proposition of dubious validity in the light of the semi-defunct nature of Willingfold Cricket Club ahead of this match.

It was no ordinary lawnmower. It lived in its own little hut. Locating it, finding the key to the hut and then identifying the key to the machine itself might have put off a lesser man, but Ray Burrill was driven to do good works. He ogled at what he finally discovered. It was a magnificent beast. The silver and blue put Ray Burrill in mind of the Coronation Scot. It was not just a rotary ride-on mower. There was a grass-collector and a range of other accessories. This was a machine capable of a large variety of garden duties. Its powerful headlights suggested that it could be used day or night. It was the acme of garden tractors, a claim reinforced by the stencilled legend 'gran turismo' on its sleek bonnet. No proud lawn-keeper and gardener could have asked for more than this top-of-the-range de-luxe piece of equipment. What Ray Burrill did not know as he wheeled it into the open was that it had a fault.

Ben Harding felt fidgety. It was all very well. His change of bowling had kept the scoring fairly well in check. At the twenty-over mark the Outcasts had scored sixty-eight, much less, he reckoned, than Willingfold at that stage (they had got ninety-eight, but had lost four wickets). There were twenty-five overs left and one hundred and twenty-eight runs needed at a rate of around five an over. The Outcasts had ten wickets left. Their openers were looking secure. Four bowlers had been tried. Ben Harding could see the match slipping away from him. Perhaps he had no real alternative but to try what he increasingly regarded as the nuclear option. He thanked Henry Pickard for a steady start and waved at Elvis Coombes.

The ideal of Elvis Coombes was leg theory (he had been heavily influenced by those old newsreels). He liked to see batsmen ducking or being felled. However, he had never been able to find a captain willing to accommodate his tastes. The result was inevitably a compromise. In this case Ben Harding conceded two backward short legs and a short square leg, but insisted on a slip, third man and fine leg. The first two were an insurance against faulty radar. Trevor Edgefield told him that he was being a bloody fool before trudging off towards deep mid-wicket. Elvis Coombes paced out an extravagantly long run. Glasses recharged, the crowd was back in full numbers and expectant.

The first ball was a long way from conforming to the prescription which Ben Harding had enjoined on his bowler. It was neither short of a length nor particularly quick. It was wide, very wide of leg stump and was duly called a wide. Trevor Edgefield smirked. Ben Harding frowned. At least one of the backward short legs was given something to do in capturing the erring ball before it cost any more runs. The next delivery was faster, but veering towards the leg side. Jon Palmer let it go and was disappointed that Colonel Crickhill did not brand it a wide. Elvis Coombes's second legitimate ball held a better line, but was much too short. Jon Palmer, pivoting, hooked it crisply into the crowd, who cheered. Trevor Edgefield continued to smirk. Ben Harding frowned again. The bowler scowled. The batsman felt a fifty coming on. These contrasting moods were soon to alter.

'A party, sir?' It was Grouse who asked the question. No-one enjoyed a party more than Grouse. Not only did it give him a copper-bottomed excuse to draw from the cellar, but under cover of general consumption, Grouse knew that he could secrete for himself one of the vintage bottles. Even so this did not strike Grouse as being the most appropriate day for a party. A wake possibly, but that customarily followed the funeral. It was unusual to mark the removal of the body in this way. However, Lawrence Phypps was insistent. There were house guests, weren't there? Grouse nodded. There was the rest of the visiting team, wasn't there? Grouse agreed. And a few chosen friends from the village? Grouse supposed so. Lawrence Phypps could not contain his enthusiasm born of what he saw as his deliverance. He explained that there had been a 'recent' delivery of a 'very reasonable' champagne. Grouse knew nothing of this, but allowed himself to be persuaded. The only edible accompaniment would be nuts and crisps. Invitation would be by word of mouth, Lawrence Phypps's own. He set off for the cricket ground.

Lawrence Phypps did not arrive in time to witness Elvis Coombes's moment of glory. Another wild ball with which Jon Palmer failed to connect was followed by one of sublime perfection with which he also failed to connect. Elvis Coombes could not credibly claim that it had been by design, because those on the field who knew him were only too well aware that full-length balls pitched roughly in line were not the most regular feature of his repertoire. When additionally they were swinging yorkers, it was an occurrence in common with the moon passing in front of the sun. Even Jon Palmer, less well acquainted with the bowler's history, was unprepared for the exocet which removed his leg stump. The surprise was universal.

Normality was swift to return. Dean Faulds was greeted with one which went over his head by a comfortable margin. The next was punched back over the bowler's head by a similar margin and earned four. After such an over the bowling of Brian Leyton-Brown at the other end seemed small beer to a crowd which had had its entertainment threshold raised. Another over of distinctly medium pace achieved nothing of note. Each batsman took a single and Ben Harding was prepared to settle for that whilst he wondered what surprises Elvis Coombes might have in store for him during the next over. He wondered whether to have a word, but decided to let one more over pass. He was partly reinforced in this decision by hearing Trevor Edgefield mutter to another fielder, 'He's a bloody lunatic.' Ben Harding hoped he meant the bowler, but was not entirely sure.

Petrol and oil dutifully checked, Ray Burrill was aboard the garden express. It had started instantly and within a few seconds the engine had settled to a steady purr. Ray felt that he needed to get to know its handling characteristics and so he released the clutch and took the vehicle on a wide arc to the further end of the Towers' lawn. He engaged the cutting arm and returned diagonally across the grass with increasing confidence and increasing speed. Approaching his original point of embarkation and turning to examine the effect, it was hard to say which was killed faster, Ray's confidence or the machine's engine. What he saw was more nearly ploughing than mowing. The lawn was torn up from one end to the other in consequence of a fault in the blade mechanism. The tractor had been awaiting repair. Ray Burrill felt that he too was in need of repair as he surveyed his unwitting handiwork. At that moment the burglar alarm sounded.

Elvis Coombes's second over had its defenders and its detractors. The atavistic element amongst the spectators were perhaps disappointed when no flesh was bruised nor blood drawn especially when it seemed that such possibilities were at the front of the bowler's mind. On the other hand, amusement was derived from the gymnastics and gyrations of Dean Faulds in thwarting injury from those of the short-pitched balls which actually came near him. This also helped to explain why the over was inexpensive although Colonel Crickhill's inability to spot likely wides and no-balls was another contributory factor. From the captain's point-of-view a maiden over was something for which he could readily settle.

Stewart Thorogood had watched Elvis Coombes rampage unchecked through his over with some dismay. He admired his partner's ability to keep out of trouble and wondered whether he himself would be so agile. Suddenly his appetite grew to sample more of the bowling of Brian Leyton-Brown. As the field changed over, he murmured words of sympathy to Dean Faulds. He found him in a state of belligerence and in no way intimidated. 'Charity match, I'll give him charity match,' he was growling. To remove any ambiguity that he might be thinking of Uncle George or even Phil Cole, he added, 'He won't get away with another maiden. You wait. Just you let me take his next over.' These last were sentiments which Stewart Thorogood could easily share. He had already made up his mind on that point. He was not to be disappointed.

As the ball was thrown to him for another over, Brian Leyton-Brown thought he heard a groan from around the ground. This only stiffened his resolve. He was unaware that Stewart Thorogood's resolve was similarly stiffened. Whilst extremely content that his partner had a masochistic desire to take on Willingfold's wild bowler, Stewart Thorogood was at the same time a team man. At this stage the Outcasts were behind the asking rate. Runs were needed and it was by no means assured that any pyrotechnics manufactured by Dean Faulds would match those of Elvis Coombes. For his part therefore, Stewart Thorogood felt he had to get on with it. Brian Leyton-Brown was unprepared for the first ball of his new over to be sent skimming through the covers for four. It had been of good length, just outside off stump, and intended to contain the batsman. The next was a little quicker, maintaining the same line and length. It should not – at least in the bowler's estimation – have received the same treatment, but it did. For a moment the cheers of the crowd riled him and he bowled a short-tempered, short-pitched ball. With adrenaline flowing, Stewart Thorogood went on the back foot and cracked it square for a third consecutive boundary.

Brian Leyton-Brown counted to ten (twelve would have been more appropriate) as he returned to his bowling mark. He pulled himself together and sent down a delivery identical to the one with which he had started the over. The difference lay with the batsman. By this time Stewart Thorogood was up for it. Encouraged by the onlookers he drove to the covers again. With too much eagerness and too little footwork, he failed to keep the ball on the ground. Even so it was a good catch which forced his dismissal. Henry Pickard flung himself to his left and held on to the ball at ankle height. Not for long. He was soon flapping his stinging hands, but Umpire Breakwell, who had been completely unsighted, ruled that it was a valid catch. No-one thought to dispute the decision as attention almost instantly transferred to the nature of the strange sound emanating from somewhere in the village. 'It's probably the warning of imminent nuclear attack,' quipped Stewart Thorogood as he marched off. However audible and insistent, the siren was not allowed to disrupt the cricket nor the determined ranks of real-ale drinkers to which Stewart Thorogood was about to attach himself.

Ray Burrill stared at the burglar alarm in dismay. It was undeniably the source of the noise, but this noise was unreal. It was quite unlike any burglar alarm warning that Ray had ever heard. At close quarters it penetrated the brain. It was excruciating. The only saving grace was that it took Ray's mind off the scarred and ravaged lawn. He was not familiar with burglar alarms. His small pad did not possess one. It was Coombes, who, in one of his few useful comments of the day, pointed out that it was probably necessary to key in a code. Such a code is not usually kept handily visible by the apparatus and so the suggestion did not immediately alter things. Having retreated outside, an exercise which did little to reduce the aural pain, Ray Burrill remembered numbers he did have. He rushed to telephone the Haverscombes' son. Keeping the explanation as minimal as possible and warning Mark Haverscombe not to let his father anywhere near the phone to hear the awful noise, Ray obtained a four-digit code. In a matter of seconds he had punched it into the machine on the wall. The noise remained unabated. Only the picture changed. The legend in the tiny window now read 'Call Engineer.'

This was more easily accomplished. The telephone number of the alarm company was prominently affixed to the box from which the disturbance came. It was a Newcastle-upon-Tyne number, which did not inspire confidence in a rapid response time, but at least Ray Burrill was speaking to someone after no more than two rings. He was promised that 'one of our trained service engineers' would be on site as soon as possible. When Ray said that he felt like taking a hammer to the equipment to stop the appalling racket, the voice at the other end of the line became agitated and said that this would only make matters worse. However, he was told not to worry as it was bound to be a battery problem and the battery would be exhausted in 'a quarter of an hour or so'. Ray had to be content with that, but he forbore from mentioning that the noise had already lasted that length of time without any sign of weakening.

The incoming batsman was Alan Birch. What he had seen of Brian Leyton-Brown's bowling told him that he was facing a useful club bowler. After two immaculate defensive strokes saw out the rest of the over, Brian Leyton-Brown recognised that he was up against a useful club batsman. The contest about to be staged at the other end was of a different order. In fairness to Dean Faulds he also merited the description of being a useful performer at club level. He also had temperament. Steadiness could sometimes give way to a blaze of glory in a do-or-die approach. Elvis Coombes could

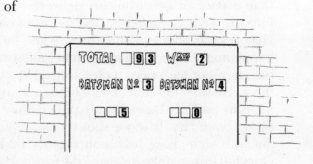

have this effect on people. Dean Faulds had donned a helmet and was ready to go. It was an over to remember. Some said that it was equally as entertaining as the games in 'It's a Knockout'.

It has been observed that batsmen of smaller stature are often the best hookers. Even so Dean Faulds was not entirely proud of his first riposte to the whirlwind fast bowler. The ball was short and rising. Dean Faulds had had to reach for it. He had not been in full control of the shot. It still earned him six runs as it sailed out of the ground. The sound of a shattered car windscreen was almost lost against the background of the continuous blast of the siren sounding from the Towers. The ball took a while to retrieve. It was soon lost again. Elvis Coombes' second ball was distinctly quicker and travelled appreciably further. Dean Faulds was pleased. Technically it had been a better shot. Elvis Coombes was less pleased. His irritation grew as he was kept waiting for the ball to be returned to him. Everyone agreed that the next delivery was the fastest so far bowled. Unlike its predecessors it favoured the off side. Although Dean Faulds flung himself at it like a dervish with blade flashing he failed to connect by a comfortable margin. So too did the wicket-keeper. Four byes resulted. Not learning from his errors, but more by mistake, Elvis Coombes sent down a ball of yorker length which Dean Faulds took painfully on the boot, but sufficiently distant from the stumps that Colonel Crickhill was not troubled with an appeal. Dean Faulds hopped around in pain. To the crowd the entertainment seemed unabated.

After a few moments Dean Faulds pronounced himself fit to resume. By now his sense of adventure had been inflated by killer instinct. He wanted revenge. As he studied Elvis Coombes charging towards him Dean Faulds made a decision. With the bowler no more than a pace or two from his delivery stride he made his move – forward. Elvis Coombes at first did not grasp what was happening. His arm was about to come over when he realised what might be happening. There was a momentary faltering before he released the ball. It might have been a chest-high full toss had it got that far, but the batsman's advance had continued. With great strength and pent-up passion Dean Faulds pulled the ball high over the mid-wicket boundary. It was a shot received by spectators with rapture, but with something less than rapture by Elvis Coombes. Umpire Crickhill fortunately misheard the words which escaped the bowler's lips. It was no longer a game. War had been declared.

Allied to the police intention to stem the flow of vehicles trying to reach Willingfold from either the east or the west was a determination to clear the approach roads of those who were already committed to the last phase of their journey. This was seen as the essential pre-requisite to phase two of the operation which was to get people out of Willingfold once the afternoon's entertainment had ceased. Execution of the plan was less easy than its authors had envisaged. Willingfold had become saturated with cars. The village organising committee had designated a couple of fields as parking areas and these had been marshalled. As numbers grew, gates were thrown open to other fields where there was no-one to supervise orderly parking. Manpower had been confined to what was seen as the more essential task – taking money at the gate. When the organisers' ingenuity ran out, that of the drivers came into play. Every space and every strip of verge was filled. When further progress looked bleak, motorists began to abandon their cars whether out of determination to see whatever it was which attracted so many people or just to get away from the crowded and complaining atmosphere within them.

Joe Metrome was made of sterner stuff. He had never wanted to come to Willingfold. He had intended to go fishing. After a stressful week at work with many call-outs he had wanted a period of peace and solitude on the bank of his favourite stretch of river. He damned the clock radio which his mother-in-law had bought them for Christmas. With their old alarm he could have been up, out of the house and on his way. He reproached himself for lingering in bed long enough to get the news headlines. Hard on the heels of the news headlines came an interview with Darcey De'Arth extolling the wonders of Willingfold. Joe was almost through the bedroom door when his wife sat bolt upright in bed and said, 'That's where we'll go. The children'll love it.' After a tense stand-off, her view prevailed. An inwardly seething Joe Metrome had eventually driven them into a heaving traffic maelstrom. The children were hating it. He was raging. Even his wife's enthusiasm was beginning to die. A long blast of the horn from the car behind, to remind Joe that he had not moved forward three feet, was what finally did it. They were going home, he decided. Their car had other ideas. Overheated and under-serviced, it was made of less stern stuff than its owner. On the first leg of an attempted three-point turn at the narrowest part of the road from the east, it expired. A key part of the police action plan expired with it.

Elvis Coombes turned, stared and hated what he saw. Mischievously Dean Faulds affected to take a step down the wicket although this time he had no intention to give it the charge. The bowler leapt into his run as though pushed by an invisible hand. Onlookers agreed that any one of a quartet of West Indian Test bowlers would have admired for its ferocity and penetration the delivery which Elvis

Coombes produced to end the twenty-fifth over of the innings. Whether Dean Faulds had an opinion on the subject could not immediately be ascertained. He was lying flat on the ground, temporarily unconscious. Of extreme speed the ball had reared sharply off a good length and completely defeated the attempted hook. The bad news was that it clattered into the batsman's helmet just by his right ear; the good news was that Dean Faulds did not clatter into the stumps as he slumped to the ground. An element in the crowd thought that this too was part of the entertainment. A cheer rose and then faded.

What had not given any indication of fading was the noise given off by the Haverscombes' burglar alarm. Ray Burrill's mood had not improved on learning from Coombes that his industrial driers must have overloaded the system, causing the trip to go with consequent interruption to the power supply. The system now minus the driers was once again in operation, but this had had absolutely no remedial effect on the burglar alarm. It was a noise impossible to ignore, but for a short while Ray Burrill's attention was diverted from it. This was on discovery of a pool of water. It was spreading from beneath the chest freezer in the utility room. By then it was too late to rescue the contents, but not too late for a spell of animated but fruitless recrimination as to who had removed the plug.

A man clad only in a pair of baggy shorts of loud design and colour had run on to the field of play. At first Ben Harding wondered if this was a drink-inflamed but half-hearted streaker. The same thought occurred to members of the watching public. They were to be as disappointed as Ben Harding and the other players were relieved. By the time he reached the middle Dean Faulds was stirring. With helmet removed, an inspection took place. The first-aider who had volunteered himself so readily went through an elaborate routine. Parts of Dean Faulds's head were prodded, fingers were held up in front of him and his pulse was taken. The sequence was repeated. Finally the stranger opined mild concussion and recommended a minimum of a half-hour's rest. Dean Faulds who, after this period of attention, felt fine, was nevertheless led from the field. As he retreated, one fielder (John Tod) remarked to another (Jim Abbs) how fortunate Dean had been that it was not the local general practitioner who had been on hand. It was a moot point. Whilst Dr Olgate's diagnoses veered towards the apocalyptic, seeing in any knock on the head the potential for brain damage, cancer or degeneration, the man who attended the felled batsman was in actuality a vet and one of the country's leading experts on BSE.

Winston Jenkins was next in the batting order. In the delay caused by the attention being given to Dean Faulds, Phil Cole hesitated. At what seemed a critical juncture he asked himself whether it was not the captain's responsibility to step into the breach. There were twenty overs left in which to get eighty-one runs. Steady play was all that was required. Phil Cole felt sure that he and Alan Birch could supply cricket of the right tempo. Winston Jenkins's (erratic) big hitting might better be held in reserve. And then Phil Cole reconsidered. The appearance at the wicket of the powerful-looking West Indian-descended third-generation Welshman might have a counter-intimidatory effect in relation to Elvis Coombes. It would, of course, be pure illusion. Phil Cole glumly recognised that Winston's efforts with the ball might already have tarnished the image. Then again, if he was allowed much longer to continue his efforts with the beer, his utility might be totally expended. So Phil did not promote himself.

When after a civilised over between Brian Leyton-Brown and Alan Birch off which two runs were scored, Elvis Coombes was removed from the attack, Phil Cole thought that his stratagem had worked. Not so. The switch to Edward Townsend at the pavilion end owed everything to a facetious exchange between the old captain and the new. Still not wholly reconciled to his demotion for this match, Trevor Edgefield asked Ben Harding whether the blow to Dean Faulds's head had produced any blood. Without waiting for a reply he added, 'If Elvis has seen blood, he'll be ten times worse.' Ben Harding had had the length of an over to think about this. The evidence provided by three overs of Elvis's bowling added sufficient credibility for him to take Trevor Edgefield's mordant comment at face value.

At this point in the innings, the police action plan to decongest the area of traffic suffered its second blow. No-one who knew them would say that the Kidsgrove brothers were a bad lot. Brought up 'proper', as their proud father would say, they never went out looking for trouble. Nevertheless, trouble did not seem to have difficulty finding them. There were four of them, all hefty lads. This was an attribute not unhelpful in the bustle of street and market trading. They took good care not to be on the wrong side of the law. They may have skirted the boundaries on occasions, but they knew to avoid the big transgression. In other ways, their sense of values was unimpeachable. They loved their cricket. They liked nothing better than to go out into the countryside, find some village cricket match and settle down with a few cans of ale. Where the Kidsgrove brothers were concerned, a few cans of ale amounted to trays of several dozen purchased at knock-down prices from their local cash-and-carry. On this first Saturday in June, they had been delayed in their rural foray by picking up three mates and a commensurate amount of ale. One of Darcey De'Arth's interviews had been repeated for the umpteenth time and they had settled for Willingfold on the basis that 'It could be a bit of a larf.' It was not much of a 'larf' at all to find themselves stuck in a barely-moving queue of traffic and no 'larf' at all when, under the weight of their dilapidated and overloaded van, the Muckersby Bridge collapsed. Bureaucrats at county hall were not always wrong.

Although arrived at by not the purest of cricket reasons, the choice of Edward Townsend to take over the bowling at the pavilion end proved to be inspired. At first demurring on the grounds that he was only an occasional bowler and that, 'Well, really I am rather rusty,' Edward Townsend was prevailed upon to take the ball. It emerged that he bowled orthodox left-arm ('rather slow, I'm afraid'). Unusually for a bowler, he seemed to take little interest in field-placing, but when Ben Harding had completed the task on a predominantly defensive basis, his new bowler approached him to say that, if he did not mind 'terribly much', he would like a silly mid-off, which three overs later was precisely where Winston Jenkins was caught.

Occasional Edward Townsend may have claimed, but tidy was what he proved. Phil Cole might have been right in ensuring that Winston Jenkins came to the wicket in his appointed place, but the clock had already advanced marginally too far. Away from the marquee and the comfortable boozy atmosphere which had been its defining feature for most of the day, Winston Jenkins needed time to adjust. It was not available. He was off the mark first ball stabbing involuntarily at a delivery wide of off stump which fortunately also went wide of slip. On a roar from his partner he took a single. Back on strike for the last ball of the over he just managed to keep out a straight ball which deceived him in the flight. Off the next Leyton-Brown over, Alan Birch took a cultured two, but failed to manipulate the strike.

Phil Cole marched out to the middle mentally chastising himself and Winston Jenkins. He realised that he might have been wiser to have been the replacement for Dean Faulds and to have put Winston Jenkins under strict instructions to sober up. It might not have paid off, but Winston Jenkins's game might have been more effective had he been more sober or more drunk. In reality Winston had been caught in a no man's-land between the two conditions. To the first ball of Edward Townsend's second over he prodded. The bat made no contact with a gently turning leg-break. Winston Jenkins tried another approach. He swung mightily at the second, achieved the contact and collected two runs over slip's head. Another change of tactic. Another leg-break. This one turned too and lifted. Taking the batsman's glove it rose gracefully and was easily pouched by Geoffrey Jarr, who had somewhat uncomfortably found himself exposed in the silly mid-off position without what he felt was full protection.

Having watchfully played out the rest of Edward Townsend's over, Phil Cole took stock with Alan Birch. Just over seventy runs to go with sixteen overs left. It seemed a reasonable equation. There needed to be no heroics. Steady accumulation should do it. This was Phil Cole's game and he knew he could rely on his partner not to indulge in anything extravagant. They both agreed that on what they had seen of the bowling so far they ought not to be in any difficulty. With half the ration of remaining overs gone, they would be forced to re-assess.

Willingfold did not have a lot to offer the discerning visitor. The church of St Broderick the Elder was far from being any kind of architectural or historical gem. More patched up than kept up, it displayed more corrugated iron than slate. The turreting on the tower was barely recognisable through decay and the church clock had stood at ten to three for seventeen years. Some of the houses in the village opened their gardens to visitors on six Sundays a year. But this was Saturday. It was said that the duck pond in Willingfold was one of its most attractive features. After a spell of hot weather and a defect in the local drainage, it was both malodorous and dry, a condition rapidly being approached by both pubs whose patrons were spilling through the doors. The queue for the village tea-room stretched fifty yards along the road. Eighty-two-year-old Ethel Mason struggled to cope with the unprecedented demand, having only seventy-five-year-old Clara Ford to help her in the kitchen. Considering her reliance on a walking frame, the turnaround of cups and saucers was remarkable.

For want of anything else, shopping fever seemed to grip many of those who packed the centre of the village. It is hard to understand the rationality of behaviour in such circumstances. There were two shops in Willingfold. One was a grocery-cum-convenience store; the other would have been taken for a junk shop but for the legend 'Gifts' on the signboard. Items which were immediately edible disappeared first from the grocery store. They were followed improbably as the afternoon wore on by tins of marrowfat peas, jars of raspberry jam and packets of powdered soup. Attention later turned to self-raising flour, parsley-and-thyme stuffing, wine vinegar, candles and airing racks. Gradually the shelves of the grocery-cum-convenience store were picked as clean as the carcass of an impala in the African bush. The gift shop fared no worse. All manner of objects, some of which had lain undisturbed for years, finally began to move. These included copies of a book published (privately) by a former village resident some fifty years ago entitled *Cricket with the Cannibals – the memoirs of a sporting soldier*. As he saw them disappear, the proprietor hoped that he was not indirectly contributing to a further fall in standards in the game. He put such thoughts aside and turned his attention to a customer who was contemplating a particularly hideous green-painted, glass-fronted wardrobe.

The avid cricket follower can admire almost any aspect of the game where the contest between bat and ball is truly engaged or where fielding skills are on display or where the overall situation of a match lends its own tension. Other more occasional watchers of cricket seem to be satisfied only by the biff-bang variety in which the batsman has ascendancy and the ball is struck hard (and preferably high) to all corners. The measured caution of Phil Cole and Alan Birch began to displease the crowd. Having committed themselves latterly to this game of cricket, people wanted action and a result. Nudging singles off bat or pad and stealing the occasional two did not conform to specification. The displeasure made itself increasingly audible despite continued competition from the Haverscombes' burglar alarm.

Between the second and third kicks which Joe Metrome administered to his defunct vehicle out of sheer frustration at yet another vile turn of events, its two-way radio crackled into life. Increasingly desperate duty clerks in the control room of the Eziguard Burglar Alarm Company were by now calling all their agents to see if any of them could crack what had become the impregnable fortress of Willingfold-in-the-Myre. By luck they had at last found their man. By luck he needed almost any excuse to get away from his present scene of embarrassment and family quarrelling. He seized his case (which he was duty-bound to carry at all times) and marched off to look for the Towers. Perhaps inadvertently, he had pocketed the car keys and these too marched with him, leaving his wife to cope with a growing number of angry motorists. The Metrome estate car was just long enough to block the entire road. To add further to the difficulty, it was an automatic.

The mid-pitch conference had a note of urgency about it. The equation had changed. Fifty-six from eight overs was now the challenge facing the Outcasts. It ought not to be beyond them, but the bowlers being used by Willingfold, both imports for the occasion, were bowling, if not above themselves, certainly above the standard to which the village team might ordinarily aspire. Alan Birch, one of the Outcasts' most reliable although not most flamboyant batsman, was finding it hard to force the pace. It was not a natural part of Phil Cole's game to force the pace. He was usually the steady accumulator with pushes and pokes mingled with dabs and deflections. Even he had not kept the scoreboard ticking at any kind of pace. The bug of caution had taken hold. In such circumstances the captain did what a captain has to do. He surrendered his wicket.

No-one who witnessed what happened in Willingfold on that afternoon of the first Saturday in June could honestly say that the spirit of enterprise in Britain was dead. Trestles and tables began appearing outside houses, bungalows and cottages. Soon they were adorned with village memorabilia of every description. Mrs Pidbert was offering home-made jams 'produced from local fruit' while Mr Pidbert was recapping and relabelling Co-op jars in the back kitchen. Wickerwork in unappealing shapes and colours was displayed by Mrs Wildhorn with a sign claiming that it was woven by patients at the cottage hospital. Most potential customers were unaware that the cottage hospital had closed twenty years ago and that the proceeds would go no further than Mrs Wildhorn's purse. Across the street, Mrs Dowder was selling shortbread proclaimed as being fresh from her own oven when in fact it was fresh from being repackaged from a large seven pound tin which her grandmother had given her at Christmas – sadly not the most recent Christmas. Next to Mrs Dowder sat Gypsy Peg with her trinkets. No-one had heard Margaret Alsom ever previously describe herself in this way. She was as far removed from the Romany culture as her trinkets were from taste and authenticity.

Nor could the young be kept idle. Once gridlock was established, out came squeegee merchants with their buckets. Some were as young as five and six, needing to stand on a box to reach the windscreen. The older children volunteered a complete car wash for which there was no shortage of time. In their wake came the wax

polishers. One imaginative fourteen year-old – doubtless a Branson of the future – armed with cloths and a battery-driven vacuum cleaner and teamed with his younger sister (she carried the vacuum cleaner), hawked a complete valet service up and down the line of stationary cars. One driver, deserted by his wife and children, bought it.

Word spread. Sloshing muddy water over car windscreens with the possibility of being paid became far more tempting to Sophie Crossley's little helpers than manning the scoreboard for nothing. The Skynn brothers sped away taking other recruits with them. Sophie was beginning to feel the strain despite the almost sleepy pace of the cricket. There were aches where there had been no previous aches. She would have liked to have sat down, but when she had last stood up, her stool had been taken by one of the increasing number of spectators. Her husband turned to her with an inquiring look. She smiled. She knew that Simon was in seventh heaven when engrossed in tending his scorebook. Not long now, Sophie reflected. Soon the game would be over. In the event, very much sooner than she or anyone else expected.

Henry Pickard bowled the thirty-eighth over of the innings. What had persuaded Syd Breakwell, who had so far spent a quiet match, to direct his attention to where the bowler placed his feet no-one could have guessed. Pitted as he thought he was against the Haverscombes' burglar alarm, Syd Breakwell's cry of no-ball was the more ear-piercing for the fact that at that precise moment the alarm ceased. Henry Pickard was almost knocked over by the bellow. His shock was obviously sufficient to shake his equilibrium for he transgressed again with the next delivery. Syd Breakwell pointed emphatically to where his foot was landing. Henry Pickard re-marked his run-up and proceeded to bowl a woefully short ball which Alan Birch failed to get hold of and could do no more than scoop over square leg's head for a single. The next was too full. The old-style Phil Cole would probably have pushed it for two; the new-style Phil Cole swatted at it, missed and narrowly escaped being bowled. Another full toss followed. This time Phil Cole got bat on it, but only just; the ball flew off the edge, narrowly clearing cover and the batsmen ran two. Syd Breakwell's intervention had clearly cost Henry Pickard his length. A rank long-hop attracted Phil Cole's swat stroke. Connection was made and the batsmen again ran two before the ball dropped into the hands of Elvis Coombes on the mid-wicket boundary.

A gust of beery breath caught Phil Cole as the incoming batsman passed him. During the remainder of his steps back to the canvas pavilion, the captain was forced to wonder whether his sacrifice had been worth it. His doubts did not last long when he saw the remaining members of his side not only pad-less, but well on the way to being leg-less. As he steered an unsteady Charlie Colson towards the changing-room, Phil Cole had no option but to hope that Harry Northwood would prove the better bet after all.

Harry Northwood himself had no doubts. He had not in fact consumed so much beer that his ability to bat was seriously impaired. He had been canny enough to recognise that he had little to do to persuade his new-found friends about his capacity for drink. What still had to be more fully tested was his capacity to bat. He was fortunate in the timing of his arrival at the crease. Steadiness had deserted Henry Pickard. The wicket had done nothing to restore it. Two balls of poor length completed the over. To the first Harry Northwood played a watchful defensive shot; to the second a fierce drive straight past the bowler for four. Spirits in the crowd rose as more action was sensed. Anticipation would be more than fulfilled.

A sort of eerie calm had descended over the Towers. The contents of the freezer had been ditched. Mopping-up operations had been conducted. More importantly, silence had been restored although not without the news that the alarm system would need to be completely re-wired. 'Damp penetration' was Joe Metrome's analysis and he would doubtless have expounded on his theory had he not been hastily conducted off the premises by two police officers keen to re-unite him with his vehicle. Expressing doubt as to whether he could get it to start, Joe Metrome was pursued by words shouted from the doorway: 'My Elvis is good with motors.' Shortly afterwards, Coombes had left with the promise (or possibly the threat) that having done all he could (here he underestimated himself) he would look in on Monday. Ray Burrill, left on his own, gave a traumatised Boycs his tea. He idly flicked through Wisden again, noting that the year's leading wicket-taker had been Derek

Shackleton with 172 whilst all the time wondering how he was to confess the full scale of the disasters to the Haverscombes when their son rang again. He dreaded the phone ringing although he wanted to get the call out of the way to enable him to escape to the cricket ground for the climax of the contest and the gallon of beer which he felt by now he was owed. However, the sound he heard next was not a phone ringing.

From a maximum of seven overs, forty-seven runs were needed to win the match. Despite an air of urgency being conveyed by both batsmen, the equation was no better by the end of Edward Townsend's next over. There was more subtlety to his bowling than at first had been apparent. Edward Townsend had been very modest in admitting his talents. He had once had a trial with a first-class county. This extra bit of quality was brought to bear as he tied down Alan Birch and Harry Northwood to a single apiece. The Outcasts had passed one hundred and fifty at the crawl. The scoreboard showed only one hundred and forty for four wickets, the Skynns' signing-off point.

Henry Pickard had not had a trial with a first-class county and lacked the experience to overcome the handicap which Syd Breakwell had so unexpectedly placed in his path. He excused himself from bowling a ninth over. His mumbled apology was quite unnecessary as Ben Harding had already made up his mind on that point. However, the alternatives were not full of promise. Determinedly ignoring the claim from Elvis Coombes that he would soon blast them out, Ben Harding eventually came to the same sort of conclusion that a little earlier had motivated Phil Cole. The captain had to rise to the challenge. Ben Harding put aside the nightmare of his last over which had cost twenty-one runs and psyched himself up by recalling that he had bowled his first five overs at a total cost of only three runs. Harry Northwood had seen only the sixth over.

Not everyone around the boundary had their concentration fixed on the calculating moves being made in the middle. Near the marquee another drama had been unfolding. As if the effort of overcoming the scoreboard backlog had been, so to speak, a plate too far, Sophie Crossley had suddenly gasped and sat down very heavily on the ground. She knew what was happening and her husband, albeit belatedly, cottoned on with some speed. Even he had not been faster than Uncle George. Seeing the collapse he had sped to a phone and made a 999 call. This call was more fruitful than his earlier attempt to establish dialogue with the MCC, but only after persistence on Uncle George's part. Having been told that no ambulance could reach Willingfold on account of road congestion, Uncle George moved a gear upwards. Another of his contacts was brought into play and minutes later so was the air ambulance.

In no doubt as to where his duty and concern resided, a scorer of Simon Crossley's calibre suffered pangs. To desert his post did not come naturally to him. His eyes swivelled despairingly from his distressed wife to the match in progress. His dilemma was resolved when Winston Jenkins weaved an uneven way towards the scorer's table. Not entirely believing that his worries were over in the one department, he nevertheless devoted himself to ministering to his very expectant wife. His opposite number, Tom Haresmith, whose reliability as a scorer was entirely untested, was left with the responsibility of bringing Winston Jenkins up to date.

Despite this inconvenience, the game had proceeded. The principal protagonists and most of the crowd were unaware of the alternative theatre to the side. A close result to the match was anticipated. Harry Northwood set out to whet their appetite. Ben Harding's first ball to him was impeccable. The second erred down the leg side. Harry Northwood went down on one knee and lifted it over the boundary. The crowd responded with enthusiasm. Ben Harding corrected his line and offered the batsman no further liberties. This did not prevent a scuttled leg-bye off the last ball.

When later he was asked to describe what happened, Ray Burrill said it started as a creak which turned into a groan which became a splintering sound which was followed by a scraping noise which was overtaken first by a crash and then by a splash. It was a case of after Coombes the deluge. The insurance inspectors argued afterwards whether the load-bearing properties of the loft floor had been fatally damaged more by the effects of the blow-torch or the foot. On either theory Elvis Coombes was considered to be a key witness.

Nor was the result in dispute. The new water tank had gone down in the manner of the Titanic. In this case the survival rate was one hundred percent: Ray Burrill and Boycs. And that was when Mark Haverscombe chose to ring again.

It was generally reckoned that Edward Townsend teased Harry Northwood throughout his next over. He cleverly varied his pace. A beautifully disguised slower ball almost resulted in a return catch, but the bowler could not quite get his fingers under it. Another ball missed off stump by a whisker. The fifth might have produced a leg before wicket decision, but Colonel Crickhill's attention had wandered towards the increasing disturbance by the marquee and so the batsman benefited from the doubt even if there was none in Edward Townsend's mind. This may have affected his last delivery because it was a little full and deserved to be hit. It deserved to be hit better than Harry Northwood managed, but still three runs were earned. Thirty-five more runs were needed with only four overs remaining.

Ben Harding felt confident. He was sure now that the task was too great for the Outcasts. He wondered whether he should bring John Tod back into the attack. It might, he reasoned, look better to have one of the true locals bowling at the death. In a wild moment he even wondered about Elvis Coombes, but a wicked leer from the mid-wicket boundary dissuaded him. Had he not overheard a sardonic comment from Trevor Edgefield, he might well have made a change of bowling, but he did not like to hear himself described as he had been and so he persevered. It proved to be a crucial over.

Ray Burrill looked upon it as a cathartic conversation. The news from Mark Haverscombe was not good. His mother had gone to hospital and had been advised to stay overnight for further tests to be completed. This had produced an anxiety reaction on the part of his father. This was diagnosed as angina and he too had been admitted to a ward. Ray Burrill asked for the name of the hospital partly with a view to sending flowers, but also out of curiosity to know an NHS hospital with as many as two spare beds. Then he told his story. When he had ended and after assurances as to the welfare of Boycs, the explosion at the other end was of laughter, not anger.

Ray was told not to worry. Insurance would pay. It would be a very good deal. The Towers could have the makeover it had long needed. Ray could be sure of this. Mark Haverscombe was in the business. There would be no mistake. In more than one sense, Ray Burrill felt released. Leaving Boycs with a chewy, he set off at a run for the cricket ground. At the end of the drive he overtook Coombes in his imprisoned truck unable to gain access to a road full of stationary vehicles. The third youngster who had attempted to clean his windscreen had been seen off with a singularly vulgar gesture which, sadly, he had all too well understood.

If Harry Northwood had had the worse of the previous over against Edward Townsend, he came out on top against Ben Harding. Perhaps the extra pace suited him; possibly he had decided that it was now or never; or maybe he had sobered up. What followed was impressive. The first ball of Ben Harding's over was drilled between point and cover in a beautifully executed cricket stroke. The second was driven straight for another four. With the third ball Ben Harding got in his sole gesture of retaliation. Short-pitched and rising, it flew past Harry Northwood's helmet-protected nose in a manner reminiscent of his school's match against Rockcliffe. But Harry, under the Outcasts' aegis, was cooler now. When Ben Harding pitched short again he was hooked one bounce to fine leg. The climax of the over was provided by neither batsman nor bowler. The remaining two balls were played cautiously if not apprehensively as the noise and proximity of the air-ambulance helicopter cast an increasing shadow over proceedings.

The majority of spectators believed that the arrival of the helicopter was somehow connected to the earlier parachute drop. The impression may have been heightened by the way in which the cricketers suddenly raced towards the marquee when it became evident that the pilot saw the strip as the centre point of his landing. It was reminiscent of the fleeing Morris dancers. The fact that twenty-three runs were needed off three overs to win the match was largely lost on the crowd because the scoreboard was still lagging. In any case, Harry Northwood's efforts notwithstanding, a helicopter suddenly arriving lent a bigger element of drama to the day, particularly as it became apparent that a medical emergency was involved. There were even those so carried away that they were put in mind of 'Miss Saigon'.

In reality, only the Crossleys were being carried away. Labour had begun, but not crisis. At any rate she was now in safe hands which was probably more than could be said for Simon's scorebook and his accompanying bag of cricket data and information. The helicopter lifted off with cheers of goodwill from those who knew what it was all about and with inane hoots from the rest who were still inclined to believe that it was a late boost to the entertainment. Poised for the resumption of play, Winston Jenkins was relieved to find that he and Tom Haresmith were in agreement over the total. Batsmen four and seven were at the crease. There were four batsmen to come (had this been put to the test there would only have been three as Colin Banks had succumbed to temptation thirty minutes ago – and again five minutes ago for that matter). So the score on the board was updated to 173–5.

WILLINGFOLD

Townsend	c. Jenkins	b. Banks	0
Leyton-Brown		b. Banks	1
Harding	run out		89
Abbs	c. Newton	b. Thorogood	21
Ryesmith	c. Birch	b. Thorogood	0
Jarr	c. Thorogood	b. Cole	36
Edgefield	not out		26
Forbes	c. Northwood	b. Colson	8
Tod	lbw	b. Colson	0
Pickard		b. Colson	0
Coombes	c. Newton	b. Colson	0
Extras			14
TOTAL	**(all out)**		**195**

Bowling	o	m	r	w
Banks	4	1	20	2
Thorogood	9	3	33	2
Jenkins	7	0	52	0
Cole	9	3	28	1
Redman	5	2	38	0
Colson	4.2	1	11	4

OUTCASTS

Palmer		b. Coombes	45
Thorogood	c. Pickard	b. Leyton-Brown	34
Faulds	retired hurt		23
Birch	not out		13
Jenkins	c. Jarr	b. Townsend	3
Cole	c. Coombes	b. Pickard	10
Northwood	not out		26
Colson	did not bat		
Newton	did not bat		
Redman	did not bat		
Banks	did not bat		
Extras			19
TOTAL	**(for 4 wickets)**		**173**

Bowling	o	m	r	w
Tod	6	0	25	0
Harding	8	2	42	0
Pickard	8	1	23	1
Leyton-Brown	9	2	27	1
Coombes	3	1	29	1
Townsend	8	0	17	1

Willingfold won by 1 run (D/L method)

CLOSE OF PLAY

There was no resumption. Precision landing by the helicopter pilot it might have been, but the machine had bounced slightly before settling. The boots of paramedics in a hurry had shown no greater respect for a surface prepared for cricket and not for civil aviation. Alan Birch was the first to pronounce: 'We can't play on that.' Confronted with a situation unique to his experience, Syd Breakwell could see his point. Colonel Crickhill, who had absolutely no experience to contribute, expressed solidarity with his colleague. Disappointing though this turn of events was, Ben Harding was not disposed to argue. In any case, the memory of the last over still rankled. However, as it became apparent what was being decided in the middle, there was someone at the boundary edge who was extremely disposed to argue. Uncle George was hopping up and down in agitation.

'We can't have a no result,' boomed Uncle George. 'That's no good to me ... us,' he quickly corrected himself. And then rather lamely he added, 'The crowd will be very disappointed. We've got to give 'em a result.' Phil Cole said light-heartedly, 'Well, we could always call on Duckworth/Lewis.' A moment later, he wished he had not said it. Uncle George was galvanised. Although he was more familiar with George Duckworth and Tony Lewis than an academic scoring system, he grasped at anything which might be a lifeline. He bombarded Phil Cole with questions. Phil was in no position to provide answers. The man who might have been able to satisfy Uncle George had flown away some minutes ago. Winston Jenkins joined the discussion at this point. Thrusting Simon Crossley's bag into the circle, he suggested that there might be something there to help.

Curious to see what had been taking place which had turned the village into a shambles, Lawrence Phypps had moved on from the cricket at its point of interruption into Farmer Pegley's field. Apart from hearty life in the beer tent there seemed the air of a deserted battlefield about the place. The turrets of a polyurethane and plasterboard castle hung askew. The obscene bouncy castle had subsided. Stalls were being dismantled, almost it seemed in slow motion. Rubbish lay everywhere. Piles of corpses, Lawrence Phypps thought to himself grimly, and the scene would have been complete. Suddenly there was a scream followed by sobbing and a young woman emerged from a striped tent which a second or two ago Lawrence Phypps had cast as the army leader's command post. In fact it was Madam Arcadia's grotto of grief.

The girl ran away across the field. Lawrence Phypps, shaken from his musing, strode towards the tent. Bursting his way in, he was confronted by an elderly lady with a pound and a half of make-up on her face. Any actor, who prided himself on playing a pantomime dame, could not have failed to be impressed by the cacophony of clothing in which Madam Arcadia was attired. All that was missing was the washing basket. By way of substitutes, Madam Arcadia had in front of her a crystal ball of yellowy hue, a set of dog-eared tarot cards, a feather duster, two packets of high tar, no filter cigarettes and a bottle of vodka which was two-thirds empty. 'Hello, dear,' she greeted her latest client. 'You seem a nice boy. Let's see what Madam Arcadia can foretell for you.' What was obviously a ritual mantra had by now become somewhat less clear in enunciation. Her tongue tripped heavily over the last four words. For no good reason, Lawrence Phypps sat down on the stool to which he was waved.

Examination of Simon Crossley's bag showed that he was abreast of the Duckworth/Lewis system of determining the result of limited-overs matches which were interrupted by the weather or helicopter damage, whatever the case may be. Whether Simon actually understood the formula and its application could not at that moment be proved. In the history of Outcasts' cricket, Simon's knowledge in this respect had never been put to the test. The only formula which had been applied in previous Outcasts' matches spoiled by rain had been calibrated in pints. The word 'drawn', when it had appeared in the scorebook, had had two meanings.

It was with his last thrust into the bottom of Simon Crossley's bag that Winston Jenkins's hand had fastened on a fat volume which by its feel he had assumed to be the current edition of the *Good Beer Guide*. In fact in the light of day it proved to be *All you ever wanted to know about Duckworth/Lewis and were afraid to ask*. Many people would contend that this was the best ever, easiest to read and occasionally jocular account of the Duckworth/Lewis system. Its five hundred and fifty-five pages were packed with information and interpretation. Interspersed in the text were copious charts with often hilarious cartoon illustrations. It has to be said that purists regarded this book very much as the rough guide to Duckworth/Lewis. Scholars preferred *The Limits of Cricket: the social and sporting impact of Duckworth/Lewis*, which had been published the previous year in two volumes by the Bovine Press Institute. For ready reference, however, this tended to be confined to the scoring boxes at first-class grounds. It was rumoured that Talk Radio would not accept anyone in its commentary team who could not show passing familiarity with this academic work.

No-one of such acumen was available at Willingfold-in-the-Myre on this first Saturday in June. Uncle George had tried the MCC once more, but with no more success than on the first occasion. The conscientious lady at Lord's, who had moved on to polishing the silverware, said she was sure that there was no Mr Duckworth or Mr Lewis there, but wondered whether the caller would like to be put through to the Museum. On second thoughts she was not sure that she could manage that on this phone, but she could run over there except that it was raining. Uncle George had hung up. One of the clearer heads belonged to Ray Burrill, who had closed in on his colleagues and his first pint of the day. When he mentioned that he had a friend who worked as an administrative assistant at the County Ground (he sold score-cards), someone produced a mobile phone with a flicker of a signal. By happy chance, imperfect contact was made. Ray Burrill, who had minimal knowledge of the detailed story of the match, gave the Willingfold total and relied on the scoreboard for the Outcasts' score. The friend promised to ring back as soon as possible. He did not like to say that he could not return to the pavilion until he had sold his present batch of scratch cards on behalf of the supporters' club.

The number of people seeking to leave Willingfold now comfortably exceeded those trying to reach the village or more accurately those whose cars were pointed towards the village, but were at this hour without hope or ambition of reaching it. What proved literally to be the key to unlocking the Chinese puzzle which the centre of the village represented was the one which Joe Metrome brought back to his vehicle. Impatiently his wife seized it from his hand. With a flourish she started the engine. At that moment Joe Metrome realised how much he hated this car. Nor was he feeling particularly charitable towards his wife who had brought them on this wretched expedition. Without stalling, the car was manoeuvred into exit mode and a slow flow of vehicles began to move away from the village.

Vodka or no vodka, Madam Arcadia had not lost her touch. Her musings had become if anything more mournful. A death in the family featured fairly early in the litany. Lawrence Phypps was impressed, but he was not to know that death in the family was part of Madam Arcadia's stock-in-trade. As she got into her stride, one disaster after another was recounted. Each grim forecast alternated with terms of endearment towards her client. After being warned that he would have three children all of whom would fall prey to a deadly virus, Lawrence Phypps could have sworn that their knees touched. Taking another swig from the vodka and wiping a sweaty hand over the crystal ball, Madam Arcadia regaled Lawrence Phypps with a disabling car accident, destruction of the family home, failure of his business and the onset of early dementia. At first Lawrence Phypps was disdainful, inclined to mock the absurdity of it, but as the doom-laden prophecies went on almost (swigs of vodka apart) unabated, Lawrence Phypps finally lost his temper. To a scream from Madam Arcadia he hurled the vodka bottle into the corner and swept the crystal ball and other paraphernalia to the floor. Then he turned over the table forcing her chair to give way and deposit Madam Arcadia on the grass. 'You wicked old crone – they should lock you up,' was Lawrence Phypps' valedictory message as he turned to the flap in the tent. But Madam

Arcadia was not yet done. She too had a valedictory message: 'They'll get you, they'll be back for you, you can't defy them.' And as Lawrence Phypps disappeared, she laughed a long, hysterical laugh which followed her erstwhile client as he stamped his way home. He dismissed her from his mind as he thought about his forthcoming party, but she was to be proved not entirely crazy.

The mobile phone erupted into its signature tune, the waltz from 'The Merry Widow'. This was the eagerly awaited news from the County Ground. The reception was still poor, but it seemed clear to Ray Burrill that, if the side batting first had scored one hundred and ninety-five, the side batting second with five wickets down needed to have reached one hundred and seventy-four to win. The Outcasts had one hundred and seventy-three at the end of forty-two overs and so Willingfold were declared the winners by one run. The announcement was greeted in silence by the mystified and frustrated crowd which dispersed muttering. At the time and in the hubbub, no-one noticed the flaw in the calculation. No doubts assailed Uncle George's very obvious sense of triumph. Nor did anyone wish to put in jeopardy the night of celebration which Uncle George emphatically promised.

The grip of traffic paralysis which had spread across two counties had at last eased. Diversionary measures implemented earlier by the police had made chronic what had previously been acute. Once the half-way point in the afternoon had passed, some motorists had been sensible enough to take any route which steered them away from the vicinity of Willingfold. Far too many people had not shown this degree of sense. Theirs proved to be a long day. The final unravelling of the situation owed a lot to a flash of inspiration by Jim Dukes of the Road Services Association.

In his RSA office, Jim Dukes had never known such pressure on the first Saturday in June. Slumped over a large-scale map of the area and constantly speaking through his telephone headset, he had not even had time to eat the cheese, celery and sweetcorn sandwiches with the hint of horseradish which many hours earlier his wife had devotedly prepared. Carelessly, instead of re-wrapping them in the foil which had protected their freshness, he had left them exposed. They were now dry, curling and, dare he admit it, unappetising. He swept them from the table in front of him into the office bin and returned his attention to the map. The answer was then staring him in the face. Previously obscured by the cheese, celery and sweeetcorn sandwiches with the hint of horseradish was Bletchworth Lane, leading to a disused Second World War airfield.

Bletchworth Lane had been closed for years. It had been the main access road to the airfield. It ran from the eastern approach road to Willingfold and was carried across the main road by a bridge which, because it had been built to a Ministry of Defence specification, was grossly over-engineered. It could bear tank transporters let alone the heaviest lorries which the European Union could supply. To the east of the airfield it ran on to another principal road. Whereas the entrance on the Willingfold road, no more than fifty yards from the main road junction, was barred by a gate and obscured by overhanging branches, access at the other end was denied by no more than oil drums and a beam placed across them. This had allowed television production companies to bring in crews to use the location to film scenes for various drama series.

Unbeknown to the authorities, one company, Staylust Productions, had pushed the frontiers rather wider than drama suitable for family consumption. Consternation was shared by actors, cameramen and producers alike when the Dukes plan was put into operation. This involved opening the Willingfold entrance to north and eastbound traffic. To ease the flow back into the main road system, vehicles were obliged to circle the airfield buildings in a giant detour. The extra fuel consumption might have offended the Minister for Environmental Protection, but the extended journey provided unexpected previews of what Staylust Productions next intended to release on video (only to selected outlets). For some it was a startlingly bright interlude in what had otherwise been a tedious day.

Clearing the road to the west of Willingfold was not so straightforward and much more dull. Vehicles between the broken bridge and the village had to be moved forward at the crawl to the place which had been denied them all day. To the dismay of the village entrepreneurs, their passengers were not in a mood to buy either goods or services. Those who had got no further than Muckersby Bridge had to reverse all the way to the main road.

Finally, a recovery vehicle reached the Kidsgrove brothers and their wrecked van. It was surprisingly a scene of tranquillity with seven unharmed bodies draped unconsciously over a heap of empty beer cans. A disembodied voice from a transistor was announcing the close-of-play cricket scores. When the nation was told that Essex had beaten Gloucestershire by two wickets, one of the rescuers thought he saw a smile cross the face of Glen Kidsgrove.

Willingfold was left to clear up the débris, count its money and celebrate into the night. By far the largest amount of money was assembled in Willingfold Cottage where Uncle George was supervising every new deposit. By far the largest quantity of real ale was in the same place (Uncle George wisely had kept a second barrel in reserve). Despite the attempt to establish exclusivity, many unauthorised people had penetrated the marquee and helped to drain it dry of real ale.

The plan for the evening, Uncle George informed the Outcasts, was to take advantage of Lawrence Phypps's party by way of cocktails, to return to the Cottage for a barbecue (the original ox roast downgraded) and, in the absence of stocks at the Oak and Yoke, to dispose of the barrel with him. It sounded good. First there were other arrangements to be made. The Redman brothers and Ray Burrill needed to be re-billeted. As did Boycs, for the Towers was no longer fit for a dog. Except in Boycs' case this turned out to be a wholly unnecessary provision.

The party at Willingfold Hall was very wet. Grouse was amazed at the stocks of wine uncovered by his boss. The event was crashed by several people from the village, but Lawrence Phypps did not mind. He was in fine form, Madam Arcadia's ramblings long forgotten. Had he been aware of the identity of two of his uninvited guests, he might have felt less easy. However, by this time Lawrence Phypps was flying. He was drinking only a forty-year-old white Chateauneuf du Pape discreetly served by Grouse. His other guests drank less nobly, but pleasantly enough. Forced like so many others to stay in Willingfold longer than intended, the men from HM Customs and Excise had decided to make a virtue of necessity.

By the time the Outcasts had moved on to Uncle George's home, Colin Banks had reappeared, entwined though he was with Virginia

Crickhill. They found their host in expansive form. It was late in the evening before Phil Cole found a discreet moment to tackle Uncle George. He needed to know the real story behind Uncle George's over-enthusiastic partisanship in relation to the afternoon's match. At first Uncle George protested innocence. Phil Cole persisted. 'A bet?' he eventually exclaimed. So that was it. A £10,000 wager. 'It was the only way I could get some money out of that sceptic, Stephen Dolbee,' confessed Uncle George. 'He refused to believe that we could revive the village cricket team. I was determined to prove him wrong.' He went on to say that with his inside knowledge of 'your lot' he thought that he was on a certainty. Plaintively he added, 'I didn't think you'd take it so seriously.' Phil Cole was convulsed.

What the Outcasts did take seriously was drinking, especially when there was good real ale in close proximity. No beds were needed for their second night in Willingfold. One by one they crashed out on Uncle George's lawn. By this time Colin Banks had disappeared. He certainly had no intention of missing out on bed.

In Willingfold-in-the-Myre, the first Saturday in June ended late.

AFTERMATH

Before it actually ended, Sophie Crossley gave birth to a baby boy, Brian Sachin. It was too early to say whether he would bat left- or right-handed. To his surprise (in view of his earlier doubts about Simon) and pleasure, Stewart Thorogood was asked to be Godfather.

On the morning after the night before, Colin Banks woke alone. Virginia Crickhill had gone as silently as she had arrived. It was just another notch on the handle of Colin's bat – and her gun.

On the following morning, a combined police, Customs and Drug Squad swoop on Willingfold Hall led to the detention of Lawrence Phypps on suspicion of multiple offences including, ludicrously, the murder of his father. Eventually, the forces of the law took apart the van in which Lawrence Phypps had returned to Willingfold to discover that it had held more than just liquor and tobacco products. Grouse and Mrs Enzyme were arrested as accessories, but later set free.

The health of Mr and Mrs Haverscombe continued to deteriorate. It was eventually decided that they would be better off in sheltered accommodation two miles away from their son and daughter-in-law. Thus they never did see how well the 'nice young man' had looked after their property. Boycs had to be prised away from the Towers – the only home he had known – with much the same reluctance as his cricketing namesake had shown in leaving the crease, even when all three stumps had been flattened. The Towers was later sold to a charitable organisation and became a rest home for distressed cricket administrators.

Willingfold Cricket Club was reborn under the twin leadership of Trevor Edgefield and Ben Harding, happily reconciled. In view of the huge sum raised on the first Saturday in June, the village had no difficulty embarking on a bid for a Lottery grant. It was proposed that the magnificent new pavilion, built on the site of the old one, should be dedicated to Uncle George for his inspirational leadership. He demurred and insisted that it should be named in memory of what had happened on the fateful evening of the collapse of the old building. So it was called the Sir Cliff Richard pavilion.

After sorting through the cards, letters and telemessages wishing them well and after dealing with the mass of other duties which attend upon the birth of a child, Simon Crossley eventually met up with his team-mates in their headquarters, the Sink and Plumber, to celebrate the birth of Brian Sachin. Wetting the baby's head was a grossly inadequate description of the alcoholic deluge which took place. It was there that Simon Crossley was reunited with his precious scorebook. He glanced in fond memory at the page for that important day, the first Saturday in June. 'Hang on, guys,' he said, straightaway sensing that something was not quite right (it was still early in the evening). His protest went unheard as another pint was thrust into his hand on a further wave of cheering. Before his senses became completely clouded, he managed to pin Phil Cole into a corner and explain his misgivings. Phil listened half-hearing for a few moments, drained his glass (not before reaching for another) and said in judgment, 'It was Uncle George's day – we can't possibly take it away from him. Now, for God's sake, get drunk with the rest of us. You've just brought a new cricketer into the world.'

Simon Crossley had got very drunk. By the time he was deposited at home, he was as helpless as his baby son, but not half so quiet. It was the next afternoon before his senses returned. And then he placed a pink adhesive note in the scorebook. Dean Faulds may have been knocked out, but he had not been bowled out. The Outcasts Cricket Club had beaten Willingfold-in-the-Myre by six wickets. Uncle George need never know. But the official record had to be correct.

The will of Mortimer Dalrymple Phypps was read in July. His entire estate was left to Willingfold-in-the-Myre Cricket Club which in an instant became the most well-endowed cricket club in England. The whole of the effort encapsulated in the great festival day had turned out to be unnecessary. Uncle George chuckled. The Outcasts need never know.

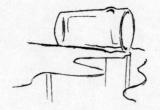